Leadership Challenges in High Schools

Leadership Challenges in High Schools

Multiple Pathways to Success

W. Norton Grubb

Routledge
Taylor & Francis Group
LONDON AND NEW YORK

First published 2011 by Paradigm Publishers

Published 2016 by Routledge
2 Park Square, Milton Park, Abingdon, Oxon OX14 4RN
711 Third Avenue, New York, NY 10017, USA

Routledge is an imprint of the Taylor & Francis Group, an informa business

Library of Congress Cataloging-in-Publication Data

Grubb, W. Norton.
Leadership challenges in high schools : multiple pathways to success / W. Norton Grubb.
p. cm.
Includes bibliographical references and index.
ISBN 978-1-59451-910-9 (hardcover : alk. paper)
ISBN 978-1-59451-911-6 (paperback : alk. paper)
1. High schools—Administration—United States. 2. High school principals—United States. 3. School improvement programs—United States. 4. Educational leadership—United States. I. Title.
LB2822.2.G78 2011
373.1200973—dc22

2010047324

ISBN 13: 978-1-59451-910-9 (hbk)
ISBN 13: 978-1-59451-911-6 (pbk)

Designed and Typeset by Straight Creek Bookmakers.

Contents

Acknowledgments

This book has provided me an opportunity to combine two apparently disparate interests. One of them is high school and its reform, specifically ways of integrating rather than continuing to separate academic and vocational education (now being called CTE for "career technical education," to avoid the disparagement associated with "vocational"). Through the 1990s, as part of the National Center for Research in Vocational Education at the University of California at Berkeley, I and others labored long and hard (if not always fruitfully) to define what it might mean to integrate academic and vocational education, to describe the advantages of doing so, to profile schools that had been successful in doing so, and to document the effectiveness of these approaches. Since then, the idea of integrated programs has morphed into the conceptions of multiple pathways and linked learning, described more fully in the introduction and then in chapter 3, and it's gratifying to see these practices increasing in large numbers of high schools and districts.

A second interest of mine, especially since 1999, has been school leadership. As a result of several events, I became the faculty coordinator of the Principal Leadership Institute (PLI) at UC–Berkeley, a program to prepare urban school leaders that opened in summer 2000. From its inception, the PLI has attempted to adopt relatively innovative practices: an emphasis on instructional leadership; a focus on equity and social justice, including forthright discussions of class, race, ethnicity, and language backgrounds that make so much difference to students in urban schools; an emphasis on problem-based learning, including a problem-solving action research project described briefly in this book; the integration of research and practice; and a cohort model with high levels of cooperation among students, mimicking the need for cooperation within schools. With the extraordinary work of Lynda Tredway, the program coordinator, the PLI has thrived for just over a decade and has expanded its leadership activities into other areas through the Leadership Connection for Justice in Education. The PLI shows up in various parts of this book, and the induction program—the Leadership Support Program—forms the basis for recommendations on ways of strengthening leadership development, found in chapter 4.

However, these two interests remained separate until discussions held by the Irvine Foundation about supporting the further development of pathways. In the course of these discussions, it became clear that pathways probably require new kinds of teachers and teacher preparation. The direct result has been the creation of a teacher program at California State University at San Diego, with a multiple pathways emphasis or linked learning "lens," mentioned in chapter 3. I asserted—without much evidence—that if pathways need new kinds of teachers, they probably need new kinds of leaders as well. But neither I nor anyone else had much idea what this meant. Fortunately, Anne Stanton and the Irvine Foundation provided me a grant to figure out what it meant, for which I thank them.

As I began thinking about what leadership for multiple pathways might entail and how to go about carrying out empirical research on the subject, I slowly became aware, to my astonishment, that there is virtually no writing on leadership in high schools and virtually no special attention to high schools in leadership programs. (The introduction documents this apparently outlandish statement more carefully.) The general issue of high school leadership was one that I needed to understand before I could examine the particular challenges of leadership for multiple pathways. This book therefore examines both the general issue of high school leadership, especially in chapter 2, and then the particular challenges of pathways, especially in chapter 3. Some readers may be interested in the first but not the second, particularly if they support high school reforms other than pathways. But many lessons of pathways—for example, the need for explicit attention to instruction, the necessity of keeping the vision of any reform, the attention to potential inequities among students, and the crucial roles of districts (in chapter 5)—are just as important to other high school reforms, such as early college high schools. In this sense, both the general and the specific demands on leaders in high schools must be understood if we are ever to reshape this difficult institution.

In addition, it's crucial to understand the high school in some depth in order to know what kinds of reforms and what kinds of leadership it requires. The high school provides a fine example of Larry Cuban's (1990) contention that we engage in "reforming again, again, and again," with nearly every generation fighting over what high schools should be, and many commission reports arguing about their favorite recipes for reform. Some readers will find the material analyzing these debates, particularly in chapters 1 and 6, academic and irrelevant to getting on with the business of reform or of running these enormously complex high schools. But Cuban's point is precisely that we often engage in reform without fully realizing what we are doing or how it differs from what has gone before. Leaders and reformers need to understand the deep issues surrounding the high school more than anyone else, and so this volume provides them with these historical and conceptual perspectives.

In carrying out the research for this book, I have incurred a number of debts. My greatest thanks go to the many principals, vice principals, and district officials we interviewed in the course of this study. They must remain anonymous, but their experiences and insights provide the basis for this book. In addition, I want to thank Anne Rardon, Carol Robie, and Jane Stern, coaches for PLI and themselves former principals, who carried out the interviews of graduates from the PLI; Daphannie Stephens, director of the Leadership Connection for Social Justice, who coordinated these interviews and the project in general; Arlene LaPlante, who organized interviews in one particular district; Kathy Harris, Roman Stearns, and Gary Hoachlander of ConnectEd California, who suggested other schools to visit; Libby Gil, who provided additional information about one particular district; and Ben Grandy of PLI, who organized interview files and transcriptions. Several individuals read parts of the manuscript and made helpful comments, including Ted Barone, Joe Flessa, Annie Johnston, Ben Levin, Anne Rarden, Jon Schmidt-Davis, Roman Stearns, David Stern, and Lynda Tredway.

I also want to thank the aspiring leaders of PLI. Through my contacts with them, particularly through my supervision of many Leadership Action Research Projects related to high schools, I have come to appreciate the dedication and persistence that real leadership in schools requires—especially in schools that have endured rounds of teacher-bashing and school-bashing in the reform movements since *A Nation at Risk*; especially in urban schools, where we concentrate the greatest inequities in this inequitable country; and especially in California, where the citizenry and the politicians have undermined the education of our children for thirty years. The dedication of PLI students to equity and improvement is remarkable, and I hope that the perspectives of this book can improve leadership a fraction of what they do.

W. Norton Grubb
Berkeley, California
August 2010

INTRODUCTION

THE "PEOPLE'S COLLEGE" OR "PATHWAYS TO NOWHERE"?

Americans seem to have contradictory views about high schools. In their 150 years of existence, they have been called "the people's college," the egalitarian heir to Horace Mann's "balance wheel of democracy, the great equalizer of the conditions of men." Some fifty years ago, at the end of the 1950s that are sometimes seen as the golden age of the high school, James Bryant Conant (1959) declared that "[high school] has come into being because of our economic history and our devotion to the ideals of equality of opportunity and equality of status ... whose programs correspond to the educational needs of *all* the youth of the community" (5). The imposing school architecture of the nineteenth century has led to comparisons with cathedrals or temples, unlike utilitarian grammar schools. High schools have also been called "citadels of learning," the protectors of knowledge against the onslaught of trivia and popular culture.

But they have also been excoriated as "pathways to nowhere," as "dropout factories" failing large numbers of students, as "obsolete—they cannot teach our kids what they need to know today" (by Bill Gates). At the same time that Conant worried about the segregation of youth in one institution and the potential for "social dynamite," his observations about the dreadful state of education for black students led him to declare that "the fate of freedom in the world hangs very much in the balance"(Conant 1961, 34). At the same time, Paul Goodman (1956), in one of the most trenchant criticisms ever, declared that nothing of intrinsic importance took place in high school because it was just a way station on the road to college. Now, in the age of College for All, when some educators think that every student should be prepared only for college, completion of high school—*successful* completion, with graduates ready to take on the challenges of college and university—is more necessary than ever. This is particularly so because high school dropouts fare poorly in subsequent employment and in their health, marital status, political participation, and many other outcomes. But high schools seem to be failing too many of their students, and an avalanche of commission reports reviewed in chapter 1 has demonstrated the complaints about many different aspects.

There are also contradictions when individuals look back on their high school years. Some individuals remember that "those were the best days of my life," as Bryan Adams sang in "Summer of '69," when they grew toward adulthood and tried all kinds of new activities and personalities. Others remember a period when they were unpopular, picked on, treated as losers and jerks and dweebs. The vocabulary of personal distinctions has changed over time, but Penny Eckart's *Jocks and Burnouts* (1989), an ethnography of a high school in the late 1980s, describes a contrast that has been present for a long time. On one side are the jocks (or preps, or collegiates), with high levels of participation in extracurricular activities, real commitment to their schools, and adequate if not spectacular grades (unlike the nerds, the brains, and the dweebs). On the other are the burnouts (a.k.a. greasers, punks, hoods, stoners, skaters, Goths), with low levels of participation, disaffection for everything in school, and marginal if not failing grades. The cliques in high schools, endlessly forming and reforming, represent various hierarchies of class, of race and ethnicity, of physical attractiveness, of athletic ability, of "cool." They describe countless ways of ranking students—all with winners and losers. Even if the grown-ups in high schools didn't create status differences, particularly on the academic side through tracking, the students would create them on the nonacademic side.

Teachers come in for their own kinds of mixed feelings. Most people can remember an enormous range of teaching, and my own children—in one of the most diverse high schools in the country—came home with tales of inspiration as well as pedagogical neglect and abuse. On the one hand are those teachers who have inspired students—awakened them with love of particular subjects, or provided them with visions of life beyond high school or outside the confines of a narrow community, or assured them they could make it to college. In popular culture we have images of wonderful teachers—Jaime Escalante teaching calculus to working-class students in *Stand and Deliver*; Michelle Pfeiffer, the angel/Marine, winning over hostile students in *Dangerous Minds* by defying the conventional curriculum; an inspiring music teacher in *Mr. Holland's Opus*; and the characters in *Blackboard Jungle* and *To Sir, with Love,* where hero-teachers win the respect and the participation of cynical working-class students. But we also have endless stories of teachers who by turn mistreat their students—especially their African American and Latino students—or simply neglect them, or demand so little that students find themselves graduating without the competencies necessary to find a job or move into a community college without remediation. For every inspiring teacher in the movies, there's another like the history teacher in *Ferris Bueller's Day Off,* droning on endlessly while students fall asleep; the weak, meddling teacher played by Matthew Broderick in *Election;* or the sarcastic, needling teacher in the semi-documentary from France, *The Class* (with a better title in French, *Entre les Murs* or *Between These Walls,* suggesting the captivity of high school).

The portraits of schools we have also reflect this dichotomy. Michael Rose's *Possible Lives* (1995) depicts a number of schools with exhilarating work going on, including high schools in Chicago struggling to teach in serious ways despite students' lack of basic skills and the district's fiscal and political struggles and high schools in New York creating small learning environments. Deborah Meier's *The Power of Their Ideas* (1995), often considered the bible of the small-school movement, similarly describes an urban school with racial minority students held to high standards. Amy Ryken's (2001) description of a career academy linked to a bio-tech firm is one in which students are committed to learning from many different sources, from teachers as well as managers and coworkers in their work settings. But the more common portrayal, of urban schools in particular, is one of places where almost no learning takes place, where personal relationships are toxic, and where teachers and students battle for control of classrooms (Payne 2008). Frederick Wiseman, one of our greatest documentary filmmakers, portrayed one of each. In *High School* (1968), he presented a large Philadelphia school with authoritarian administrators and teachers berating their students endlessly. He contrasted this with *High School II* (1994), showing Deborah Meier's Central Park East as a center of serious academic effort for its low-income Latino students of East Harlem. Sometimes the split occurs within a school: I visited an all-black traditional vocational high school where students were working diligently and purposefully in their occupational specialty classes, dedicated to subjects and projects they had chosen, while the academic classes in the same school accomplished almost nothing—two separate schools in one building.

So too for the principals we interviewed for this book. Many of them were committed to their work and described it as "inspiring work: I think this age of young people—they are really at a point in their lives where they are figuring out who they are, where they want to go with their future—and so it is absolutely fulfilling work," said one. Another said,

> If you're a person that likes excitement, it's a great job because there's always something happening. You get the feeling of accomplishment, although you can never finish everything you do, but the time just flies by ... It's rewarding. When you stand up there graduation day and those kids walk across that stage, it's just awesome. I always tell the kids it's my privilege to serve you as your high school principal.

The principals in charge of theme-based pathways—one of the most promising high school reforms, described in the third section of chapter 1—talked about their efforts in glowing terms; one said,

> One of the things that I do at graduation is just brag, brag, brag, brag, and so I talk a lot about where our kids are going and how they got there. One of the taglines that I always say is, "Whatever your kids want, we can get them there. This school can get them there." And the academies,[1] they're just the jewels in our crown—they're excellent.

On the other hand, many of them also acknowledge that the work is exhausting. One declared that "I love being a high school principal," and then went on to acknowledge: "There's so much to love, you know? More budgets, more people, more events, more involvement in the community—the high school is so central to the community." Another admitted that "It takes an enormous amount of time, sunup to sundown and beyond—it certainly doesn't foster great family relations." A district official, trying to keep several pathways in operation, reported that "these programs are extraordinarily toll-taking on teachers and administrators. It is exhausting work, so another part of my job is to keep everybody motivated and keep us thinking about why we decided to do this in the first place—which was to make sure that more of our students who are in high school stay in high school." Others described the bewildering variety of their responsibilities; one assistant principal described his role as

> Assistant principal of in charge of public services, that means disciplinary stuff. I oversee the counseling department. I do a lot of student services stuff. I'm also in charge of attendance counseling, and I'm the testing coordinator as well. I am also de facto head, or overseer, of the Academy of Arts and Sciences.

As we will see later, the sheer variety of responsibilities often means that leaders cannot get around to all of them—"you can never finish everything you do"—and some activities, especially those related to instruction, don't get much attention.

The high school is a contradictory place, or at least a place of enormous variation, for its leaders as well as its teachers and its students.

So the high school is a contradictory place, or at least a place of enormous variation, for its leaders as well as its teachers and its students. Some reasons are obvious: high schools are larger and, because of the variety of their offerings, are more complex than middle schools or elementary schools—an issue to which I return in chapter 2. They are more heterogeneous than middle or elementary schools because they typically bring together students from several middle schools. The differences among students in interests, ambitions, mastery of school subjects, and commitment to the schooling are therefore greater, with obvious implications for status variation ("jocks and burnouts"), for academic and nonacademic performance, and for success and failure. And in a society with high levels of inequality compared with other developed countries—inequalities of income and class, inequalities associated with race and ethnicity and immigrant status, differences among regions of the country and between urban and rural areas, political differences in a country with an increasingly polarized citizenry—it's not surprising to see these differences reflected in high school, in success and failure, and in perceptions of how well or badly the high school is doing.

Other reasons for our differing perceptions are less clear. In the history of the high school, developed briefly in chapter 1, a number of dilemmas have been debated without clear resolution—or more precisely, with varied resolutions along a continuum of possibilities. But because there are many alternative directions high schools can take, there is almost endless bickering about what high schools *should* be. And there's also endless bickering about what high schools *are,* about how well they carry out the roles expected of them that almost everyone agrees about—ensuring completion for all students, enhancing equity, and preparing students adequately for a next stage of either work or further education or other dimensions of adult life. This arguing occurs with parents and students dissatisfied with their high school experiences, of course, but also appears in an endless series of commission reports and reform proposals—the subject of the second section of chapter 1.

LEADERSHIP IN HIGH SCHOOLS

With all this debate and reform energy, there has been virtually no attention to the special challenges of leadership in high schools and to reforming high schools.

With all this debate and reform energy, there has been virtually no attention to the special challenges of leadership in high schools and to reforming high schools. Elsewhere in the vast landscape of school reform, a consensus has emerged that the quality of school leadership is crucial to reform, second only to the quality of teachers.[2] Indeed, in recognizing the variety of leadership responsibilities, they might be the *most* crucial factor in improving high schools, not just second fiddle to teachers. Principals are called on to be instructional leaders, diagnosing and improving the quality of teaching—and therefore crucial to solving problems with teaching. They are expected to lead "data-driven" reforms, using information about students to identify which reforms are most necessary; to create schools as small learning communities where teachers and leaders collaborate around instruction and learning; to take responsibility for closing the various achievement gaps, themselves hideously complex forms of inequality; and to find the non-academic supports (such as health and mental health services) that many students need, particularly in urban districts with high concentrations of low-income students. The current reforms emanating from Washington also seem to assume that principals are centrally responsible for the quality of a school because the first step in "reconstitution" to "turn around" failing schools is to replace the principal.

But in the vast literature on leadership in schools, and on the problems with current high schools, there is virtually nothing on the leadership challenges in high schools. Most writers have treated leadership as a generic requirement for reforming schools, not one with special characteristics in high schools.[3] For example, the National Association of Secondary School Principals—which one might think would clarify the demands on high school principals—instead resorts to bromides applicable in any educational institution, such as "the principal will provide leadership in the high school community by building and maintaining a vision, direction, and focus for student learning" (*Breaking Ranks* 1996, 99). Their *Field Guide for Leading Change* has many worthwhile recommendations about analyzing data, establishing collaborative leadership, developing communication, and supporting the oft-mentioned "buy-in" by teachers, but nothing at all about conditions particular to high schools—except for a passing reference to keeping student/teacher ratios under 90:1, an acknowledgement that high school teachers often face as many as 180 students a day. Its successor, *Breaking Ranks II* (2004), discusses "four steps to change"—establish an action planning team, use data, assess conditions for change, and report the results—but these are again generic elements of change, not challenges specific to high schools.

A reform manual such as "Reinventing High Schools"—a source that several principals we interviewed mentioned—has ten sections on such important elements as personalization, adaptive pedagogy, and democratic decision-making (an oblique reference to distributed leadership[4]), but nothing about the special demands of high schools (Darling-Hammond, Ancess, and Ort 2002). The authors subsequently examined the issues of preparing school leaders, but again without any particular attention to high schools (Darling-Hammond et al. 2010). A report with the promising title of *Profiles in Leadership: Innovative Approaches to Transforming the American High School* (Alliance for Excellent Education 2004) says virtually nothing about the conditions in high schools, with most of its articles portraying leadership as relatively generic. The exception, a piece by former secretary of education Richard Riley, acknowledges the difficult transition to high school, the need to create smaller learning environments, and the waste of the senior year, and then leaves the reader with the recommendation to "choose [not develop] caring and smart leaders"—a pallid response indeed. Most commission reports on high schools say very little about leadership, and the most recent in this long series—a volume on America's High Schools, part of the series on *The Future of Children* (2009)—says nothing at all. A burgeoning literature about high school reforms and their effects is, with one exception, silent about the leadership dimensions of reform.[5] The practitioner literature (as distinct from research or policy literature) is full of titles on leadership, but leadership is again treated as a generic capacity, the same in elementary, middle, and high schools.[6] Virtually the only exception to the profound silence about high school leadership is an organization called the Principals' Partnership, supported by Union Pacific and dedicated to high school principals.[7] And very few leadership preparation programs do anything special for individuals interested in becoming high school leaders.[8]

Given the widespread belief in the power of principals, a working hypothesis is that the greater difficulties in reforming high schools, and in improving instruction and learning in particular, are due in part to the neglect of leadership.[9] Of course, several structural conditions make high schools difficult to reform—especially their sheer size, the complexity of their offerings, and the challenges of teaching in a faculty dominated by disciplinary allegiances. But many of these structural conditions could be overcome—that's what such reforms as smaller schools, multiple pathways, and early college high schools are intended to do—if leaders and teachers were able to work collectively first to identify and then resolve them. This requires, however, that leaders be well prepared to address the special challenges they face in high schools. Certainly the principals we talked to think their jobs are quite different from those in elementary and secondary schools—"It's not a mystery: high school students, teenagers, are different from children"—and many of them acknowledged that they had to get most of their preparation by trial and error on the job: "There's nothing like screwing up on the job to teach you the really hard lessons about how to develop consistent practices and to be able to implement in the face of controversy or challenge," a new principal commented. But there must be a better way than trial and error.

> *Given the widespread belief in the power of principals, a working hypothesis is that the greater difficulties in reforming high schools, and in improving instruction and learning in particular, are due in part to the neglect of leadership.*

The purpose of this book, then, is to correct the neglect of high school leadership by analyzing the challenges rooted in conditions distinguishing high schools from middle and elementary schools. I first examine the history of the high school in chapter 1, to clarify some inescapable dilemmas that continue to affect high schools and reforms. I also review recent commission reports critiquing the high school, to indicate how broad these critiques are and to suggest that many reforms proposed for high schools cannot respond to these critiques. I then describe one particular reform—the creation of multiple pathways, sometimes called "linked learning"—that responds both to recent critiques and to the historic dilemmas of the high school better than other reforms—because a secondary purpose of the book is to understand what leadership for pathways requires. In chapter 2, I examine the special conditions in high schools *and* their implications for leadership; for example, it is obvious to say that the high school is larger and more complex than elementary schools, but precisely how that affects leaders—and how it might be incorporated into leadership preparation—requires greater specificity. Then I turn in chapter 3 to the special challenges of high schools with multiple pathways because any major reform—and certainly pathways—requires different characteristics of leaders (as well as teachers). Chapter 4 summarizes the implications for high school leadership preparation, both preparation in pre-service programs and in-service (or induction) programs, as well as—because many principals don't think they can be fully prepared except through experience—carefully structured sequences of experience. Chapter 5 addresses the roles of districts in supporting high schools, high school leadership, and multiple pathways—because district policies are crucial and are all too often unsupportive of these reforms. Chapter 6, the conclusion, speculates about the potential future of these developments.

In addition to the material presented in these chapters, each one ends with questions appropriate for teachers, leaders, district officials, and researchers to contemplate. The issues in this book have been generated by a particular kind of research, involving both current and historical sources, but they are in no way academic. Nearly every high school needs to confront these questions, and high schools with multiple pathways confront others of them—particularly those in chapter 3—every day. And for district- and school-level reformers contemplating how to reshape high schools, the benefits of pathways presented in chapter 1, and also the special challenges examined in chapters 3 and 5, provide a series of issues to contemplate ahead of time.

Throughout this book I take an expansive conception of leadership. Principals are leaders, of course, the individuals that most people think of first as being in charge of schools—and, under the policies of the Obama administration and Arne Duncan, the secretary of education, the first to be replaced if a school is judged a "failure." (As one district official in charge of high schools put it, "you [the principal] are the target every time.") Assistant principals or vice principals are leaders too, particularly when they are in charge of some dimensions of a school's operation as part of a leadership team. Often teacher-leaders are crucial to a school, particularly when principals have shared responsibility for operating a school with teachers by establishing various decision-making committees and school-site councils, the practice often known as "distributed leadership" (Spillane 2006). Teacher-leaders are particularly important in multiple pathways because individual pathways may be headed by a teacher-leader rather than an assistant principal. All of these individuals need to be aware of the special challenges of leadership in high schools, and the preparation for high school leaders examined in chapters 3 and 4 applies to all of them.

THE METHODOLOGY OF THIS BOOK

The information in this book about conditions in high schools comes from several sources. Because there has been virtually nothing written about leadership in high schools, I decided to take a simple and direct approach: asking those individuals in leadership positions what their particular challenges are, and how they differ from the challenges in elementary and middle school. A series of interviews with principals and assistant principals from forty-three high schools and five district officials in charge of high schools (all of whom had previously been principals) constitute the most basic information for this book. (The Appendix provides more information about the sample of leaders interviewed and about the focus of the interviews.) About half the leaders we interviewed had experience at several levels of the education system, so they had sufficient information to make comparative statements.

Inevitably, there are limitations in these interviews: given that there are about 14,000 high schools in the United States, a sample of forty-three principals seems small—though we reached the point of "saturation" mentioned by qualitative researchers, where we were no longer learning anything new. For reasons of convenience, and to develop a sample with many pathways, we confined our interviews to California; however, the commission reports reviewed in chapter 1 indicate that the issues in California are precisely the same as those across the country (though perhaps exacerbated by the low level of funding in California, low National Assessment of Educational Progress [NAEP] scores, and the chaotic nature of state policies). We also concentrated on urban and suburban high schools because that is where the challenges seem especially acute; as a result, the high schools we visited are larger—between 1,500 and 4,000 students, even while high schools average 819 students.[10] Of course, other approaches are possible, including interviews with teachers as well as leaders about leadership issues; ethnographic study of high schools in the midst of reform, to see what role leadership plays in successful reforms; and various surveys of principals or other leaders. But given the lack of any writing on leadership in high schools, and the lack of any empirical understanding of what the special issues in high school are, the simple approach of asking those in the best position to know about their challenges seems appropriate.

In addition, I have supplemented this information by other materials on high schools, especially the history of the high school in chapter 1, the complaints in a long series of commission reforms later in that chapter, my own statistical analysis of high school outcomes and the resources leading to them (Grubb 2009b), and my research on theme-based pathways over two decades.[11] Recently, there has been a flurry of reports examining reforms in high schools, especially the efforts to create small schools,[12] and these evaluations provide other sources of information about the crucial features of high schools.

Finally, I am the founder and faculty coordinator of the Principal Leadership Institute (PLI) at UC–Berkeley, a program that prepares leaders for urban schools in the Bay Area. As coordinator and instructor in this program, I have substantial opportunities to see the special challenges in high schools. In particular, these aspiring principals undertake action research projects to improve their schools, and every year I supervise about a dozen such students working in high schools. Some of these research projects are cited in this volume, but more important, working with PLI students on their action research has clarified in many ways the difficulties aspiring leaders in high schools face, particularly in a time of scarcity.

There is, of course, no way to fully capture the richness and variation of more than 14,000 high schools around the country—each of them with its own history and culture, each with its own leadership structure, each with its own potential for reform—in one book. My hope is that the analysis here will stimulate at least two communities—those concerned with educational leadership, and those intent on reforming high schools—to pay more attention to leadership in high schools.

QUESTIONS FOR THE INTRODUCTION

1. Think back to your own high school experiences—academic, extracurricular, and social.

Which of them were positive, either in the sense that they were enjoyable or in the sense that they helped you develop as an individual and student?

Which were negative—either unenjoyable or harmful to your development?

Which of these elements are quite similar to the experiences of high school students today? Which are quite different?

What do these comparisons suggest about the needs for reforms in high schools? Which reflect practices or events that are simply different, not better or worse?

2. For those individuals who are leaders—principals and assistant principals, teacher-leaders, district leaders:

What about your preparation has prepared you specifically for the challenges of high schools?

If you went through an induction program of any kind, what about it prepared you for the challenges of high schools?

What has been the most useful aspect of your preparation, induction, or experience on the job in getting you ready for the challenges of high schools?

What does this imply about programs to prepare high school leaders?

See also the questions at the end of chapter 4.

Chapter 1

"Inspiring Work," "Sunup to Sundown and Beyond"

The Enduring Dilemmas of the American High School

As the introduction clarified, our views about high schools seem to be contradictory or at least are so varied that there seems to be little consensus about their role in American society. In fact, when we look beyond our current stereotypes about high school teachers and student experiences and examine the history of the high school more closely, the main theme seems to be constant battle over what high school should be. Recent commission reports critiquing high schools are similar, particularly because their purple prose and exaggerated claims make it seem as if American society will crumble unless we reform high schools: "Nothing is more important to the welfare of this society and its students than the reinvention of the American High School," thundered the National High School Alliance, at a time (2004) when the war in Iraq, the evidence of torture by American forces, the further dismantling of the welfare state, the divisiveness of politics, and an overbearing education reform (No Child Left Behind) divided the country in ways that make the future of the high school seem trivial.

But even though there might be other issues important to the welfare of the country and education, for all the students whose educational lives lead them inexorably to and through high schools, and for the leaders, teachers, district officials, policy-makers, and researchers who struggle with the conditions of high schools, these battles are all too real. In this chapter, I therefore describe both the historical dilemmas of high schools, and the recent critiques, to clarify the substantial challenges that high schools face. Only then can we make sense of the many reform proposals that have been offered and understand the challenges confronting leaders who hope to reform their institutions.

THE HISTORY OF AMERICAN HIGH SCHOOL: CONSTANT REFORMS, CONSTANT THEMES

It's worth starting with a little history because current reforms so often look like past failures. Following George Santayana, those who ignore the past are condemned to repeat it unknowingly, or—following Larry Cuban (1990)—policy-makers and leaders are likely to engage in "reforming again, again, and again" without understanding why previous reforms haven't worked. The history of the high school has been written many times, and I summarize it only briefly to extract several themes.[1] We will then be able to see how these themes turn up in the most recent commission reports urging reform and how they affect the reforms currently being tried.

The conventional history of the high school begins in the mid–nineteenth century with its predecessor, the academy. Academies were somewhat like charter schools today (Beadie and Tolley 2002; Sizer 1964): they were directed by independent boards rather than public bodies such as school boards; they received most of their funding from private sources; their curricula varied widely; and—although they were intended to follow grammar schools ending at grade 8—the levels of work in academies varied enormously, from grammar school to college-level. They did prepare students for entry into college, but most of their graduates did not attend college; the notion of clear prerequisites for college and university taken in secondary school did not emerge until later.

Slowly, public high schools developed to compete with academies—starting in 1821 with Boston English Classical School, spreading during the 1850s in large cities of the East Coast, during the 1860s in smaller towns, and in the 1880s and 1890s elsewhere and in rural areas. Where high schools developed, they tended to restrict the range of the curriculum to subjects established in the service of mental discipline—the doctrine that the mind, like a muscle, needs to be exercised by the most difficult subjects, including math, rhetoric, and logic. They also promoted the civic and moral education that dominated the public grammar schools, such as history, Greek, and Latin, so that students could read the classics in their original languages. "Modern" subjects, such as science, and current languages, such as French and German, came into the curriculum only toward the end of the century.

The nineteenth-century high school in many ways was codified by the Committee of Ten, a group appointed by the National Council of the National Education Association to standardize the high school curriculum so that colleges might count on more or less uniform preparation. The report of that committee has been widely cited for its curriculum, one that looks amazingly like the conventional college prep curriculum today. It also reflects a hostility to differentiating the curriculum to suit the needs or interests of students: "every subject which is taught at all in a secondary school should be taught in the same way and to the same extent to every pupil, no matter what the probable destination of the pupil may be." So those bound for college and those bound for other pursuits (such as the work of homemaking) were all to take the same curriculum. It allowed only two variants—a classic and a modern version, the latter with more science and modern languages. As of 1900, approximately 10 percent of the age group 14–18 were enrolled in high school, and only 6.4 percent of 17-year-olds had high school diplomas, so it was quite an elite institution by current standards.[2]

In many ways, however, the report of the Committee of Ten was the dying gasp of the nineteenth-century high school. The transitional programs of manual training in the 1870s and 1880s provided aspiring engineers with "hand skills" in metalwork and woodwork, and new commercial courses developed to compete with private commercial schools for the new clerical occupations. Toward the end of the nineteenth century, high schools began to adopt more overtly vocational courses and programs—commercial and clerical programs for girls, then industrial programs for both skilled and production-line workers, agricultural programs for those in rural areas, and home economics for middle-class girls likely to stay at home. Ability grouping followed this kind of vocational grouping, and by the 1920s the outlines of a watered-down "academic" track—the general track—emerged. All this differentiation was justified by a change in the conception of equity: in place of the nineteenth-century common school idea of sameness—with all students taking the same subjects for the same length of time—a differentiated concept of equal opportunity emerged, emphasizing different learning for different students. As two elementary educators declared (Elson and Bachman 1910, 361):

> Instead of affording equality of educational opportunity to all, the elementary school by offering but one course of instruction, and this of a literary character, serves the interests of but one type of children and neglects in a measure the taste, capacity, and educational destination of all others, and of those, too, whose needs are imperative and to whom the future holds no further advantage. In a word, what was intended to be a school for the masses and afford equality of educational opportunity to all ... serves well the interests of but the few.

The new conception of equal educational opportunity achieved enormous support because at the time it seemed appropriately democratic. As the Commission on National Aid to Vocational Education put it in 1914, "Widespread vocational training will democratize the education of the country ... by recognizing different tastes and abilities and by giving an equal opportunity to all to prepare for their life work." The other important strand of the Committee of Ten—a restricted curriculum based on nineteenth-century ideas of mental discipline and civic education—was quickly repudiated by the continued elaboration of the curriculum. In 1917, yet another committee of the National Education Association (NEA) released the *Cardinal Principles of Secondary Education,* declaring the "main objectives of education"—of all education, elementary and secondary—to include:[3]

1. Health.
2. Command of fundamental processes.
3. Worthy home-membership.
4. Vocation.
5. Citizenship.
6. Worthy use of leisure.
7. Ethical character.

Some nineteenth-century standards—citizenship and ethical character—were included, along with the newer purpose of vocation, but intellectual purposes had vanished into "command of fundamental processes." The other purposes—health, worthy home-membership, worthy use of leisure—would have made the Committee of Ten apoplectic.

In many ways, the *Cardinal Principles* created an early justification for the *comprehensive* high school with a variety of academic and nonacademic activities, a development that was going on anyway with the expansion of sports, clubs, and other extracurricular activities in the early years of the century. Many observers have portrayed battles over the high school as a continued reflection of the Committee of Ten and its narrow emphasis on an academic curriculum versus the *Cardinal Principles* and their expansion of purposes. But several other developments have been crucial to the emergence of the current high school. One is the enormous increase in enrollments, first in the 1910s as the youth labor market dried up and compulsory attendance laws were enforced, and then in the 1930s with the Great Depression. By the 1950s, the high school was a mass institution, quite different from the elite institution it had been in 1890, with the enrollment rate hitting 83.5 percent by the middle 1950s. Since then, dropouts—a subject of concern ever since the early years of the twentieth century, when educators worried that "laggards" (those falling behind grade norms) would be an enormous social problem—have been even a greater subject of concern, with dropout prevention a nearly constant issue.

In the late 1940s and 1950s, another reform came and went, one that highlights a continuing dilemma of the mass high school. In the various efforts to wrestle with what public education should be after World War II, those on the side of the Committee of Ten and those following the *Cardinal Principles* contended for control of the curriculum. In discussions around an NEA report wrestling with *Education for ALL American Youth,* George Stoddard, the commissioner of education for New York, painted the image of the high school as a bulwark against the onslaught of trivia in the curriculum:[4]

> If we give up this last little citadel, in the high school, in terms of health and social relations, and getting along with people, and visiting, and being nice, and the rest of it, and forget the glory of the human mind ... I think we are cheapening education. Nobody will teach anybody any algebra whatsoever outside of school, but everybody will teach everybody else a good deal about social relations, about health, about personal contact, about work, about travel.

But Charles Prosser—earlier a supporter of vocational education—confronted a serious dilemma of the comprehensive high school in making the case for life adjustment education:

> The vocational school as a community will be able better to prepare 20 percent of the youth of secondary school age for entrance upon desirable skilled occupations; and that the high school will continue to prepare another 20 percent for entrance to college. We do not believe that the remaining 60 percent of our youth of secondary school age will receive the life adjustment training they need and to which they are entitled as American citizens—unless and until the administrators of public education with the assistance of the vocational education leaders formulate a similar program for this group.[5]

So the 40 percent of students going into managerial and professional work or into the skilled trades were well prepared in academic and vocational tracks, respectively, but the mass of students who wound up in unskilled work needed something else, especially in a school preparing students for future occupations. In practice, the program for life adjustment education for this third group included "functional experiences in the areas of practical arts, home and family life, health and physical fitness, and civic competence," as well as work experience programs. Some of the courses developed under the life adjustment program were truly silly—"How to Find a Family Dentist"—and the movement quickly came under attack for its shallowness. But as debased as life adjustment education seems now, it posed a question as difficult currently—when only 31 percent of jobs require any postsecondary education at all, a figure that will rise only slowly to 32.4 percent in 2018 (Lacey and Wright 2009, Table 3)—as it was in 1950. And though life adjustment courses themselves disappeared, their heirs remain ubiquitous in "life skills" courses still found in many high schools (especially in the general track), in job training programs, in welfare-to-work programs, and in youth development efforts. For the vast numbers of individuals in our unequal labor markets who can find only minimally skilled employment, life adjustment, or life skills, or "soft skills" solve the problem of what education and training institutions should teach.

Hard on the heels of life adjustment and its demise, the Sputnik crisis of 1957 provided another twist to the agenda of the high school. The fear that the Russians were beating us in the space race led to increased interest in science and math, as well as short-lived additions to the curriculum, such as Russian language. Changes in course-taking were not as dramatic as the changes in rhetoric surrounding schooling,[6] just as changes with vocational education and life adjustment were less dramatic than the rhetorical changes, but the incident affirmed again the centrality of an academic curriculum—in the "modern" subjects of science and math—rather than nonacademic pursuits.

But another shift during the 1950s moved high schools in precisely the opposite direction. Extracurricular activities, such as sports and clubs, had mushroomed since the early years of the century, and in many ways they dominated the concerns of students.[7] But these efforts were always under the control of adults, and their goals were reasonably close to those of the school's—not, of course, to the academic curriculum of the Committee of Ten, but to the expanded agenda of the *Cardinal Principles.* Sports promised to teach the blend of competition and cooperation characteristic of corporate capitalism; clubs expanded student interests ("worthy use of leisure"); student government allowed adolescents to try on leadership roles; and all of these occupied the free time of adolescents who might otherwise run amuck. But in the 1950s, the early signs of youth culture untethered from adult control emerged, a culture more oriented to sex, drugs, and rock 'n' roll.[8] Music developed a distinctively teenage audience, sexual experimentation started to take off (though pregnancy remained highly stigmatized), and some students—the "cool kids"—began using marijuana. This was the era of Elvis Presley and black-influenced rhythm and blues, of *High School Confidential!* and *Rebel Without a Cause.* It started a wave of teenage movies—more recently *The Breakfast Club* (1985), *Fast Times at Ridgemont High* (1982), and *Clueless* (1995)—in which students are entirely engaged in the dilemmas of adolescence, and school fades away to nothing, apparently pointless except as a place to meet. The high school might be a citadel against the assaults of the curricular barbarians, but it couldn't protect against youth culture, which took place during the free time of students, outside the school's control. The directions of youth culture and that of science and math in the wake of Sputnik could not have been more different: Dionysus versus Apollo in the high school. The educators of that period had little to say about these developments—as they have continued to have little to say—but youth culture, friendships, and the thrills of adolescence provided very different reasons for going to school.

The concerns of earlier years with dropouts, of *Education for ALL American Youth,* and of life adjustment were all focused on finding something worthwhile for everyone to do in the comprehensive high school. But the 1960s focused more on equity, or more precisely—in a country with high levels of inequality but persistent concerns with equity (Pole 1978)—on equality of educational opportunity, a slippery concept indeed. Convinced that education was the most powerful antidote to poverty, Lyndon Johnson pushed through not more rhetoric or curricular changes but more resources for low-performing students: Title I funding for "disadvantaged" (low-income) students, Head Start to prepare little children for the elementary grades, job training programs for high school dropouts, and financial aid for college students. Very few of these resources affected high schools directly—Title I money overwhelmingly funded elementary grades, and the other programs funded preschool and post–high school programs—but the issue of equal opportunity was securely on the educational agenda.

Since then, the barrage of reforms seems constant. The late 1960s and early 1970s saw a brief period of experimentation with alternative forms of education, some of them quite (John) Deweyan in reshaping pedagogy, others (like community control of schools in New York) inspired by the desire to counter the obvious inequality of public schools. Career education, aspiring to orient every activity in the school around ideas about careers, made a brief appearance and then died, leaving behind only a few work experience programs and a few efforts to bolster guidance and counseling about careers. Then *A Nation at Risk,* with its histrionic language about the failure of schools ("the educational foundations of our society are presently eroded by a rising tide of mediocrity that threatens our very future as a Nation and a people"), burst onto the scene in 1983. It promoted the new basics—really the old basics (English, math, science, and social studies) plus computers—but it was probably more important for starting a period of reform that has not quit. There were many counter-reports, of course. One, *Our Students at Risk,* excoriated *A Nation at Risk* for paying so little attention to equity issues. Another, *What Work Requires of Schools,* from the Secretary of Labor's Commission on Achieving Necessary Skills (or SCANS), reemphasized the vocational purposes of schools and the challenges of international competition. It added an augmented list of "necessary skills" (sometimes described as "twenty-first-century skills," or now "deep thinking") for high-performance work: "foundation skills" (the three R's plus speaking and listening); thinking skills (creativity, decision-making, problem-solving, conceptualization, reasoning, knowing how to learn); and personal qualities, such as individual responsibility, sociability, and self-management (sometimes labeled "soft skills," and first cousin to the "life skills" of life adjustment education). Once again, it's easy to see in this debate yet another battle between the Committee of Ten and the *Cardinal Principles.*

But developments in accountability became more important than this war of words. First states and then the federal government in No Child Left

Behind (NCLB) imposed accountability systems, with schools penalized in various ways for failing to make progress. In theory, accountability might encompass any of the valued outcomes of education—civic and moral goals, the multiple "intelligences" championed by Howard Gardner (1983), the various SCANS skills, or whatever a state might decide its goals should be. In practice, accountability was measured by student performance on tests of math and reading, usually basic skills tests. In some schools with high proportions of low-performing students, the curriculum has collapsed to math and reading, with subjects not tested given little attention.

Despite these many debates, a standard version of the high school has dominated since the early years of the twentieth century: the comprehensive high school, with many offerings to suit the variety of its students; different formal and informal tracking mechanisms undermining the promise of equity; an array of extracurricular activities adding their own support and distraction; and—at least since the 1950s—the added temptations of youth culture. Comprehensive high schools have accommodated all of these—that's what makes them comprehensive but also bewildering and inchoate, more like cafeterias or shopping malls than coherent institutions (Powell, Farrar, and Cohen 1985). They are by now deeply rooted in American culture, in most students' and parents' concepts of what high school should be. Therefore substantial reforms, such as the multiple pathways described at the end of this chapter and then in chapter 3, always face skepticism about the idea that they can be superior to the comprehensive high school.

A standard version of the high school has dominated since the early years of the twentieth century: the comprehensive high school, with many offerings to suit the variety of its students.

Even this brief history reveals a number of themes, debated for more than a century, that remain unresolved:

- The question of purpose: The Committee of Ten, building on nineteenth-century ideas of mental discipline and civic education, argued for a relentlessly academic curriculum. Its argument emerged again in the reaction against life adjustment education, in the emphasis on science and math after the Sputnik crisis, as well as in present concerns with STEM subjects (science, technology, engineering, and math) as a way of maintaining the country's competitive edge. The *Cardinal Principles* justified a range of other, less academic subjects, including vocational education and personal interest courses. These reappeared in life adjustment and in life skills, soft skills, and SCANS skills, which emphasized the personal qualities necessary for work. And though educators have debated the content of the formal curriculum, the expansion of extracurricular activities and of youth culture beyond the control of educators has meant that the high school, in fact if not in principle, has become the locus for a wide range of nonacademic activities.

- The theme of differentiation: In the nineteenth century, the Committee of Ten, showing its commitment to the common school, articulated the need for a relatively unitary curriculum, one that we would now call the college prep curriculum. Its concept of equity was based on providing the same education to all students. But developments after 1900 brought a differentiated curriculum to the high school that were, as stated in the *Cardinal Principles,* differentiated by "taste, capacity, and educational destination"—that is, by whether students were continuing to college or not. Life adjustment education also reinforced a differentiated curriculum, in the process identifying a group of students—those bound for unskilled work—who posed a particular dilemma for the vocationalized high school. Subsequent calls for the new basics; more stringent high school graduation requirements in many states; the antitracking movement with its demonstration that tracking almost inevitably leads to inequality (Oakes 1985); and now the notion of college for all, implying a college prep curriculum for all students, all reinforce a more or less unitary curriculum. In practice, however, the development of special education, the continuation of the general track, the creation of honors programs and advanced placement (AP) courses, and the development of remedial courses and alternative education for those who have fallen behind their peers have continued tracking in new forms.

Differentiation in high schools has always been *vertical* differentiation—that is, different curricula with different status rankings; different class and racial/ethnic composition of students; and different outcomes, including employment, community college, and four-year colleges of different rankings. The possibility of *horizontal* differentiation—of different programs of study of equivalent status, separate but equal, differentiated but equivalent—has rarely emerged. But when I turn in the last section of this chapter to multiple pathways, horizontal differentiation will surface again as one way of reconciling the value of differentiation with that of equity.

- The rhetoric and reality of equity: As private academies gave way to public high schools, the new institution was often called "the people's college," open to all students in ways that academies, colleges, and universities were not. The undifferentiated curriculum celebrated by the Committee of Ten also reflected the dominant belief of equity and access to a common curriculum for a common period of time.

  But with high school enrollment encompassing perhaps 4 percent of the age cohort by 1890, and only 10.6 percent by 1900, the high school in reality was an elite institution until the 1930s. High dropout rates—unequal by class and race—meant that high school completion was always more unequal than initial enrollment. The twentieth-century idea of equal opportunity justified vertically differentiated tracks, and the continued differentiation as the high school became a mass institution guaranteed that the high school would remain inequitable even as rhetoric about equal opportunity continued and strengthened during the 1960s. Currently, the rhetoric of No Child Left Behind—demanding that all students be "proficient" by 2014 and that racial and ethnic achievement gaps be eliminated—far outruns the reality, with NCLB so far having little detectible effect on either levels of test scores or variation in outcomes (Cohen 2009; Fuller et al. 2007). Ever since Horace Mann declared that public schools were "the great equalizer of the conditions of men," it has been popular to claim equity for public schooling but much harder to do anything about it.

- The dilemma of standards: The history of the high school has been one of periodic efforts to enhance rigor and standards. The Committee of Ten articulated one concept of rigor, represented by the academic curriculum. Those protesting the banalities of life adjustment education denounced the decline of these standards and, like the advocates of science and math after the Sputnik crisis, articulated an idea of rigor represented by a conventional academic curriculum. *A Nation at Risk* and its promotion of new basics more or less repeated this call for standards. Recently, a new wave of reports has condemned low standards in high schools, exemplified by the work of the American Diploma Project and its call to "restore value" to the high school diploma, and by the New Commission on the Skills of the American Workforce. Two ideas about rigor dominate: test-based rigor, requiring higher scores on conventional tests; and course-based rigor, requiring more demanding courses (such as algebra II and AP or International Baccalaureate courses). However, these conventional academic standards neglect other potential approaches: depth rather than superficial breadth and "coverage"; and more sophisticated levels of understanding, including such "higher-order skills" as problem-formulation and solving, analytic and synthetic abilities, the ability to apply learning to unfamiliar settings, and the ability to integrate learning across different subjects. Ultimately, the arguments for rigor call for high schools to do a better job of college preparation for all students, in ways reminiscent of the Committee of Ten (Grubb and Oakes 2007). But at the same time that we lack any different ideas about rigor, observations of classrooms clarify how little most high schools demand of most of their students, defined either by conventional concepts of rigor or by alternative concepts (Cohen 2009; Powell, Farrar, and Cohen 1985).

- The role of outside activities: Most reports about high schools have treated them as self-contained institutions, where the curriculum (and to a lesser extent extracurricular activities) provide all the education that adolescents would receive. Periodically, however, reformers have criticized high schools for being overly insular, denying students the advantages of learning in settings outside the high school. In experiments of the 1930s, a number of colleges agreed to relax their academic admissions standards. Nearly all of the thirty high school that participated developed internships programs outside the schools (*Thirty Schools* 1943)—some vocational, though most of them oriented to civic participation (as service learning is today). In the 1970s, several commission reports critiqued the high school for isolating students from adult life. Aside from a few examples of experienced-based career education, there was little response to these reports. In the early 1990s, yet another wave of interest in the German apprenticeship system, with its substantial periods of work-based learning, developed (Hamilton 1990). The School-to-Work Opportunity Act of 1994 emerged from this discussion, with its provisions for work-based internships. However, the results were disappointing, to say the least: most high schools used federal funding to support conventional guidance and counseling, rather than developing new internship programs (Hershey et al. 1998; Stull 2003). At the same time, service learning developed, providing students internship experiences in public organizations and community-based organizations dedicated to civic improvement. But despite widespread support for the civic goals of education, there appear to be relatively few service learning placements—certainly no more than work-based internships.

Consistently, then, critics of the insular high school have called for incorporating learning in settings outside the high school, either in occupational settings or in civic organizations. However, the responses have been both inadequate and short-lived. One problem has been the lack of strong employer and union support, which is a necessary component of the apprenticeship systems in German-speaking countries. But another consistent problem has been the difficulty of articulating the conventional academic curriculum with either work-based learning or service learning. Until the curriculum of the high school changes, the likelihood of integrating out-of-school learning with school-based learning seems remote.

- The uneasy relationship with postsecondary education: For much of its history since 1890, the high school's relationship to college and university has been contested. In the era of the academies, students might enroll in college without having completed an academy program; there were no fixed college admissions standards as we know them today. As public high schools took over from academies, they became prerequisites for college admissions, and indeed the Committee of Ten was intended to standardize the high school curriculum so that colleges could count on certain preparation—what we now might think of as "college readiness." Other forms of standardizing the high school came in the form of Carnegie units—the blocks of time of about fifty minutes—and then standardized tests: the SAT and the ACT. As a result, colleges and universities were often accused of dominating the high school,[9] and for some students high school became only a way of preparing for college (the critique of Paul Goodman 1956). This became increasingly true over the twentieth century, as average levels of formal schooling and the proportion of high school graduates continuing to college both increased.

Currently, with the domination of college for all—the idea that every student needs at least some postsecondary education for personal advancement and economic opportunity—every high school student seems to be trapped in an institution whose sole purpose is preparation for college. The transition between high school and college has become the latest "crisis" in education because many students—and disproportionate proportions of low-income, African American, Latino, and immigrant students—fail to make this transition successfully (Grubb 2008c). From a historical perspective, this is not surprising because only a small proportion of students were ever destined for college (only 20 percent, according to life adjustment ideas), and the transition was never designed to be easy because colleges and universities have always set their admissions standards independently of secondary schools. But for the students who don't complete high school, for the roughly 40 percent of graduates who don't even attempt college, and for the enormous numbers who drop out of both two- and four-year colleges, it remains unclear what high school is for.

- The neglect of instruction: From a historical perspective, there has been remarkably little discussion about the central issues of teaching and learning and about the effectiveness of different approaches to instruction. Of course, John Dewey and the pedagogical progressives developed alternative approaches to teaching after 1900, but their efforts concentrated on elementary schools, with child-centered teaching most common in kindergarten. The experiments of the 1930s also brought some innovation into high schools, with the development of more project-based learning and interdisciplinary coursework and more activities outside the school. But by and large, the teaching innovations that influenced elementary schools, and to lesser extent middle schools, passed by the high school, and high school teaching has remained remarkably unchanged over the past century (Cuban 1993).

These seven issues have no clear resolution—or rather, they have different resolutions in different schools. Sometimes the lack of resolution can be explained by the absence of explicit attention to these issues; the neglect of instruction and the dearth of internships are the most obvious examples. In other cases—the question of purpose, or the dilemma of whether to differentiate the curriculum—there isn't one "right" answer because the possible answers are so value-laden and often so related to class and racial differences. Continuing to think in conventional dichotomies—a vertically differentiated curriculum versus a unitary curriculum, college preparation versus "terminal" vocational preparation with little chance of going on to college—limits choices to those that are unsatisfactory for many students. But reforms that neglect these issues are doomed to failure because they fail to understand—much less to redress—the persistent dilemmas that have made the high school so embattled.

COMMISSIONITIS AND THE HIGH SCHOOL

In addition to battles over the high school itself, another source of critique has come from commission reports urging reform. The commission report is a peculiarly American vehicle for promoting school reform. Unlike government white papers and policy commissions in Europe, commission reports rarely lead in any direct way to legislation or policy changes. But they do summarize public opinion at specific points in time, and they often lead indirectly to reforms. Perhaps the clearest example is *A Nation at Risk* (1983), which has sparked almost three decades of reforms. And when commission reports do not lead to reform, they often highlight simmering problems that will not disappear without some direct attention.

Commission reports and their rhetoric of crisis[10] have been prominent in the history of high schools, of course. The report of the Committee of Ten, various reports supporting the development of vocational education, the *Cardinal Principles of Secondary Education,* the Prosser resolution and the declamations of the life adjustment movement, and the reports of the 1970s critiquing the isolation of high schools from daily life have already been mentioned. These documents have partly represented positions about what the high school should be and have partly outlined reforms that (according to their authors) should take place. During the 1980s, another round of critiques charged that the high school curriculum was superficial and fragmented, that schools were inequitable because of various forms of tracking and the resulting curricular differentiations, and that schools were too large and impersonal.[11] There has been another surge of reports since 2004, with at least a dozen appearing that year and even more since then.[12]

It's sometimes difficult to articulate the themes of these reports because they overlap with one another, and many of them offer only garden-variety recommendations, such as strengthening the quality of teaching, linking schools to communities, and engaging all students. Similarly, there's a great deal of familiar rhetoric about success for all students, the need for strong leaders, and the power of learning communities—though much less about how to create such success, leaders, and communities. Reports with such urgent titles as *Crisis or Possibility?* are saturated with purple prose ("High school is the Waterloo of the current round of school reform") and exaggeration ("Nothing is more important to the welfare of this society and its students than the reinvention of the American High School"), while practical strategies are notably absent.[13]

From the thicket of commission reports—what one commentator during the 1980s called "commissionitis"—at least five themes emerge. One, not surprisingly, is that *the high school curriculum, and particularly the conventional college-prep curriculum, is boring, irrelevant for many, incoherent, and poorly taught.* The conventional curriculum, an amalgam of college entrance requirements, has been critiqued for lacking any focus or coherence; others note that it is irrelevant for many who won't or don't want to go to competitive colleges.[14] A related problem is the disjunction between the academic character of the standard curriculum and the essentially vocational orientation of most students, including college-bound students who understand college as professional preparation (Grubb and Lazerson 2004). And when high school is only a mechanism for getting into college, nothing of intrinsic importance takes place during the four long years of high school; as Paul Goodman (1956, 41) said several decades ago: "If there is nothing worthwhile, it is hard to do anything at all."

The problems with mediocre instruction have often been expressed as problems with the motivation and engagement of students, but these in turn are linked to instructional approaches and curricular choices. The National Research Council's Committee on Increasing High School Students' Engagement and Motivation to Learn (2004) developed several recommendations for creating engaging schools:

1. *Students are more likely to be motivated in programs with close adult-student relationships.*
2. *Students' engagement increases where they have some autonomy in selecting tasks and methods and where they can construct meaning, engage in sense-making on their own, and play an active role in learning.*
3. *Motivation and engagement are enhanced in well-structured educational environments, with clear purposes.*
4. *Motivation is enhanced in settings with a challenging curriculum, high expectations, and a strong emphasis on achievement.*
5. *Motivation and engagement are enhanced when students have multiple paths to competence.*
6. *Helping students develop education and career pathways can enhance their understanding of school and its relation to future goals.*

But most high school teaching doesn't look like this. Other than the recommendation for challenging programs, none of these precepts are met in conventional high school teaching nor with the traditional methods of teaching academic subjects. The obvious implication is that overcoming the basic problem of motivation and engagement requires substantial changes in both curriculum and approaches to instruction, rather than additional exhortations for students to take high school more seriously.

A second theme of many reports concerns *equity*. Everyone agrees that dropout rates are atrociously high, affecting 20–30 percent of students, with much higher rates for Latinos especially and also for African American students. The qualitative literature clarifies that dropping out is a lengthy process, starting as early as third or fourth grade as some students experience failure, poor relations with teachers, and sometimes racial prejudice or misunderstanding, and then begin to draw away from schooling. Solutions in high schools may therefore be too late, but common proposals include various interventions for ninth graders who are behind grade level (many of the interventions small-scale, fragmented, and poorly planned); better personal relations (again); smaller schools (again); alternative curricula (again); improved instructional methods (again); various support services; and an endless array of such specific reforms as Puente, ASPIRE schools, and First Things First. Overall, however, dropout rates haven't improved much since the 1950s, and the current climate of accountability and exit exams is likely to make things worse.

A related critique is that high schools engage in too much inequitable tracking and sorting. Although some traditional tracking systems related to vocational education have largely vanished, and de-tracking is all the rage following Jeannie Oakes (1985), newer informal mechanisms of tracking (Lucas 1999) exist. Tracking at the upper end in honors and AP courses, the continuation of the general education track, practices of remediation when students enter high school below grade level, and "push out" to continuation schools and alternative education all constitute other forms of tracking. The solutions include renewed efforts at de-tracking, pathways and other schools-within-schools that incorporate wider varieties of students, open enrollment in honors and AP courses, and college outreach programs to identify and work with promising students.

A third area, usually from a different group of critics—on the educational right instead of the educational left—expresses *the need for standards and rigor.* As I mentioned above, the only concept of rigor we have in this country is a conventional academic standard, expressed either as course rigor—taking more advanced academic courses—or test rigor, performing better on standardized tests. Advocates for standards have consistently lamented the supposed decline of standards in high schools; as Bill Gates said:

> America's high schools are obsolete.... Today, only one-third of our students graduate from high school ready for college, work, and citizenship. The other two-thirds, most of them low-income and minority students, are tracked into courses that won't ever get them ready for college or prepare them for a family-wage job ... This isn't an accident or a flaw in the system; it is the system.... Once we realize that we are keeping low-income and minority kids out of rigorous courses, there can be only two arguments for keeping it that way: either we think they can't learn, or we think they're not worth teaching. The first argument is factually wrong; the second is morally wrong.[15]

The common response insists on higher standards and increased rigor for all students as a counter to what George W. Bush infamously called "the soft bigotry of low expectations." All states have established minimum graduation requirements, and they are slowly increasing them; twenty-five states police their standards through exit exams—though these exams are not necessarily closely connected to state standards. The two most prominent organizations advocating standards propose adding to these examinations. The American Diploma Project supports specific academic courses that include new, standards-aligned assessments, as well as more rigorous exit exams. The New Commission on the Skills of the American Workforce proposes to embed its standards in two board examinations, one at the end of tenth grade, and the second at the level of AP courses or the International Baccalaureate (IB) program. But, as with most systems of accountability—including state accountability and NCLB—these organizations focus their efforts on devising tests to drive standards higher, not on improving teacher capacity through improved preparation so that teachers (and instructional leaders) can develop their own standards and teach accordingly.

A fourth critique is that *the personal relationships in high schools are dreadful,* especially in urban high schools (see also Payne 2008). One complaint is that high schools are so large that teachers cannot know students well; students feel anonymous, unknown, and uncared for. The main antidote has been the proposal for small high schools, or schools-within-schools, where presumably teachers can know students better. (A related view is that students in smaller settings cannot "hide out" or avoid real work.) Another complaint, from teachers and some leaders, is that their authority, largely unquestioned in the nineteenth and early twentieth century,[16] has been undermined by movements for student rights, by more student-centered teaching, and by the general decline in adult authority after the 1950s. Teachers now have to earn their authority, and one element is the admonition that teachers must treat students with dignity and respect, contrary to the observation—particularly prominent in the ethnographic literature about African American and Latino students—of how badly students are sometimes treated. Everyone now agrees that teachers and leaders must be selected in part based on such personal attributes as caring and genuine empathy for adolescents, but how that gets put into practice is unclear. The various high school reports are largely silent about how school systems might either develop more caring and respectful teachers through professional development or improve the conditions of teaching so that teachers are not so stressed. And the racial/ethnic dimensions of teacher-student interactions are simply missing from these high school reports, even though some aspects of the "crisis"—particularly the high dropout rate and the various achievement gaps in test scores—are powerfully related to race and ethnicity.

A more complete view acknowledges that relationships among students are also often poor (Payne 2008): many students are angry, brittle, and quick to explode at fellow students as well as teachers, sometimes because of the conditions of their lives outside of schools but also because of treatment within schools. Often, the "solution" is some kind of enhanced discipline, with rules for treating other students with respect; but such rules clearly don't work, don't help students develop their own moral codes, and instead lead to battles between students and adults about the fairness of the rules.[17] There have been some efforts to develop high schools as moral communities, where students participate in creating and adjudicating rules, but they seem to be few and far between.

A fifth critique is that *high schools are places of captivity*, stressing order and containment over exploration and learning—precisely at the moment in their lives when students are struggling to express their independence.[18] This critique has emerged from students themselves (Cushman and Students 2003) and is implicit in the freedom many students celebrate when they get to college. The structure of classes meeting every day, the bell schedule, the requirements of being in a confined space, and the relative lack of choice within the conventional college prep curriculum are all part of the sense of captivity.

The solutions have been to recommend greater flexibility in scheduling (National Association of Secondary School Principals, *Breaking Ranks I* and *II*, recommending "the look and feel of college"), but aside from creating double periods and a few experiments with college-like schedules—classes meeting on alternative days, for example—this hasn't gone very far. And no doubt many educators and parents fear that greater freedom would result in chaos and misbehavior. The idea of contingent freedom—for example, having ninth graders attend on conventional schedules, followed by increasing freedom for students whose diligence and accomplishments merit it—has never been proposed, to my knowledge. An alternative solution has been simply to truncate high school and get students into college earlier through dual enrollment programs—the California High School Proficiency Exam giving students diplomas as early as age sixteen—and related proposals, such as Marc Tucker's (2004) first gateway, an exam allowing entrance into the freshman year of "the bottom tier of state higher education institutions," presumably community colleges and regional universities or state colleges. Some of these look like proposals to substitute institutions of greater variety and freedom for high schools.

A broader analysis of the captivity of the high school might contrast the restrictions of school with the greater freedoms of adolescents outside of school. The various high school reports almost never mention life outside school, but the development of a rich youth culture implies a greater variety of lifestyles and roles, many employment opportunities (even if low quality), more discretionary spending, sexual freedom, freedom to experiment with drugs and alcohol and music, a culture of cool that supports resistance to convention, and an ethic of fun that makes schoolwork even more tedious. The contrast between the excitement and freedom of real life outside high school versus the rigidity and constraint of school life must have some influence, though none of these high school reports mention this. My own view is that schools can't compete with Disney culture on the dimension of fun, and the attempt to enhance students' interests with sports and cheerleading and drama club doesn't help with their interest in the academic component of school. That can only be addressed by giving students academic activities that are serious and intrinsically meaningful and by providing teaching that follows the precepts of motivation and identification noted above, in place of conventional dreary academic instruction—returning us to the problems with boring and irrelevant instruction already noted.

A few other themes emerge with less frequency in recent commission reports. Some have complained about the lack of support services, including health and mental health services. Some have called for better articulation of high school and postsecondary education—for example, through P-16 commissions that better articulate secondary and postsecondary education—though with relatively few suggestions about what needs to change in high schools to prepare students for college-level work.

Finally, several high school reports have mentioned the importance of leadership (Alliance for Excellent Education 2004; *Breaking Ranks I* and *II*). But—like the literature on leadership mentioned in the introduction—they do not articulate how leadership challenges are different in high schools from those in elementary and middle schools or what should be done to prepare high school leaders differently.

Several high school reports have mentioned the importance of leadership, but they do not articulate how leadership challenges are different in high schools from those in elementary and middle schools.

Even a brief look at recent commission reports suggests an enormous agenda for change. However, some of the recommendations are contradictory; for example, the movement for higher standards and more conventional testing would—in the absence of special attention to instruction—reinforce conventional teaching and thereby exacerbate the boredom and irrelevance of high schools. Advocacy of a unitary purpose for the high school, particularly college for all, contradicts the efforts of reformers to develop more motivating programs whose connections to adult life are clearer. Some critiques—such as the lack of support services—extend the idea of the high school as encompassing a variety of intellectual and nonintellectual development, while others cling to the Committee of Ten and its insistence on a rigidly academic curriculum drawn from the nineteenth century, though now in the twenty-first century. Many recommendations—calls for more flexible scheduling, the reforms that get students outside schools in alternative learning arrangements, efforts to create alternative pathways, the issues of changing pedagogy, the attempt to increase standards and rigor—have emerged over and over again, but with little sustained progress. So we seem to lament the "crisis" of the high school again, again, and again, making little progress despite the profusion of alternative visions.

Finally, the historical dilemmas of the high school developed in the previous section and the recent complaints in commission reports are not completely consistent with one another. To be sure, the neglect of instruction arises in both, as do equity and the question of standards and rigor. The historical issue of outside activities, such as work-based learning, and the complaints about schools as places of captivity are quite congruent with one another. The historically contested relationship with postsecondary education shows up in the current angst about the transition from high school to college, the inequity of this transition, and the emphasis on "college readiness." But the historical issues of purpose and differentiation—often linked to one another—are not particularly prominent in recent commission reports, and conversely the personal relationships, "classroom management," and the overall climate of the school is more prominent in recent reports than in historical debates. Together, the historical dilemmas and the more recent complaints provide a long list of challenges for reshaping high schools—not always consistent with one another, to be sure, but enough to provide a substantial agenda for reform.

THE PROMISE OF MULTIPLE PATHWAYS

In response to the constant "crisis" of the high school, advocates have proposed many reforms—some small and marginal, some challenging the conventional high school in more substantial ways. Each of these reforms addresses some of the complaints about the high school in recent commission reports, and they take particular stands on the century-long dilemmas of high schools. One of the most prominent, backed by enormous sums from the Gates Foundation, has been the movement for smaller high schools or schools-within-schools. Presumably these correct the anomic conditions in high schools where teachers don't know their students, and students don't know one another. But size by itself cannot address the question of purpose and may not improve the state of equity if, for example, differences *among* small schools develop. Unless it is accompanied by other reforms, small size does not confront the issue of standards, or the neglect of instruction, or the relationship to postsecondary education and outside activities. As we will see in chapter 3, small size may *facilitate* some of these other reforms, but it is insufficient by itself to address most dilemmas of the high school. Indeed, the Gates Foundation abandoned its support for small schools rather abruptly, finding they had not increased test scores quickly enough.[19]

Another widespread reform has been the development of early college high schools (ECHS), where high schools develop a "college-going culture" and stress preparation for college over everything else. Students usually take some courses on a college campus, enabling them to earn up to two years of college credit while in high school. An ECHS is most obviously a way of reducing dropouts and enhancing the equity of access to college; secondarily, it is intended to enhance rigor by adhering to college standards. The early evaluations appear to be relatively positive in terms of attendance, state proficiency exams, and creating positive environments. But the ECHS model has made decisions about the historical dilemmas of high schools that can't please everyone: it focuses on the sole purpose of preparing for college, the curriculum is dominated by the conventional courses of the Committee of Ten, it does not incorporate outside activities except conventional trips to colleges, and it has largely ignored the improvement of instruction and the changes that are necessary to enhance motivation and engagement (Berger et al. 2007). Compared to the watered-down tracks of the comprehensive high school—the general track, the remedial track, and the few leftover traditional vocational tracks—the ECHS is surely an improvement, but it is hardly a mechanism for moving beyond the high school of 1894.

Other reforms respond to specific dilemmas. The Talent Development High School started as a way of introducing multiple pathways, but it quickly began to emphasize a ninth-grade academy as a way of helping students who are far behind grade-level norms. It has been somewhat successful (Kemple, Herlihy, and Smith 2005), but other than this practice, the model leaves the conventional high school in place, with its conventional instruction, a traditional academic focus, and the lack of motivation and engagement unchallenged. First Things First is also an attempt to improve completion rates in high schools and thereby address equity problems; it operates by changing instruction through intense staff development and enriched language and math curricula and through greater support for students in small learning communities and a system of family advocates. Because it addresses both the quality of instruction and the personalization of the school, it is one of the few reforms to improve *both* progress through high school *and* learning (Quint et al. 2005). But many other aspects of the comprehensive high school remain unchanged, including its solely academic purpose, its isolation from the world outside, and many of the precepts of motivation and engagement. Back to basics schools with presumably high standards, which can be found among charter schools and private schools, simply replicate the high school of 1894, ignoring most issues of the last century and the critiques of recent years.

In contrast, multiple pathways are attractive reforms in part because they address many more of the historical dilemmas and recent complaints about high schools. Pathways go by many different names—majors, theme-based approaches, "college and careers," sometimes school-to-work programs, "linked learning"[20]—and they can take many specific forms, as we will see in chapter 3. (Some reforms calling themselves "multiple pathways" have little to do with the theme-based approaches for high schools I emphasize here; after all, the word "pathway" is quite generic.[21]) Whatever their names, their distinctive feature is that they replace the standard curriculum of 1894 with coursework and external activities (like internships) focused either on broadly occupational themes (such as business, health occupations, biotechnology, or information technology) or on such nonoccupational themes as the environment, international developments, or social justice. Where schools choose broadly occupational themes, the goals of "college *and* careers"—preparing *either* for college, *or* for employment after high school, *or* for the combination of employment and further education that has become so common—expand the purpose of high school beyond college for all and strengthen the "relevance" of its coursework because it is oriented to a broad area of economic and social importance. Students normally take courses in a pathway for two, three, or four years of high school. Choosing a specific pathway among *multiple* pathways offered in a school or district usually involves guidance and counseling that allow students to see the future consequences of current choices. The small size of most pathways—in our sample, they ranged from eighty to four hundred students, in contrast to high schools of between two thousand and four thousand students—facilitates certain methods of improving instruction, reduces the anonymity associated with most high schools, and helps improve personal relationships, as we will see in chapter 3; the adoption of a theme supports collaboration and integration across subjects. Finally, most pathways have tried to create internships, work-based learning, and service learning opportunities in placements related to the pathway theme, and these external activities are therefore consistent with the pathway curriculum in a way that is not possible for the conventional academic curriculum.

Multiple pathways are attractive reforms in part because they address many more of the historical dilemmas and recent complaints about high schools.

Multiple pathways therefore respond to many of the recent criticisms about high schools. They offer a clear sense of purpose related to the theme instead of the diffuse purposes of the Shopping Mall High School. They provide ways for making the curriculum exciting and relevant by tying it to issues of substantial importance in the world outside the high school—issues that students themselves have chosen to address. If they are correctly designed, with roughly equivalent status among pathways and all allowing access to both college and career, they promise to "give an equal opportunity to all to prepare for their life work" (Oakes and Saunders 2008, 5) at the same time that they lead to college as well. In effect, pathways create horizontal tracking where students choose different but equivalent pathways depending on their interests—though the challenges of making pathways truly equivalent are substantial, as I clarify in chapter 3. As long as the connections to college are not forgotten—and all the pathways we visited made sure that their courses were eligible for college admissions—they cannot sink back into traditional vocational education, with its "terminal" curriculum providing no access to college. Pathways also offer the possibility of developing new standards and rigor, related not to the nineteenth-century progression of academic subjects but to mastery of cognitive requirements and non-cognitive abilities—sometimes manual dexterity, sometimes the ability to work in teams, sometimes visual abilities—appropriate to broad occupational and social areas (as I will elaborate in chapter 3). In most ways, then, they create strong alternatives to the comprehensive high school.

Indeed, some districts have adopted pathways precisely because their comprehensive high schools have worked poorly. In one district we visited, and in several other districts across the country, large, dysfunctional, comprehensive high schools have been broken into small learning communities or autonomous small schools, most of which have a theme.[22] This is a different form of "reconstitution" from those championed by the U.S. Department of Education. It creates multiple pathways on one school site, each able to focus on a different theme, each with a different curriculum, each attracting students (and teachers) with different interests, each able to capitalize on the advantages of small size.

To be sure, just as small size does not guarantee that certain changes take place, restructuring a high school into pathways does not guarantee that instruction improves or that the changes are equitable—particularly if multiple pathways recreate vertical tracking—or that pathways are able to find work-based learning or service learning for their students. When I return to the special challenges of pathways in chapter 3, therefore, I will clarify the dimensions of pathways that still need emphasis, even if their structure accomplishes some of the reforms called for in recent reports.

Finally, any such substantial reform as multiple pathways also changes the demands on teachers, leaders, and district officials. As will become clear in chapter 3, teachers in pathway programs need to be able to work in ways different from their discipline-bound peers in conventional high schools—better able to coordinate their content with other courses; able to teach with a variety of approaches, including problem- and project-based learning; and willing to collaborate with other teachers in overseeing students. Leaders, including the teacher-leaders who are often the heads of individual pathways, face not only the general challenges of high schools—the subject of chapter 2—but an additional set of challenges specific to pathways—the subject of chapter 3. And just as pathways require new forms of teacher preparation—with a promising model now being developed in San Diego, described in chapter 3—so too the preparation of leaders needs to change, the subject of chapter 4. Finally, if pathways are to survive as a distinct alternative to the comprehensive high school, they require certain district support, the subject of chapter 5.

There are, then, two sets of challenges for leadership not widely recognized: those associated with high schools in general, and those associated with pathways in particular. These are in addition to the dimensions of strong leadership that are consistent across different levels of the K-12 system—indeed, across all educational settings. This book assumes that leaders have mastered them as well as—not instead of—the special capacities required in high schools and in pathways. For me, and for the Principal Leadership Institute, these include at least the following:

- The centrality of all leaders serving as *instructional* leaders, able to direct all other administrative activities (such as budgeting, hiring and dismissal, and school procedures and policies) toward the improvement of instruction.
- The crucial role of *distributed leadership*, implying more active roles for teacher-leaders and teachers (and often students and parents) to play in the direction of a school through various committees and school-site councils (Spillane 2006; Spillane and Diamond 2007).[23] This is a clear alternative to the conventional top-down hierarchical model of schools where the principal directs the activities of teachers, and it appears to be a prerequisite for schools to reform themselves through collective action.
- The role of *school reformer and problem-solver*, first diagnosing what is going right and wrong within a school; then being able to use available data to inform themselves of potential problems; becoming knowledgeable about alternative approaches to reform, especially those interventions that help low-performing students; understanding which resources are effective in enhancing outcomes, which are ineffective, and what effective resources cost in terms of money and time, collaboration, and leadership attention; being able to lead faculty in putting reforms in place; and finally being willing to evaluate

reforms honestly, to disentangle what works from what doesn't as a precondition to continuing reform efforts.

- The role of *advocate for all students and for social justice,* incorporating different dimensions of equity in all their complexity. In urban schools, this means recognizing the roles of race, ethnicity, class, and immigrant or language status in shaping students and teachers' reactions to students; being able to carry on "courageous conversations" with faculty about race, ethnicity, and the other tough topics of American education; and knowing about the educational and noneducational strategies for improving outcomes among the lowest-performing students, including such approaches as culturally relevant pedagogy, multicultural education, contrastive analysis and code-switching, and other ways of addressing head-on the dilemmas of race and ethnicity. I will return to the racial and ethnic dimension of inequality near the end of chapter 2.

There are, of course, oceans of words written about school leadership, and there are hundreds of leadership preparation programs across the country. But this writing and these activities are usually generic and say almost nothing about high schools specifically. The rest of this book is devoted to the special challenges for leadership in high schools and then in multiple pathways—challenges that have so far generated only trickles of attention.

QUESTIONS FOR CHAPTER 1

1. From the first section of chapter 1, on the history of the high school:

What conflicts in your school, community, district, or state have reflected the implicit debate between the Committee of Ten, with its insistence on a conventional academic high school, and the *Cardinal Principles* of 1917, with its idea of a broader array of purposes and subjects?

2. On the subject of what "skills" students should master:

The Committee of Ten had one list of skills; the *Cardinal Principles* another; life adjustment a third; the battle after Sputnik stressed math and science; *A Nation at Risk* stressed the new basics; the SCANS report had a broader array of skills, including some that are now called "higher-order skills" or the "skills of the twenty-first century."

In your state, district, or school, what are the debates (plural) over skills? Make sure to consider implicit debates—for example, embedded in state exams, graduation standards, or exit exams—as well as explicit debates over the curriculum.

3. What are the discussions in your community over standards and rigor, and how is rigor defined?

4. What kinds of differentiation or tracking among students takes place in your high schools? What are the mechanisms (for example, tests, grades, student choice, or teacher recommendations) that determine who gets into what track?

Chapter 2

"You Can't Do It All"

The Special Conditions of High School Leadership

High schools are different from middle and elementary schools in many obvious ways—their size, the complexity of their course offerings, the age of their students, and the variety of extracurricular activities, to name a few. One principal noted that

> It's not a mystery. High school students—teenagers—are different than children ... it's the social, the emotional, the fact that they're closer to adulthood—what kind of issues do adolescents have to face that the high school itself becomes involved with?

This doesn't automatically mean that leadership challenges are different. All leaders—principals, assistant principals, teacher-leaders, district leaders—have to confront similar issues: how to identify and solve problems, whether to follow older patterns of hierarchical authority or to adopt the more collegial patterns of distributed leadership, how to gain the trust of a community of teachers and other leaders, how to improve the quality of instruction for those who hope to be instructional leaders, and how to enhance equity in these inequitable institutions. Much of the stuff of leadership—the teachings of principal preparation programs, the huge literature on school leadership—remains the same at all levels.

But when we asked our forty-eight respondents to tell us about the special leadership dimensions of high schools compared to elementary and middle schools, the challenges tumbled out. Some come from the structure of the high school; others emerge from the location of high school at the juncture of K-12 education and postsecondary alternatives, either work or further schooling; and some come from the accretions of extracurricular activities and the development of youth culture. These are challenges that virtually all high schools—and the districts that (presumably) support them—need to confront, no matter what approach to reform and improvement they take. And if leadership is crucial to the success and equity of schools, as most educators now believe, the failure to confront these special challenges directly—in most leadership programs (the subject of chapter 4), in district policies (in chapter 5), and in the enormous literature on leadership—may help explain why high schools have been so difficult to reform.

This chapter raises nine special challenges in high schools, some obvious—their larger size and greater complexity—and some of them still somewhat baffling, especially the difficulty of improving instruction. Of course, not every principal or district leader mentioned all of them, and a few—such as policies to address racial and ethnic differences directly—were rarely mentioned and seem important only because of overwhelming evidence from other sources (including my own research). But these nine issues provide a kind of catalogue summarizing the differences between high schools and other levels of schooling that merit special attention.

THE SIZE AND COMPLEXITY OF HIGH SCHOOLS

Virtually every individual mentioned the larger size and the greater complexity of high schools compared with elementary and middle schools. The size comes, obviously, from greater numbers of students, between fifteen hundred and four thousand in our sample. Even though a movement for small schools has been underway at least since the 1990s—Deborah Meier's 1995 book on Central Park East is often cited as an early manifesto—many high schools are still relatively enormous institutions.

Now, it's quite obvious and somewhat banal to say that high schools are larger and more complex. The difficult question is precisely how these characteristics affect leadership and how such challenges might be overcome, and to do this we need to understand the different dimensions of size and complexity. The issue of size is relatively clear: it inhibits the ability of leaders to know many individual students, and conversely students usually don't know their teachers or counselors well. The conditions for a student-centered environment (including student-centered teaching) are poor when individual teachers face 160–180 students in a day. In response, a number of schools have adopted houses or advisories or the equivalent of homerooms to create some smaller units within a large school to facilitate some adult's knowing each student well. The problem is that these houses and advisories often have no clear purpose—unlike pathways—and tend to drift apart.

It's quite obvious and somewhat banal to say that high schools are larger and more complex. The difficult question is precisely how these characteristics affect leadership and how such challenges might be overcome.

Large size also seriously limits the ability of leaders to know all the staff. One specialist in charge of instructional improvement complained that "with eighty teachers and one of me, where do you start and how do you prioritize? ... In a school of eighty it's hard to make sure that everyone attends [professional development], to do follow-up." Another principal in an even larger school would have sniffed at her problem: "We had 170 teachers, so we didn't have really close relationships." Just as the conditions for a student-centered environment are poor, the conditions for professional learning communities—for groupings of teachers (such as for ninth-grade teachers or math teachers) who might be able to resolve problems together—are poor in large high schools.[1] Particularly in urban schools with high teacher turnover and many inexperienced teachers, the sheer size of the teaching staff is sure to create special problems:

> Specifically in urban schools, we have a lot of teachers who are new, who are on preliminary credentials; they have very little experience, they have very little background knowledge . . . you're not going to find just one person who needs a lot of help; you're going to find five people.

Furthermore, while states may have induction programs to support inexperienced teachers—in California, the Beginning Teachers Support Program, or BTSA—"that's not as strong as it needs to be," so mentoring new teachers falls on the instructional specialist (or on literacy coaches, math coaches, or master teachers). The obvious "solution"—a larger number of specialists, to reduce the ratio from 80:1 to something reasonable like 25:1—is impossible in states under fiscal constraints, so the sheer size of the staff, and of new teachers needing more support, becomes overwhelming. Under these conditions, professional development to enhance the instructional capacity of teachers becomes much more difficult.

The complexity of high schools comes partly from the greater variety of courses and academic activities: a greater range of courses covering more subjects than in middle school, the complexity of the master schedule, interventions of many kinds to help students who are behind, course requirements for graduation, course requirements for four-year colleges (called the a–g requirements in California), and high school exit exams in about half the states. One principal noted that "there's simply more to do," and then mentioned the exit exam—"kids have to be prepared for it, and you have to manage it"; accreditation visits, "which are really, incredibly time-consuming"; athletics—"nothing to do with academic student achievement, but a huge time drain—it's horrible, and . . . that takes people away from paying attention to instruction"; preparing kids for college; managing transcripts—and "none of it has to do with actual classroom practice." So leaders get pulled in many different directions. Here's an assistant principal in charge of several pathways describing her day:

> If I was to keep a diary of the interactions I have with students and teachers during the day—like going from a drug overdose to then a teacher layoff, to then a negative evaluation [of a teacher], to then a parent conference of the 504 [a special education procedure] that was horrible because I had not communicated with them, then to the technology issue of the system blowing up for all the teachers. That day feels so much more complex to me than an elementary school day.

Some of the complexity comes from the nonacademic elements we associate with the traditional comprehensive high school. As the principal of a small, autonomous high school noted, "[Leadership] is hard because we are so entrenched in the traditional view of high school in terms of athletics and the traditional idea of how we spend our time and money"—on extracurricular activities; sports, including Friday night football and Saturday basketball; such related activities as cheerleading and band; and proms and other social events ("proms are huge in this school!"). As a former high school assistant principal noted,

> We're there at all the dances, we're there at all the after-school activities. We have to organize assemblies with the teachers. We have to make sure that the police are there. It's not doable. If you want to have a family, it's not doable in high school at all with that amount of school activities.

Another said,

> You have no idea what the time sink is with the athletics piece—it has nothing to do with the primary mission. I mean, it does for the connectedness to school, don't get me wrong—that was my connection to school when I was growing up, so I'm not saying it's not important. But you don't realize when you're a classroom teacher what a time sink that becomes, from the supervision piece to the parent complaints to the drama that surrounds sports, cheer programs, and all that business.

She was referring to the ambiguous effects of the extracurricular side of the traditional high school. On the one hand, participation enhances students' sense of belonging—"that was my connection to school"—and progress through high school;[2] it is, after all, what many graduates remember most about high schools. On the other hand, it distracts students from an academic culture—it's "nothing to do with academic student achievement." For *leaders,* the need to adjudicate disputes over extracurricular activities, to attend endless games and proms and musical events "sunup to sundown and beyond," places additional demands on their time, demands that detract from their other responsibilities.

The complexity also comes, in many high schools, from the greater variety of students. Elementary schools are much smaller, often based on neighborhoods, and in such cases relatively homogeneous. Middle schools gather students from several elementary schools and become somewhat more varied. But high schools incorporate students from several middle schools, particularly in urban areas, and therefore the variety of students becomes larger[3]—the variety of races and ethnicities, the variety of family backgrounds, and the variety of academic achievement.[4] As one principal noted,

> The big challenge at the high school level is you have this huge range. You literally have kids that are going right into the UCs [University of California school system] or tier-one universities, and then you have students who come in at two grade levels below in English and math assessments, and perhaps even have been socially promoted from middle school. So you have this huge range of abilities upon entering ninth grade, and your goal is to serve all of the students well, and to make sure that all of the students receive a very high education that's going to keep doors open to them beyond high school.

Part of the challenge as an instructional leader is to get teachers to teach the variety of students, rather than ignoring some of them: "What's been a challenge is to get my staff to stop riding the aggregate [teaching to the middle of the class], and to not just write off the bottom quintile, and to say that we need to be committed to those kids." And not only is there a greater variety of class and racial backgrounds, students in high schools also have lived with the effects of their families for longer periods of time. The principal of a small school-within-a-school, himself African American and enormously supportive of his largely black students, noted:

> They continue to have the same type of family dynamics and social ills adversely affecting their home situation—by the time we get them they've been dealing with that stuff for sixteen years. So they're experts at disorganization, they're experts at all the social ills ... and by the time they get here it's extremely difficult to get the kids focused.... Many of them lack the motivation, and now they're big enough and bad enough that if they don't want to come, they don't come.
>
> Scheduling with an enormous variety of specific needs can be a nightmare; as one assistant principal described, it, "the other thing that is important is understanding the complexity of a school that has a course of study for kids at every skill set ... In my schools we have seven ELD [English-language development]students who are ready to transition into sheltered classes, but we cannot financially support a class for seven kids. So how do you meet their unique needs and not short-change them? ... And it also happens at the other end, with

> some of our AP kids: we may have forty-two students who qualify, too many for one class but too few for two, so who gets to go, or where else do you short-change your master schedule? Those are our deepest conflict questions, to ask all the time. Kids don't fall into neat little packets when they show up at your doorstep.

So principals have to worry not only about college prep programs, or about AP and IB courses, but also about remedial courses and intervention programs for those who are still reading at the elementary school level.

Sometimes the complexity of a school can be the fault of leadership, when principals take on too many small programs as a way of getting resources into a school, but resulting in a lack of coherence and in too many demands on the principals' time. This is a particular issue for high schools with economically disadvantaged students because many community-based organizations and foundations eager to support schools offer their services—but principals who know their students need additional resources are not always able to decide which partnerships are most effective. One district official who had just visited a school said about the principal:

> He's so immersed in programs that I don't know if he can sort through them. Some schools are so desperate to get things into the school site that you just keep taking them on and layering them up. I think there needs to be some kind of process by which you're choosing particular programs, and not taking every program that comes through your door.... That is a leadership role in how to discern what's best for your students, and not choose everything that flies by like a kid in a candy store.

Others have noted that schools with greater coherence are more effective (Newmann et al. 2001), and schools with too many little programs have often been derided as "Christmas tree schools," with too many shiny baubles on their branches (and more attention to the baubles than to the trunk and branches, the real capacity of teachers and leaders). So one dimension of leadership, and one way to reduce the complexity of high schools, is to concentrate on smaller numbers of effective programs. When I turn to the ninth-grade transition below, this proves to be a specific area in which there seem to be too many ineffective programs in some schools.

There is some consensus that what is lost in the crush of different responsibilities is attention to instruction:

> The priority is going to be to get rid of that horrible teacher and maybe not finishing the evaluations of the non-horrible teacher, who still might need a lot more coaching. But because of the things I'm dealing with, I can only focus a small piece of my time on the instruction.

Other principals agreed that instruction was the first responsibility to go because "you can't do it all," and instructional improvement is less pressing and less dire than responding to angry parents, coping with serious discipline issues, or participating in mandated procedures.[5] Similarly, when accreditation visits and athletics demand attention, it's "nothing to do with academic student achievement, but a huge time drain that takes people away from paying attention to instruction." When we turn to instructional issues below, then, the problem is one of greater instructional challenges, with fewer administrative resources in instructional improvement.

When we turn to instructional issues, the problem is one of greater instructional challenges, with fewer administrative resources in instructional improvement.

So the obvious size and complexity of the high school works in many ways—to undermine the conditions necessary for a student-centered climate, to make it difficult to know all students and staff, to undermine the requirements for professional learning communities, and to increase the demands on leaders in ways that take them away from instructional responsibilities. There have been, to be sure, a variety of approaches to these difficulties. One operates at the individual level: principals in high schools need to be able to set priorities and then stick to them—particularly if they want to be instructional leaders. As one principal noted,

> The elementary school principal actually does it all, and they need to know everything ... At the high school you need to know who to go to, and you very much need to be able to delegate and let go. For example, I tend not to deal with health issues—even a major health issue would be one of my three assistant principals. I tend not to deal with disciplinary issues unless it gets to the level

> of expulsion ... But it is important that a high school principal be a curricular leader and have knowledge of [instructional] strategies.

There are various activities in pre-service and in-service preparation programs that can help principals create and sustain their priorities, and induction programs can provide support for novice administrators who are trying to keep their priorities straight. But recognizing the complexity of demands on high school principals, and what elements (like instruction) are most likely to be neglected, is a necessary first step.

The obvious size and complexity of the high school works in many ways—to undermine the conditions necessary for a student-centered climate, to make it difficult to know all students and staff, to undermine the requirements for professional learning communities, and to increase the demands on leaders in ways that take them away from instructional responsibilities.

Another, more systemic approach has been the movement for small schools, mentioned in chapter 1 and examined again in chapter 3—either by creating smaller, autonomous schools or by breaking up large high schools into schools-within-schools, including multiple pathways. This hasn't made much headway—districts continue to build enormous high schools, as if the small-schools movement had never existed—and the apparently negative experiences of the Gates Foundation with their small-school initiative has clarified that size itself may not be the problem. Alternatively, smaller size may be necessary but not sufficient (NBNS) for improving high schools, and smaller size may need to be accompanied by efforts to use the smaller size to create professional learning communities focused on instruction, to improve instruction in other ways, and to change a school's climate and interpersonal relationships.

Other efforts have tried to reduce the complexity of high schools. In the early days, the Coalition for Essential Schools (now the Coalition for

Effective Schools) tried to strip schools down to their essential elements—a modern version of essentialism, the nineteenth-century doctrine that tried to find the inherent essence of any practice or institution. Most often, this has involved jettisoning peripheral curricula, such as traditional vocational education; reducing the number of electives; or eliminating extracurricular activities to focus on academic content. Some charter schools have done the same, and (as I will describe more completely in chapter 3) some pathways have also taken this road.

In addition, various other solutions have developed that require more resources, or different kinds of positions, in order to cope with complexity. For example, adding instructional specialists to cope with the huge numbers of teachers in a large high school would provide more resources in instructional improvement, at the cost of additional positions. These specialists might, for example, carry out classroom observations that are at the heart of understanding the quality of instruction and then devise the right kind of professional development to improve instruction. In a few high schools, a single principal has been replaced with multiple principals (Grubb and Flessa 2006). In some cases, this arrangement has allowed one principal to "specialize" in instructional improvement, or in student support services, or in another dimension of the principal's complex job that would otherwise be neglected. In other cases, multiple principals have been in charge of separate schools-within-schools, sometimes with a site principal or executive principal.

Another possibility developed by the Wallace Foundation is the school administration manager (SAM), when schools hire individuals to cover managerial roles and free up principals for instructional roles.[6] In some ways, this is not very different from the current practice of constructing leadership teams with one assistant principal in charge of building and administrative tasks, though a SAM might conceivably have different preparation from principals. This is, as with the idea of multiple principals, another way of increasing the resources in leadership. Finally, in chapter 5 I will return to district responsibilities for leadership development and outline many ways in which districts could create more coherent leadership policies to prepare principals better for difficult high school positions.

So there prove to be many ways to combat the size and complexity of the comprehensive high school. As long as the structure of the high school is not sacrosanct, its limitations can be modified in many ways and thereby can make the positions of leaders less "impossible."

HIGH SCHOOLS MATTER MORE (OR AS MUCH)

A substantial majority of our forty-eight respondents noted that high school matters in ways that elementary and middle schools do not. By and large, elementary and middle schools can pass their students on to higher grades, and then to high school—the "social promotion attitude of K-8," one principal described it. Some students may be poorly prepared, but this then becomes a problem for subsequent levels of schooling, where educators have to search for ways—"interventions" or remediation—to help students who have fallen behind. No one ever blames an elementary school for high school dropout rates, but high schools themselves are obvious targets. As one principal noted,

> At a high school, everything matters more, right? In middle school, unfortunately, the attitude persists in some venues that what's happening at middle school doesn't matter that much. There's no transcript of students' grades. And we all know their performance matters, but there is kind of that sense, "You're going to go on to high school almost regardless of how you do here." And so there is some pressure off. At high school, I think of high schools as a springboard for the rest of the student's life, and certainly there are many ways you can bounce from here, but it just seems like it matters a whole lot more.

This is particularly true for low-income students who don't have parents to fall back on; as the principal of a virtually all-black school-within-a-school noted,

> When they leave us, there's no other system that's designed [to help them] ... Once they leave us, they're on their own. So whether they go to fully caring and loving parents or not, they're on their own, unlike when middle schools say, "I'm going to send them up the street to the high school." Elementaries just send them to middle school. We send them out to the world ... and that's a huge weight to carry that the other grades can't begin to understand.

Another noted: "In the short span of four years, you have to bridge kids into a high school program and then get them ready for adulthood."

One principal noted how unfair it is that high schools are blamed for the dropout rate when the problem is partly one they inherit from poor-quality middle and elementary schools: "If you're looking at issues around the achievement gap, it gets wider and wider and wider. And by the time they are in high school, it is really complex to change. When you talk to high school teachers about the achievement gap, it can be almost overwhelming." (This is a direct reference to a problem in schools that I refer to as "dynamic inequality," examined below.) Another noted that "I have to remediate what did not happen at the lower levels." High school is the "end of the line," the stage of education that inherits the differences among students that have developed throughout elementary and middle school, but it is also the last chance to narrow the achievement gap or, at the very least, to prepare low-performing students so they can graduate. This has become particularly crucial in a period where the pressure for college for all is so great: "the accountability that parents hold over high schools—that all kids need to be ready for college."

High school is the "end of the line," the last chance to narrow the achievement gap or, at the very least, to prepare low-performing students so they can graduate.

Social promotion and the lack of accountability end in the high school. One principal called it "the end of social promotion," with "that high school diploma and all that it means symbolically and socially, both for educators and then for families." First of all, students in high school have to accumulate the right number of credits to graduate, and the whole credit system is unfamiliar. As one principal of an autonomous small school noted,

> It's the first time that course completion and grades have actual value to the future … the kids that get here have this mentality that they can continue to move forward if they fail, because you can fail all your middle school courses and end up in high school. [But] you can't go to a four-year college if you have a D on your transcript … or inadequate numbers of credits, so for the high school principal you have the challenge of "I've got to get these kids to understand that these courses have consequences and value."

Another noted the importance of educating students about the credit system: "They don't immediately understand the credit-based system: they've been passed along for ages, and when they start failing classes because they're not meeting the standards, it comes as a shock to everybody."

Exit exams are another barrier that prevents some students from graduating. They may be especially confusing when students think passing an exit exam is sufficient for graduation or for entering college. In addition to clarifying the role of exit exams, high schools must develop prep classes for exit exams, along with prep classes for the PSAT, the SAT, and the ACT. This means that someone in the school (and ultimately the principal) must devise a sequence of exam prep courses, find times to give them, and urge students to attend—but then suffer the blame if students don't pass their exit exams.

Grades are another dimension of pressure in high school. Students aiming for elite colleges have to keep their grades up; those hoping to get into state universities often need to pass courses with a certain grade point average. Even those planning to attend an open-enrollment community college need to master a range of competencies associated with "college readiness" (Conley 2007). Unfortunately, many students seem to believe that "I can make it up in community colleges" if they spend their high school years fooling around, though the high rates of such students having to take basic skills courses and then their abysmally low completion rates indicate that this view is simply not true. So along with clarifying the credit system to students, as well as the roles of various exams, high schools need to clarify the importance to their futures of appropriately hard work—just at a point when students seem reluctant to hear that message.

Dropping out goes on all through the high school years, but the threat of it creates a special urgency at the outset of high school: "Most of your resources are focused on ninth grade and tenth grade and getting the 70 percent of your kids who are far below basic and getting them on track [to graduate], and it's all very urgent because they basically have a two-year window, if that." So principals need to be able to diagnose which students are likely to drop out or fail exit exams, and then to develop *effective* interventions to help them. But there isn't very good information about what practices work to accelerate students who are badly behind, some of them still reading at the fifth- or sixth-grade level and some of whom have still not mastered numbers and transformations.

The pressure to ensure that students accumulate credits and make steady progress toward graduation leads to a dilemma for high schools. As the principal of a small, autonomous school admitted, "You have the pressure to graduate students. At the same time, you have the pressure to make their diploma meaningful. And so how do you balance that?" In some cases, the balance has come at the expense of content and rigor. An assistant principal in charge of several pathways—an individual who acknowledged the conflict between "rigor *versus* personalization"—complained that "the small schools will do whatever they possibly can to make sure that the students get a passing grade so that they can go to college, because it's an equity issue for them"—but also an issue of making these small schools look effective. In this particular district, a local newspaper ran a long and damning article about grade inflation in pathways.[7] Another tactic has been to develop "credit recovery" programs, where students can earn credits for a variety of nonstandard work. But this often means "being creative," as one assistant principal noted: getting credits in poorly taught continuation high schools or other forms of alternative education, getting algebra credit for construction work, or getting credit for independent study or English-language development (ELD) courses—"just finding all the loopholes." Whether these forms of credit recovery help students in the long run is unclear, but it isn't an *educational* solution to the dilemma of getting all students to graduate.

The conclusion that high school matters *more* than elementary and middle school contradicts the convention that the early grades matter the most and that reforms should emphasize getting young students to master basic skills, to prevent their falling behind in later grades. (Currently, this idea is being extended downward in the idea of universal prekindergarten programs.) However, it seems pointless to argue whether the early grades or high school matter more. A schooling system that neglects the early grades in favor of an all-out emphasis on high schools would face even greater needs for remediation and intervention on behalf of low-performing students, so this is obviously not a solution. A different approach would be to follow John Dewey, who consistently reminded us that debates framed in polar opposites—civic purposes versus occupational goals, academic versus vocational education, traditional versus progressive pedagogies—often reflect false dichotomies. In his introduction to *Experience and Education,* he wrote: "Mankind likes to think in terms of extreme opposites. It is given to formulating its beliefs in terms of Either-Ors, between which it recognizes no intermediate possibilities" (1938, 17). A Deweyan synthesis would therefore argue for a both-and approach rather than an either-or debate—that all levels of schooling matter in the overall trajectory of education, though perhaps in different ways.

This in turn implies that the exclusive emphasis of much school reform and compensatory programs on the early grades may be misplaced and that such resources should be used throughout the grades.

This perspective is also consistent with the concept of dynamic inequality (Grubb 2009b, chap. 6). Students start school in kindergarten at different levels of readiness for formal education, linked to dimensions of family background, including their parents' education levels, as well as experience in early childhood programs. Although information about patterns of inequality over time is scanty, what there is indicates that initial differences are magnified over the early grades, middle school, and especially high school, for a large variety of reasons. Furthermore, increasing inequality may develop not uniformly but instead may expand suddenly at certain points in the trajectory—"bursts" or "explosions" of inequality, for example at the transition to high school (Grubb 2009b, chap. 7, based on National Education Longitudinal Survey of the Class of 1988 [NELS88] data). And this presumably happens at other transitions, such as the shift into middle school. The result is, as the principal quoted above noted, that the achievement gap "gets wider and wider and wider."

Another principal referred to this problem using the same language of "explosions" in inequality, and went on to blame the rigid structure of the high school:

> There is a segment of our student population that does not benefit from [small learning communities, guest speakers, fieldtrips, "attempting to get the best for the kids as possible"] ... We just keep having the conversation about "yes, this isn't right," but we can't figure out at which point along the continuum it goes awry. All of a sudden the explosion of inequality becomes too apparent and yet, like right before, it doesn't seem inequitable. The pieces seem to be working, and yet, the end result is nothing like what it should look like .... And recognize that we are constrained by certain parameters that are the institution of high school in America in the twenty-first century, and so there are certain things that we can't figure out how to undo, that are so systemic that we can't figure out where we can make a shift that will change the direction exponentially. Because we have these little boxes that things have to fall into, in terms of getting funding, and getting teachers, and getting classes on your a–g list, and getting community support, so all that constrains how you can think outside of the box.

The concept of dynamic inequality implies that all levels of schooling contribute to inequality by grade twelve in learning, progress through schooling, school connectedness, and various attitudes and aspirations. In order to develop a schooling *system* where initial inequalities are not exacerbated—and might be, one hopes, diminished over time—requires attention to all levels of schooling, not just the early grades, as well as to those transitions that might produce explosions in inequality. The conclusion, again, is that high school reform is just as important as making sure that teaching in the early grades is strong.

THE NINTH-GRADE TRANSITION

The transition into ninth grade is a particularly crucial stage in educational trajectories, especially because an explosion of inequality takes place at this stage. All too many students enter high schools—particularly urban high schools—unable to do high school–level work. These are the students who have been "passed along" in earlier grades, without learning what they should have; these are also students whose commitment to schooling is tenuous. They then face a more impersonal environment, a much larger number of teachers and peers, briefer interactions with teachers who themselves face many more students each day, teaching that involves more lecturing and less discussion of students' ideas, and an increased workload and pressure to do well as the end of high school approaches (Grossman and Cooney 2009). For leaders, the conclusion that high school is a crucial juncture where students either graduate or drop out, with dire consequences for the rest of their lives, means that they must be knowledgeable about and dedicated to implementing interventions to help students make this difficult transition and catch up to grade-level norms.

Recognizing this, the principals whom we interviewed have adopted a wide range of strategies. One principal of a themed, small school noted that his ninth graders "are coming from this whole spectrum of middle schools, all over the place," with very different levels of preparation. This particular school had adopted a ninth-grade "induction process," run by a nonprofit group during the summer before high school, to "establish bonds and relationships, and start to work together as teams. And then also to set all of the behavior expectations for the campus and provide a roadmap for them, for those four years." Another school had "shifted the paradigm, where we make the first year a lot easier, a lot less strenuous and rigorous. We have more intervention classes, art classes, no foreign language classes, in a really sincere attempt to make their first-year transition easier so that we can keep them here longer. And then as they grow and mature, then we gradually increase the demands on their academics." Yet another mentioned a number of approaches for "8.5 kids," those between eighth and ninth grades: a summer bridge program with an orientation to high school, study skills, and connecting with key teachers; a learning community where all ninth graders take an art class, learn to play an instrument, perform in a drama, learn computer skills, and participate in a study skills class "for their math and English that they were lacking"; a program to identify "the worst of the worst kids"—the worst in terms of behavior—and develop a mentor program for them; and support materials and interventions, including an English program that incorporated the skills of sixth-, seventh-, and eighth-grade English. Another principal developed a program called the Link Crew, training juniors and seniors to work with first-years "around the whole-school concept," reinforced by various related activities in ninth grade as well as multiple pathways; she was also working with teachers on engagement strategies, especially questioning techniques beyond standard inquiry, response, evaluation (IRE) questions ("asking a question, waiting for the same two or three kids to respond, and assuming everybody got it"). Another received a special grant for ninth- and tenth-grade teachers to have parent conferences for "borderline students," and adopted an AVID program. ("Advancement via Individual Determination" is a system of college readiness that is intended to increase the numbers of students going to four-year colleges.) This simple list shows a substantial variety of ideas and programs, with little agreement on what might be most effective.

In some cases, schools create a pathway or school-within-a-school or a ninth-grade academy (as the Talent Development High School model has) to smooth the transition and to provide ninth graders with instruction in basic skills. But if ninth graders have any choice in the matter—if, for example, such an academy has to compete with other pathways—then parents and their children are unlikely to choose such a remedial option. For example, one district tried to confront the ninth-grade transition problem by creating something called the Pathways Program. The principal described it in these terms:

> If you were a ninth grader who had bad attendance and behavior problems, it was sort of sold to them as a credit recovery program ... There is this problem in most high schools of a flood of kids who come in unprepared, and the question

> is what do you do. Some high schools have essentially set up schools-within-schools that are designed to support these kids. But they are—I don't know what pretty language you want to use—but they are basically remedial. When you talk about supporting kids, parents immediately go to, "OK, it must be remedial." So there is a sort of tension between needing to have that and not wanting to have something that looks like remediation.

The "solution" in many schools is not to give students much choice: all students, or all students with certain records of poor performance, are required to attend such a school-within-a-school.

Most schools we visited, then, have adopted something to confront the ninth-grade problem: small learning communities with linked subjects (such as English and history); different versions of ninth-grade academies or houses, where students can relearn basic skills, sometimes in free-standing classes, and sometimes (in one high school) in the context of classes exploring community, political, and racial issues; moving the best teachers to the ninth grade from the eleventh and twelfth grades; reducing class sizes in ninth grade (though the pupil/teacher ratio of 25:1 mentioned by one principal hardly seems adequate); specific curricula like Read180; and summer bridge programs and orientation periods before school starts, to smooth the transitions from eighth grade. One principal with a variety of transition mechanisms said his school

> has embraced this "whatever it takes" mindset ... it's easy to judge those [students] who do not [do everything you ask of them] as being lazy bums, and you write them off because you have so many ... And I think what has been a challenge is to not just write off the bottom quintile, and to say that we need to be committed to those kids ... What's been a challenge is to get my staff to embrace leadership positions where they're not being obstructionist to educating all kids.

Most schools we visited, then, have adopted something to confront the ninth-grade problem; one principal with a variety of transition mechanisms said his school "has embraced this 'whatever it takes' mindset."

Unfortunately, we know very little about the effectiveness of these different strategies. Some approaches—ninth-grade academies or houses or orientation programs—may well be effective, though the evidence so far is not particularly strong.[8] But other common approaches—requiring two or three periods of basic skills courses in math and English, preparation focused on passing a low-level exit exam, some dubious credit recovery options—cannot possibly help enhance motivation and engagement or "make the diploma meaningful." Indeed, remedial pedagogies—drill and practice on subjects that students should have mastered earlier in their schooling—are associated with *lower* test scores and *slower* progress through high school.[9]

What high schools need is both better information about effective intervention strategies—in better-developed versions of the What Works Clearinghouse or in more active forms of translating research into practice, such as the proposed Educational Extension Service (Grubb 2010a)—*and* leaders who are knowledgeable about these strategies and ways of implementing them. I will return to both these points in subsequent sections, particularly chapter 4 on the development of high school leaders and chapter 5 on the responsibilities of districts (and perhaps states) to provide better information about the effectiveness of programs, so that principals don't have to discover this information for themselves.

THE SPECIAL DIFFICULTIES OF INSTRUCTIONAL IMPROVEMENT

Improving the quality of instruction is as crucial in the high school as it is in elementary and middle grades, particularly if students are to pass their courses with decent grades, to pass exit exams, and to master the conceptual abilities associated with college readiness. If college for all has become a major requirement for individual success, then learning and grades become all the more important (and we need to hope that grades reflect the quality of learning). Yet high schools have been more resistant than elementary and middle schools to instructional reform and improvement (Cuban 1993), and overall high school teaching seems worse—more conventional and traditional, more concerned with information transfer and less with conceptual and other higher-order abilities, more teacher-driven and less student-centered, and more concerned with content and coverage than understanding—than teaching in elementary or middle schools. One assistant principal noted that

> the biggest challenge at the high school level is teachers who are fossilized in their pedagogical positions, and their willingness to say publicly, "it's the kids, because there's nothing wrong with the lesson plan" . . . and not see that they may need to shift their instructional strategies and instructional content in order to serve a different population.

An instructional coordinator in a school with multiple pathways illustrated just how bad teaching can be. She complained that

> We haven't been able to move in a constructivist direction because our basic direct instruction is so poor. You need to really understand direct instruction well, and then you can flip it to that constructivist perspective, because that's a lot harder . . . but we have so many teachers who are so bad at basic direct instruction that we haven't been able to move to that [constructivist] model.

Many of her teachers were just teaching by the seat of their pants, without going through the steps necessary for high-quality direct instruction—careful framing of the issue, demonstrating new material, practicing with students, scaffolding or supporting their initial efforts, and gradually having them work more independently. Given that teachers had not mastered these basic teaching methods, they were far from able to use complex constructivist practices or the combination of direct instruction and constructivist approaches that is often called "balanced instruction."

Many other respondents complained about the problem in roughly the same terms. One admitted that "I have passive teaching and passive learning on this campus—it is rampant." Another complained that "I don't need any more social workers . . . too many [of the teachers] are saying 'isn't this great, that I am here doing it for these kids,' when a staff believes that students can learn, but hasn't mastered the pedagogical alternatives that would enable students to learn." Between the teachers who have not mastered basic approaches to teaching and those who believe that "social work" or caring for kids is sufficient, the quality of instruction in many high schools is quite mediocre.

A number of conditions explain why it is more difficult for principals and assistant principals to serve as instructional leaders in high schools. First, elementary schools are better linked to the early childhood tradition of child-centered teaching and the "whole child"; middle schools have recently focused more on early adolescence as a developmental stage in its own right and also have shifted to more interdisciplinary and theme-based teaching. But, as many principals we talked to noted, high school teachers are wedded to their disciplines much more than elementary and middle school teachers are. Their egos are involved in being subject-matter experts rather than expert teachers: "high school teachers think they are content area teachers—that they are math teachers, science teachers, teachers of the Civil War—but not necessarily teachers of language, or teachers of critical thinking ... At the elementary school it's more a kind of holistic approach to teaching." Some of them want to be teaching at the college level ("a little delusional," cracked one principal) or teaching AP, so they don't want to be teaching remedial courses or low-performing students. Furthermore, they aren't prepared to do so. One individual who had been in charge of several pathways and was now a middle school principal noted that "high school teachers are mostly subject-matter experts and aren't necessarily trained in how to accelerate students"—that is, in the instructional methods necessary to help students catch up. As a principal noted, "They expect students to come with certain skills and they say, 'Well, it's not us. They came like that from junior high. And how do they expect for us to build all these skills if they send them like that?'"

A number of conditions explain why it is more difficult for principals and assistant principals to serve as instructional leaders in high schools.

In addition, teachers wedded to disciplines are less familiar with a variety of pedagogical methods. There's no logical necessity for this. Shulman (1987) in particular has stressed the importance of "pedagogical content knowledge" among instructors, or knowledge of how different pedagogical approaches can be applied to various subjects (as well as content knowledge, not instead of it). Little (2006) has stressed the importance of pedagogical content knowledge in professional development. Certainly all the major subject-matter organizations for teachers—the National Councils for Teachers of Mathematics and Teachers of English, the National Council for the Social Studies—have developed various pedagogical approaches for their subjects. But these discussions appear to have reached relatively few high school teachers.

Furthermore, both the preparation of high school teachers in subject-specific credential programs and their subsequent lives within discipline-based departments has reinforced content expertise over pedagogical exploration. Most high school teachers receive single-subject credentials, preparing them to teach one discipline-based subject. Their preparation programs do include courses in pedagogy or how to teach these subjects, but these are the courses that are often criticized as "theory" or perspectives far from classroom requirements; they appear to be less powerful in single-subject credential programs than in the teacher preparation that middle school and elementary school teachers receive.

Then high school teachers live in subject-matter departments, and again—while such departments might focus on the instructional debates in their subject areas—they are more likely to focus on the content of their discipline rather than pedagogical issues.[10] Even though the National Association of Secondary School Principal's *Breaking Ranks I* asserted that "every high school will be a learning community for teachers and the other professionals it employs," these kinds of communities "remain exceptions in the landscape of American high schools," and only 20 percent of teachers report that they meet regularly to share lessons plans and methods of assessment (McLaughlin and Talbert 2007). One principal complained that "the departments here have more rigid agendas ... and I don't necessarily have all the cooperation that I need [for instructional improvement]." The departmental agendas seem to be more about logistical issues—has the department prepared for an upcoming exit exam or SAT, are there enough sections of a particular course?—rather than instructional issues. Another complained in particular about the power of department chairs, "ancient dinosaur institutions," with principals sometimes unable to get departments to do what chairs do not want to do—and "people in their little small areas of expertise don't always remember the large picture."

In addition, subject-matter departments in high schools spend a great deal of energy competing with one another for control of time, personnel, money, territory and classroom space, students, and voice in the schools' policy-making—any of the scarce resources in schools. They tend to focus on curriculum issues—what counts as English or math, which specific books should be taught or mathematical procedures presented—rather than the instructional methods of doing so (Siskin and Little 1995). They may be caught up in the internal discussions of what "English" should be, what "history" should be. Even when leaders try to move them toward instructional discussions, they keep reverting to curricular debates—"backsliding" to more familiar territory (McCalmont 2010). The result is that high school departments are not usually fruitful places to improve instruction. There are exceptions, of course (e.g., Boaler and Staples 2008; Gutierrez 2000), and departments are still logical groups for leaders to work with in order to create professional learning communities focused on improving instruction. But very little in the preparation of high school teachers or in the life of departments fosters an attention to instruction over curriculum.

Very little in the preparation of high school teachers or in the life of departments fosters an attention to instruction over curriculum.

In addition, many teachers seem resistant to professional development, including that which might take place within departments. In part, the traditions of teacher autonomy are stronger than they are in elementary and middle schools, where ideas about professional learning communities and teachers collaborating around student work have become much stronger. As one principal noted,

> When I implemented some high-level student engagement strategies [in professional development] or structured oral response strategies, my teachers say, "Well, this is very elementary, and this is very middle school." They don't see that good teaching strategies are good pedagogy; they say that "Well, we don't do that because we're in high school." … At times I get stuck as to how to rephrase it so that teachers see it's also good practice to have in the high school.

From the student side, as anyone with an adolescent knows, high school students themselves can be more difficult than littler kids, and this may require a different type of teacher. One district official who had been both a middle school and a high school teacher, declared:

> I see the ability to manage and work with and inspire and motivate high school students as more of a challenge. It kind of socially becomes less cool to interact with adults, so at that point you draw upon different skills to reach them. [Good] high school teachers are more outspoken, they are strong advocates for themselves ... I just tend to see it as kind of the personality of a high school teacher and it's more—I don't want to say renegade, but just more outspoken and assertive.

Yet another contrasted elementary and high school students:

> When I go onto an elementary campus, those kids love their teachers. They're touching them, they are hanging around them, they run up to their principal—they see these people as a good thing. At a high school campus, it's not that kind of environment. For some students, it's almost like, "I dare you to teach me."

So the developing independence of adolescents and the widespread perception that school is not cool create other challenges not present in the lower grades.

At the extreme, some students are seriously alienated from school, defiant and resistant, and they may be nearly impossible to teach. For these students, schools have devised a variety of poor alternatives: continuation high schools where they are segregated with other defiant kids; "push out," when students are quietly encouraged to drop out; special education; low-performing tracks, such as the general track and, in the olden days, traditional vocational ed; and remedial tracks, when students are placed in three or four extra periods of remedial math and English, taught with a barren "remedial pedagogy" of drill and practice on small subskills rather than important competencies. But teachers are rarely prepared in how to teach these difficult students, and the combination of monotonous teaching and resistance to learning is lethal. Popular culture has tended to extreme portrayals of teachers, of course—the beautiful ex-Marine played by Michelle Pfeiffer in *Dangerous Minds,* able to overcome the challenges of her gangsta students, or the tricks played by Jaime Escalante, getting his Latino students to learn calculus in *Stand and Deliver.* But none of these depictions illustrates the difficult process of learning to teach resistant adolescents in appropriate and motivating ways. The principles of motivation and engagement in high school and summarized in chapter 1 (National Research Council 2004) require changes in instructional approaches, but these are precisely the changes that have been the most difficult in the high school.

In addition, structural conditions in high schools make strong teaching difficult. One of these conditions is the high numbers of students per teacher: if instructors teach five classes of approximately thirty students each day, they face one hundred fifty students (and sometimes up to one hundred eighty)—too many to know well, and too many to assign writing, or complex problems, or interpretive assessments rather than tests requiring only the regurgitation of facts. Indeed, William Ouchi (2009) has argued that the total student load—the total number of students each teacher faces in a school day—is a better measure of the opportunities for personal contact and enhanced learning than is the average class size. Though the underlying statistical work isn't particularly persuasive,[11] the idea that teachers can form closer relationships with their students when they face fewer students each day has some self-evident merit, and for such subjects as writing, smaller total numbers of students are crucial.

Another problem in conventional high schools is that is impossible to pay attention to the "whole student," as elementary schools like to educate the "whole child," because a high school student's day is broken into a series of independent activities. These include instruction structured by discipline-specific courses, attention from counselors unaware of classroom issues, intervention courses and after-school remediation disconnected from the regular curriculum, preparation for exit exams and SAT or ACT exams unrelated to regular classes, and extracurricular activities unconnected to the academic side. High schools place the burden on *students* to integrate these different activities, though without giving them any preparation in how to do so.

Yet another structural problem in the comprehensive high school is the large number of teachers—"with 80 teachers and one of me, where do you start?" One way to identify instructional problems and then to improve the quality of instruction is to engage in classroom observations and walk-throughs to diagnose the strengths and weaknesses of instruction, followed by conferences, coaching, and professional development with weak teachers. However, the principals we interviewed mentioned observational methods very little; although these have become common in elementary and middle schools, they seem to be rare in high schools. The large number of teachers in most high schools also means that "it's easier to hide at a comprehensive school—if you have students that complain about a certain teacher, you just move them out of their class to another teacher's classroom," whereas "in a small school they stick out like a sore thumb." So mediocre teaching can easily persist in a conventional high school because no one but students gets to see how bad teaching is. Students may complain—there's plenty of student talk about good and bad teachers in high schools—but this is not a mechanism (such as formal observations) for triggering instructional improvement.

Finally, it's important to remember that—as a previous section clarified—many leaders in high schools are taken away from instructional leadership by the many other, more pressing duties they have. As one district leader in charge of high schools noted,

> They're drawn away [from instructional issues] by compliance issues—state bureaucratic reports, and sometimes things that are designed to help, like accreditation processes—typically the principal's ultimately responsible, so they could be drawn away to spend time writing and collecting information for central office, state office-type people, and that pulls them away from kids and teachers.

Furthermore, many high schools have structured leadership teams so that one assistant principal is in charge of discipline, one in charge of building and maintenance, one in charge of curriculum and instruction, perhaps one in charge of extracurricular activities—so relatively few members of a leadership team have direct responsibility for instruction. In contrast, a few high schools in our sample have distributed the responsibility for instruction to all members of the leadership team so that, for example, every assistant principal is responsible for instruction in some grade level, or in some schools-within-the-school. This at least expands the number of leaders responsible for and attentive to instruction. In general, though, leadership attention is distracted from instructional improvement in many ways.

In addition, districts themselves are partly to blame for the inability of principals to get around to instructional improvement. One head of an arts-themed pathway stressed the importance of instructional leadership: "the whole thought needs to be, your work as a principal is in the classroom," and then claimed that "from my experience with my colleagues, I would say they want to" pay attention to instruction. But she went on to note the distractions caused by district requirements:

> What happens there, in a large school, you get called to district meetings. You have multiple committees that you have to sit on at the district. And I have to say, he [the superintendent] told us, "I want you in that classroom 75 percent of

> the time," to all principals. But yet at the same time—support us to be able to do that!

Furthermore, districts often impose specific requirements about the "crises" that pop up in all schools: "You also get a directive from the district: 'I don't want any parent complaints at the district level,'" so principals are *directed* to pay attention to small crises first, and to long-run, noncritical improvements second. When I turn in chapter 5 to district support, their interference with principals' time is one of the issues to confront.

Now, because we interviewed administrators rather than teachers, we have an administrator's view of the problem. A teacher's-eye view of instructional difficulties might be quite different, as illustrated by a story from one assistant principal—herself a teacher until quite recently—about a teacher-led effort to improve literacy instruction:

> I was asked to lead the committee [of teachers] and get all this feedback and all these ideas from teacher-leaders ... and I would take it to the administration and nothing would happen ... And they [teachers] knew they weren't being listened to ... so it was kind of this revolt, and last spring the instructional leadership team resurrected itself ... They would recommend that certain things happen, not necessarily to the administration but to the school site council. So this was a whole change in the system here because there wasn't much faith in the administrative team that they would listen.

This is a school where the administration operated in traditional hierarchical ways; where administrators made decisions and handed them down to teachers but did not listen to them; and where teachers did not participate in decision-making, even around instruction. This vignette illustrates the importance of what many have called *distributed leadership,* a sharing of leadership between administrators and teachers with communication back and forth, rather than simply from administrators to teachers. The resistance of high school teachers to instructional improvement and professional development may be, in part, a consequence of traditional methods of management, rather than being the fault of teachers wedded to their disciplines.

The overall implication is that, for a large number of reasons, improving instruction in the high school is more difficult than it is at other levels. At the same time, leaders have less time to devote to instruction because of the complexity of the high school and the multiple demands on their attention.

So the resources necessary for improving instruction—vision, leadership, cooperation from all participants, time and effort enough to engage in classroom observations and instructional improvement, as well as knowledge of what makes instruction more powerful—are largely missing in most high schools, helping to explain Larry Cuban's observation about the lack of improvement.

As a working hypothesis, the failure of most high school reform—and certainly the failure of most reforms to improve test scores[12]—may be because of the inability of most high schools to improve instruction. The further implication is that, until leaders and teachers confront the instructional problem head-on, high school reform will continue to fail, and too many high schools will remain places of lackluster student performance.

As a working hypothesis, the failure of most high school reform—and certainly the failure of most reforms to improve test scores—may be because of the inability of most high schools to improve instruction.

Now, it's not difficult conceptually to see how to improve teaching in high schools. As one district official who had been both a middle school and a high school principal declared,

> Good comprehensive high school principals work directly with teachers. They do have an instructional council … they are in the department meetings. The ones who struggle are the ones who have delegated it [instruction] all out to their assistant principals because they really gave up that influence. And at the large schools, they don't directly work with all of their teachers in an instructional capacity.

So first and foremost, improving instruction requires working directly with teachers, attending department meetings to monitor the instructional conversations there, observing classes, providing support in improving instruction either themselves or by providing coaching, or by creating instruction-focused professional development. To be sure, this approach to improving instruction—especially observing classes and then improving instruction through coaching or professional development—is easily articulated but much more difficult to carry out. The culture of isolation surrounding teaching is much stronger in high schools than in elementary schools, and so instituting classroom observations—deprivatizing instruction and sharing practices across teachers and across subjects—usually creates resistance. Creating professional learning communities to discuss instruction is a tactic with an enormous amount of how-to literature, but pulling this off requires persistence, vision, and positional as well as instructional authority. And professional development in most schools needs to be restructured, shifting away from the conventional Friday-afternoon, one-shot events with invited speakers to sustained discussions about applying different pedagogies to specific subjects (Little 2006).

This approach to improving instruction—especially observing classes and then improving instruction through coaching or professional development—is easily articulated but much more difficult to carry out.

Of course, in a large high school—but not in a smaller learning community or pathway—principals cannot do all of this themselves. Therefore they have to create teams of people to observe classes—for example, assistant principals assisted by department heads, or senior teachers or master teachers with the respect of the school, or teachers and administrators assisted by "outsiders" from other schools who can provide different perspectives.[13] Similarly, the improvement of instruction cannot be the sole responsibility of the principal, as it is in small elementary schools. It can sometimes take place with one-on-one coaching by hiring literacy coaches or math coaches, or by promoting professional development where teachers with common interests (sometimes in a department, sometimes in a pathway, sometimes with particular innovations in mind) meet over longer periods of time to discuss instructional issues, student dilemmas, and approaches to pedagogical content knowledge (Little 2006). In some cases, departments can develop their own pedagogical visions and instructional practices, and leaders can support these efforts through common planning time, occasional outside consultants, and methods of professional development. In addition, improving instruction is a process where practice and revision, based on feedback from instructional coaches or master teachers or experienced leaders, is invaluable (e.g., Tharp and Gallimore 1988, chap. 10), so finding the resources for such practice is another responsibility of instructional leaders. High school principals cannot do it all themselves, but they can organize instructional improvement by sharing authority with others—distributed leadership once again.

In terms of what to improve, all instructors in every kind of educational situation need to know some basic principles, and writing and workshops on all of them abound. One is how to develop lesson plans, with clear objectives and methods of assessing whether those objectives have been met. Another subject involves the basics of direct instruction, including a conventional sequence of presenting and illustrating new content, allowing students to try new approaches and procedures with considerable support ("scaffolding"), and then allowing them greater autonomy and choice in carrying academic tasks. Questioning techniques by instructors can be vastly expanded beyond the simple IRE questions that most teachers use, moving to various ways of asking sophisticated questions that get students to think conceptually rather than simply regurgitating factual information. A third approach that teachers can readily master is some knowledge of inquiry methods so that students start to construct meaning for themselves; another, often linked to inquiry methods, is the use of cooperative learning, including group work and projects. With an expanding portfolio of teaching approaches, instructors can begin to understand that there are many ways of teaching, not just one conventional, discipline-based method, and can then begin to use balanced methods of instruction drawing on several approaches, as appropriate, to the subject being covered. None of these improvements is particularly mysterious; all of them are the subjects of myriad how-to books and workshops.

In addition to creating systems of observation and instructional improvement, high school leaders can take other steps to improve instruction. First and foremost, leaders themselves as well as teachers need to be convinced of the value of improved instruction. A variety of evidence, plus many reviews of instruction by the National Academy of Sciences, plus the deliberations of such groups as the National Councils of Teachers of English and of Mathematics provide support for the importance of innovative instruction, and all of these can be used for persuasion.[14] Then single-subject credential programs should devote adequate time to different approaches to instruction in that subject area—that is, to pedagogical content knowledge—and high school committees and principals should look for such preparation in the hiring process. School districts should be searching for principals and assistant principals who are committed to being *instructional* leaders, as part of the larger process of developing coherent policies toward leadership development outlined in chapter 5. This may involve working with local leadership programs in schools of education to make sure that instructional methods are part of the curriculum. Finally, paying attention to instruction is infinitely easier where teacher unions are *professional* unions concerned with professional prerogatives including instruction, rather than *industrial* unions concerned only with wages and working conditions (Kerchner and Caufman 1993), and districts can work with unions to provide teachers more professional autonomy and discretion (Marshall 2008).

To be sure, none of these steps to improve instruction do anything about the structural conditions in high school that impede strong teaching. One way to conceptualize high school reform, then, is to focus on those conditions—large size, the distractions of nonacademic activities, the enormous variation in student needs—that make pedagogical improvement so difficult, *and* to work more directly on improving instruction. Without these structural changes, instructional improvement is much more difficult. We might even conclude that any reform that fails to grapple with these structural conditions—such as the various proposals to make high schools more rigorous and increase assessments of various kinds—is a false reform, "a tale told by an idiot, full of sound and fury, signifying nothing" (Bryk 2010)—and that only the combination of reshaping structural conditions *and* improving instruction directly is likely to work.

BEHAVIOR: SEX, DRUGS, DISCIPLINE, MENTAL HEALTH . . .

Virtually all principals acknowledged that behavioral issues are more difficult in high school. One principal of a small school-within-a-school noted a behavioral version of high school as the "end of the line":

> Drugs, sex, and the negative influences of the community play themselves out at schools like ours, more than anywhere else.... It's a huge weight to carry because we know what they need, and it's hard to watch them struggle through it and make decisions that so adversely impact their ability to be successful in schools. It's a hard thing to watch because when they leave us there's no other system [that's designed to help them]—they leave us, they're on their own.

One assistant principal in charge of discipline—as so many are—asserted that the discipline problems in "getting kids ready to learn" are "more pervasive in high school. You definitely see it in middle school, but I think in the ninth and tenth grade you have kids trying to explore the boundaries, pushing boundaries, figuring out who they are." He started a student group called "Gentlemen Panthers," tenth-grade males who were the most disengaged from school and appeared in repeated discipline cases, working with different male mentors about "what it means to be a man, or how to define your role as a man in today's society ... manners and etiquette, and how to look for jobs, and what to expect in relationships, and questions about who they are in general."

Similarly, fights start in elementary school, of course, but by high school students are physically larger and may have weapons, so fights are more serious:

> The danger level is more significant ... In an inner-city school, you have a lot of gang-type problems. A school like ours has a lot of psycho-emotional problems, where we have a lot of students stressed and on the verge of hurting themselves and others as a result of the stress ... The size of our campus, the size of high schools has an adverse affect on curriculum and discipline and everything.

The culture of hypersexuality in which we live has sexualized behavior in high school too. One principal complained that "pep rallies are conducted in a way that is almost vulgar, and just interferes with an academic culture"; in response, she had prohibited "the slutty Strawberry Shortcake outfit" and other "slutty" costumes for Halloween. Dress codes related to clothes—bra straps and revealing tank tops and sagging pants—are subjects of debate at many schools. Even more seriously, of course, more students are engaging in sex, many more than in middle school—"sex is talked about a lot in middle school; sex is done a lot in high school"—and the consequences for pregnancy and subsequent opportunities are dire. Drugs and alcohol are much bigger risks—again, "drugs are experimented with in middle school, but drugs inform a significant population at the high school level, how they see themselves and how they relate to school, how they relate to each other," and the combination of alcohol or drugs and driving can be lethal. Although all of these problems arise in middle school, they're much less serious: middle school referrals are for "things like they're wound up," or "annoying others," "whereas at the high school it's like possession of marijuana." Another principal drew a similar distinction: "In middle school, they're experimenting. I think when they get to high school and these things start tearing away at their ability to do classwork, do homework—there again, it gets back to the consequences." These kinds of behavior do detract from academic work: the amount of homework students do, attendance problems and absences, and their own admissions of behavior problems all influence test scores and progress through high school in ways one might expect, while a negative school climate caused by fights, drugs, alcohol, and gangs reduce most test scores; both educational and occupational aspirations; and some measures of progress through high school.[15]

A number of principals mentioned mental health problems. These are usually treated as a single category, though the specific issues may include mood disorders, such as depression and suicidal thoughts; eating disorders; rage disorders and anger problems; anxiety; such compulsive behaviors as cutting; and addiction to drugs or alcohol as a method of self-treatment. Students are going through several transitions that exacerbate these issues: the transition into full-blown adolescence, with (in our society, at any rate) anxieties about identity; a difficult transition in moving from eighth grade into high school, where there is a different schedule, more electives, and therefore some choice; and fewer people monitoring what they do. At the same time, the consequences of choices for future opportunities are more serious—the student's-eye view that high school matters in a way that earlier levels do not. Finally, a couple of principals noted higher levels of anxiety and depression because of the 2008–2009 recession; as one mentioned, "I see a lot of difference this year—the economy, I think the stress of the [2008] election ... many houses are foreclosing, our students are couch surfing." Corroboration has surfaced in newspaper articles about seniors facing uncertain futures, and postsecondary institutions are also bracing themselves for more anxiety, stress, depression, and panic disorders (Speer, McFall, and Mohatt 2009).

Other contributors to mental health problems are those issues coming from students' home lives. A majority of the principals we interviewed mentioned family problems in some way. (The sample of schools was a largely urban one, where disproportionate numbers of families are low-income, African American, Latino, or immigrant.) By and large we did NOT hear demeaning comments about these families but rather, these leaders presented family conditions as facts in students' lives, facts that made teachers and leaders sympathetic to students and desperate for ways to help them. As one principal of an autonomous, small school noted,

> A huge challenge is the sheer number of issues within the students and the families and the community and how that affects their performance at school—some of the drug, gang, poverty, absentee parents, parents that are suffering from addictions, mental health issues; in our neighborhood tons and tons of gang and violence issues ... My goal is to provide a safe haven for kids and to show them that this can be the place where they're safe, where someone cares about them, where someone can provide them with food, where someone can help them with their skill set, where people know them as individuals and understand where they're coming from.

Another noted that "the biggest impediment to learning here is relational aggression ... it has to do with the media, with tensions in the urban core, with a lot of affluent flight from public schools ... it's addiction issues, incarceration of parents. It is really this whole mass spectrum." This particular principal had engaged a community-based organization to develop a program of anger management, paid for through Medicaid. Similarly, Charles Payne (2008) has written eloquently if sorrowfully about the demoralization of students as well as teachers in urban high schools, the mistreatment of students and their subsequent disengagement, and the hostile social relationships that then impede reform.

Some of the behavioral problems in high school stem from the developmental stages of adolescence, of "kids trying to explore the boundaries, figuring out who they are." Several principals noted that at least leaders should be aware of the stresses and strains of adolescence and have suggested courses in adolescent development. Another principal, the one who noted that elementary students "love their teachers," acknowledged her perception of a changed attitude in high school students—"I feel this; I don't know if it's true":

> For some students it's almost like, "I dare you to teach me." For others it's "you can't tell me what to do." It's all those issues that come with being a teenager and their need for independence—I think all that's magnified in a high school.

This is a tale about adolescents and their developing independence coming up against the rigidity of high school; the tightly scheduled classes and the bell schedule; the conventional teacher-centered classroom; the burdens of many required courses; and, for those who are behind grade-level norms, the requirements of stultifying "interventions"—all constraining students just at the point when they are trying to assert, or at least find, their own identities. But high schools have almost never tried to develop methods to accommodate or even channel this emerging independence—for example, by adopting methods where sophomores, juniors, and seniors have greater freedom and choice as they show their ability to respond appropriately or by providing some of the instructional conditions necessary for engagement and motivation reviewed in chapter 1. This could include the ability to choose programs, assignments, and projects, potentially including activities outside the school, including work-based learning or service learning.

High schools have almost never tried to develop methods to accommodate or even channel the emerging independence of students.

Many of these problems come from sources outside the school, including the difficulties associated with families and communities; the violence and hypersexuality of popular culture; the anti-school bias of youth culture, including hip-hop.[16] However, even as the leaders we interviewed acknowledged a range of difficult behavioral issues, none of them mentioned the school's own contribution to adolescent problems. One culprit is discipline: harsh discipline systems, including zero-tolerance policies, themselves add to the stresses of students' lives, cause them to view high school as unfair and uncaring, and further weaken their commitment to schooling. A second culprit is lackluster teaching and an unsupportive school climate: large, impersonal environments in which students feel that no one cares do not promote either feelings of control over outcomes or the social connectedness that promotes mental well-being and academic engagement. Conversely, data from the National Longitudinal Study of Adolescent Health indicate that students in schools that foster feelings of connectedness and being cared for by teachers and peers are less likely to suffer emotional distress, use alcohol and drugs, engage in violent or deviant behavior, or become pregnant.[17] This suggests that the solution to various mental health problems in the high school must be a both-and approach: both reshaping the school's instruction, discipline policies, and climate *and* providing more support services for students who need them (for example, in school-based health centers providing a variety of services).[18] For leaders in traditional comprehensive high schools, this implies knowing about a range of alternative actions, both those taking place within the school and others that rely on outside agencies—issues and actions that are rarely included in principal preparation programs.

If schools are to provide a safe haven from some of the stresses outside the school, this requires schools to develop a supportive culture in place of "relationship aggression." One of the schools we visited had adopted what was in effect a new discipline policy, but it was based largely on improving instruction:

> What we created a couple years ago was a compassionate, progressive discipline policy. Someone from the district came to [my school] and said, "Congratulations, you've had the largest decrease in the number of suspensions of any high school in the district." Normally, when principals get together, that's one of the statistics we care less about because we believe that if a kid's messing up, we got to get him out of here so we can just do teaching and learning. But it was good to hear that we had systems in place that prevented us from having to suspend students. And what it was, was that we only had one new teacher last year, so everyone here had been here for two or more years—most of them five or more years. So we had a staff who knew better how to engage students in the classroom ... it's all about how we design our lesson plans and curriculum and how rigorous we create and organize our classrooms. We all sincerely believe that student discipline problems stem from teachers' inability to create meaningful, engaging lessons. And the other piece of it is the respect side of it, that if you're going to be sarcastic, disrespectful, and mean to students, then be prepared to suffer the consequences.

Another possibility is that explicit discipline systems can be changed, replacing the common systems of rules adjudicated by assistant principals in charge of discipline. One principal mentioned a school-wide discipline policy they had developed called PACT, reviewed and signed by all students and parents at the beginning of the year, based on the principles of restorative justice,[19] with a youth court as part of legal studies class so that students participate not only in formulating the rules but in adjudicating them: "In the PACT it is pretty clear as well if you violate any of these agreements that we've *collectively* created, these are the responses."

Others described their efforts to find support services in their communities and to form connections with community-based service agencies. However, this proves to be difficult for several reasons: it takes a great deal of time, and draws principals away from their instructional responsibilities. Although some communities have a wide range of service providers, including municipal services offered to teenagers, others do not. A common pattern, then, is for a few schools with hero-principals and in generous municipalities to provide support services, while most do not.[20] My own view is that until there is categorical funding for support services—for example, a distinct title of No Child Left Behind or its successor, or specific funding for school-based health centers with comprehensive health and mental health services—the problem of adequate support services will not be resolved.

Finally, to anticipate a point in chapter 3, those principals of small schools or schools-within-schools (including theme-based pathways) credit smaller size and closer working relationships between students and teachers with reducing discipline problems, decreasing the distractions of youth culture, and engaging students in their schoolwork. So changing the core of schooling, in addition to such add-ons as school-based health centers, may be the only solution to the range of behavioral issues that plague many high schools.

BUDGETING ISSUES

Numerous principals complained that budgeting issues are more complex in high schools because of the sheer size of the budget. This view first came from a principal in a district with site-based budgeting, where schools receive sums of money that they are free to allocate (within the limits of union contracts and certain district requirements, of course). But the district does not adequately prepare principals and school-site councils to grapple with the technical details of budgeting or the much broader conceptual issues of how to think about money, resources, and the relations between the two. Another principal in a small, autonomous school with a much smaller discretionary budget mentioned that "you also have to be really clever with funding sources to maintain a high school," a reference to the complexity of funding from many small categorical programs and foundation grants. One principal in a school receiving special state funding for underperforming schools complained that the amount of money received was inadequate to cover the requirements of the program and the challenge of "unfunded mandates" that occurs consistently with other programs, such as special education.

Most principals are unprepared to think about budgets and resources. There is virtually nothing in principal preparation programs about budget and finance, and indeed districts often don't understand where their resources go.[21] When districts do provide help, it usually comes in the form of technical assistance about the spreadsheets the district uses—one principal complained about inadequate training in how to use "the tool" for budgeting, referring to the software program the district uses—but not in how to think about resources. In one district we examined closely, the amount of help provided by district staff varied widely, and principals did not find any of the professional development around budgeting very helpful (Rigby 2010). Veteran principals thought the professional development was a waste of time—"I understand the budget better than she [the district official] does"—while novice principals thought professional development was not differentiated enough, felt lost, and needed more support. As one said,

> The training wasn't really helpful for me because it wasn't training, it wasn't a work session, it wasn't differentiated ... and so for me it would have been really helpful to have someone walking me through [site-based budgeting].

Another, reporting that the process was stressful, advocated special training for new principals—again, a notion of differentiated treatment of principals.

But budgeting and resource allocation are not mainly software problems. They are really issues of knowing what school resources—teachers with certain practices, other aspects of instruction, personalization and school climate, class-size reduction under specific conditions, the use of computers, tracking practices, the effectiveness of aides and resource specialists, after-school and other out-of-school-time programs, stability, coherence of the curriculum, and on and on—are effective rather than ineffective, and then how to allocate resources, including money, leadership, and teacher collaboration to develop these effective resources. Some effective resources can be readily bought—more counselors, higher-quality teachers lured by higher salaries, more adults per student to personalize a high school, or certain kinds of support services. Other resources—particularly improved instruction, a supportive school culture, or a discipline system based on different principles—cannot be bought but have to *constructed* by teachers and leaders working collaboratively.[22] This requires a focus on effective resources rather than funding, on goals and outcomes rather than the budget and its spending categories. As one principal in a district with site-based budgeting mentioned (Rigby 2010):

> The site's goals drive the budget, not the other way around. You gotta start with "what are your goals as a site? What are your priorities for the programs that you're gonna fund based on those goals?" and you create a budget based on that, not based on positions you've had forever and so you wanna keep them, even if they don't meet your goals.

But this attitude, requiring a shift from funding to effective resources, from budgets to goals, is virtually nonexistent in American schools. The consequence in all too many schools is that funds are wasted even as students have substantial unmet needs.[23] The only antidote to this problem is a different kind of preparation for principals on planning, budgeting, and resource issues—to which I return in chapter 4.

The consequence of principals unprepared for budgeting in all too many schools is that funds are wasted even as students have substantial unmet needs.

THE TYRANNY OF THE MASTER SCHEDULE

Many principals, perhaps the majority, referred to devising the master schedule as a special challenge in high schools, which elementary and middle schools avoid. The difficulty arises from the greater number and variety of courses that must be scheduled, along with teacher preparation time. Then specific scheduling needs—of athletes for morning classes, or of de facto tracks such as honors courses, or the needs of pathways to schedule all their students in the same courses—complicate the problem. Most master schedules seem to be developed through custom and may become dated as new courses and programs—such as multiple pathways—come along. The presence of many specialized teachers in high school who cannot be substituted for one another (as most middle school teachers can be)—Spanish teachers and Filipino teachers, physics and chemistry teachers with different certification—makes it more difficult to create a schedule. And one principal noted that "adult comfort" often drives the master schedule: "'Oh, I always have this fourth period prep. Oh, I always have AP English.' It takes an innovative leader to say back to a teacher, 'Wait a minute—no.'"

The odd thing about these discussions is that they usually talk about the master schedule as an external force with its own independent power imposed on schools rather than a structure that leaders and teachers devise for their own purposes. The basic problem seems to be that developing a master schedule requires a school to articulate its priorities and to order these priorities so that the highest priorities are the first to be scheduled—for example, the schedules of sports teams in one school, or the preferences of experienced teachers in a school devoted to "adult comfort" for AP classes, or pathways in a school that has given priority to creating these schools-within-schools. If a school cannot agree on its priorities—a difficult process in a large comprehensive high school, sometimes with more than 100 teachers fighting for their own prerogatives and "adult comfort," many priorities ranging from AP classes for high-performing students to interventions for students who are behind, or many extracurricular activities with their own demands for "academic" time—then the master schedule will always be viewed as a malevolent force by some group of unsatisfied teachers. When the master schedule is handed to a new assistant principal (or even a secretary) to work out, as is frequently the case, then again the discussions about school-wide priorities do not take place, and the master schedule is seen as illegitimate by many people and external or imposed by others.

High schools are complex places, of course, but the master schedule does not create the complexity—it merely reflects the difficulty of accommodating conflicting purposes—and it does not have a mind of its own. There are various computer programs available for master scheduling, and these can facilitate the process—for example, by churning out different schedules under different assumptions, almost instantly so that participants in the process can see the consequences of different priorities. But for leaders, there is no substitute for developing agreement about school priorities, and this is possible only if schools have mechanisms for weighing the voices of all participants and judging the validity of completing claims.

THE DIFFICULTY OF PARENT PARTICIPATION

Parent participation is conventionally thought to be a crucial component of education, with parents ideally supporting rather than combating the efforts of educators. However, several principals noted that a fall in parent participation occurs in high school. They asserted that elementary school parents are much more engaged with their children's schooling but that high school parents are more distant, expecting the school to be responsible for education: "Each school has a community surrounding it that is very vocal and participatory—or wants to be. At the high school level, that participation rate drops off dramatically." Many parents cannot provide much help to their children by high school, as coursework moves into mathematical and scientific areas they may not know; parents who have not been to college may not be able to provide much help on choices after high school. And by high school (if not middle school), many parents have become embarrassments to their adolescent children, and parental efforts to participate in school events may be resisted by the youth they are trying to support.

Still, principals who raised the problem of parent involvement all wanted to increase it, though most were at a loss about how to do this. One principal in a school with four pathways that replaced an earlier dysfunctional comprehensive school developed "the only parent center in the city," staffed with parent volunteers with one parent coordinator. The center opens the campus to adults (not just parents) for such activities as a book club, an exercise club using the school's athletic complex, dance nights with aerobic workouts, and college tours—activities for adults that are not necessarily tied to the education of their children. The advantage for the school is that parents do come on campus more for these activities, and there are more adults on campus—"you know children act better when older people are around."

Aside from this example, the schools where we interviewed have not addressed the problem of how to increase parent participation. Elsewhere, such innovative programs as Puente have formed parent groups focusing more specifically on the academic performance and progress of students (Grubb, Lara, and Valdez 2002), and in some schools parents sit on school-site councils and other decision-making bodies. Some have developed other centers, such as computer centers or libraries, where parents and other adults can use the facilities at hours when students are not there. But in general, the problem of low parent participation has not been solved in most high schools.

THE GREAT SILENCE: RACIAL AND ETHNIC ISSUES

The principals we interviewed obviously had a great deal to say about the special conditions of high schools, and many of them seemed relieved that someone was examining the issue. But one topic virtually never came up: what high schools might do about the racial and ethnic gaps in student performance and in dropout rates. To be sure, many principals acknowledged the gaps in performance between white and Asian American students on the one hand, and African American, Latino, other racial minority, and immigrant students on the other. The discussion of achievement gaps in this country has been thoroughly racialized, attributed to racial and ethnic differences, instead of being discussions about class differences or urban-rural differences, for example, or of the different resources that families and schools provide—and the principals we interviewed are under great pressure to moderate these achievement gaps, even to eliminate them. But—as with most other people discussing achievement gaps—they said quite little about distinctly racial or ethnic issues.

To be sure, some substantial fraction of achievement gaps are due to differences in family background, especially parental education, occupation, and aspirations for their children—because of class, not race, in the common shorthand. Other variation in achievement can be attributed to inequalities in the school resources provided to different students, and still others are caused by differences in students' commitment to schooling—rather than to other activities, such as employment, television (and now computer-based gadgets[24]), or just chillin'. But even after these other influences are considered, a substantial part of these racial and ethnic gaps cannot be explained by other variables—49 percent of the differences in math scores between blacks and whites cannot be explained by all these variables, for example, as well as 61 percent of black-white differences in science scores; 27 percent of the differences in reading scores between whites and Latinos; 45 percent of the gap between blacks and whites completing high school; and 20 percent of the white-Latino difference (Grubb 2009b, Table B.4). A substantial knot of racial and ethnic inequality remains even after considering a wide variety of other explanations, with one of the most complete data sets we have. My contention is that it will be impossible to eliminate this source of achievement gaps until schools face squarely what the racial and ethnic dimensions of inequality are, and then work to decrease them.[25]

A substantial knot of racial and ethnic inequality remains even after considering a wide variety of other explanations. It will be impossible to eliminate this source of achievement gaps until schools face squarely what the racial and ethnic dimensions of inequality are, and then work to decrease them.

But with one exception, none of the forty-eight principals and district officials described anything specific that they were doing either to clarify the racial/ethnic causes of various gaps or to address these causes. The one example was a principal on a campus with a ninth-grade academy that was incorporating a course on social justice, where "teachers work together to develop that whole activism in their writing and in their math, and in their core subject areas." Under direct questioning, he claimed that the course included the chance to discuss racial issues that students of color usually find missing from the curriculum:[26] "What we want to do is develop classes, as we did [at another high school] where we had a black studies class and a Latino studies class, and you took one during one semester and then you flipped to the other—I don't care what color you are ... we are teaching them to be [more tolerant], not just color-wise, but gender-wise." This means providing a place *in the curriculum* for discussing issues of race and starting to confront the issues of racial identity that are crucial to the performance of racial minority students.[27] But no other principal mentioned doing anything about specifically racial and ethnic issues, even though most of them described the usual achievement gaps in racialized terms.

For schools to confront racial and ethnic issues seriously, it would first be necessary to convene teachers to agree about the seriousness of racial gaps, and then to agree about the causes of these gaps and the *school's* responsibility for such differences. These are difficult conversations ("courageous conversations," as Singleton 2006 calls them) to have, particularly in a period when right-wing opposition to racial preferences has imposed an odd color-blindness on schools and other institutions. Then, assuming faculty agreement about the problem, the next step would be to adopt practices that would provide support for students of color and immigrant students, including practices drawn from multiculturalism, culturally relevant methods, and approaches to English learners and students speaking nonstandard English (such as contrastive analysis and code-switching).[28] These approaches would require the active support and encouragement of principals and other leaders, and they could not possibly take place in schools lacking trust among members of the school community. But without efforts to address racial and ethnic gaps head on, a substantial fraction of these inequalities will persist.

SHARING LEADERSHIP

In many ways, then, the demands on high school principals are greater than they are in elementary and middle schools, or at least different in crucial ways. There is only one sense in which the high school principalship is easier: a common pattern in comprehensive high schools (though not in autonomous, small high schools) is for a principal to work with several assistant principals, constituting a leadership council. Therefore, as several principals mentioned, the job is "less lonely" because of the ability to share leadership. In contrast, "the elementary principal does it all," or at most has one assistant principal.

There is, to be sure, a downside to becoming a principal with an entourage of assistant principals. An executive role may take individuals away from instruction—as so many other aspects of the principalship do. As one noted, "when you become a principal, there may be the idea that I'm now an executive, I have a big desk and wait for everyone to come in. But the whole thought needs to be that your work as a principal is in the classroom. You spend your time in the classroom, and your desk is for after the teachers are gone." Another noted that "the challenge for the high school principal is to be able to keep everything in his or her head and have that broad knowledge of everything that is happening at the school, while simultaneously not having any need to do anything about it other than to make sure that [other] people do it.... But a lot of high school principals have trouble in letting go." A little later she repeated the point about instructional leadership: "it is important that a high school principal be a curricular leader and have knowledge of [teaching] strategies."

In addition, there doesn't seem to be much thought about how to structure the responsibilities of assistant principals and therefore the leadership council. The most common structure is to have an assistant principal in charge of discipline, one in charge of facilities, one in charge of curriculum and instruction, and perhaps one in charge of sports and extracurricular activities. But as one principal in our sample pointed out, this means that only one member of the leadership council is directly responsible for the quality of instruction. An alternative, therefore, is to make sure that every assistant principal has some instructional responsibilities—sometimes divided by grades, or houses, or pathways—so that instruction is a concern of all members of the leadership council, and consistency of instruction across grades, or houses, or pathways can be monitored. We saw both kinds of leadership councils but heard very little from most principals about the rationales for these different approaches.

There doesn't seem to be much thought about how to structure the responsibilities of assistant principals and therefore the leadership council to enhance instruction.

In every other respect, however, the additional demands on high school principals are substantial. Some of these challenges are reduced in small schools or schools-within-schools, including the pathways examined in the next chapter, though other issues emerge with pathways. Very few of the challenges have been incorporated in principal preparation, or in induction programs (which are rare in any event)—the subject of chapter 4—and districts have paid almost no attention to providing any special supports for high school principals, the subject of chapter 5. So reforming high schools can take many forms, but all of them should include confronting the special challenges of leadership.

QUESTIONS FOR CHAPTER 2

1. To establish priorities in the use of time:
On a random day, keep a time diary, with an entry every time you shift from one activity to another. Then calculate what proportion of time you spend on various activities: interactions with parents; discipline; other interactions with students; sports-related interactions; other extracurricular activities; curriculum discussions, including discussions about which courses to offer; and instructional improvement, including classroom observations and instructionally related professional development.
2. What programs does your high school have to smooth the ninth-grade transition, including support or interventions for students who are behind grade level in their academic skills? Why did you choose these particular programs?
3. What programs do you have to prevent students from dropping out of school? Again, how did you choose these particular programs?
4. What programs do you have to improve approaches to instruction? Are they school-wide? Or confined to a subset of teachers, such as particular subjects or grade levels?
5. To analyze the causes of disciplinary referrals: for a period of time (perhaps a month), identify all referrals and/or suspensions by student, by teachers, and by the type of infraction. Which students—and which kinds of students (e.g., boys versus girls, upper grades versus lower grades, special ed versus general track versus honors track, students by race/ethnicity)—are responsible for the most referrals? Which teachers are responsible for the most referrals? If a small number of teachers is responsible for a large proportion of referrals, then observe these teachers to see if something about their instructional approach might be responsible.
6. How would you describe your discipline system? Have you considered alternative forms of discipline, such as positive behavioral or student-run discipline systems, including youth courts or restorative justice?
7. What are the responsibilities of different members of the school's leadership council? How many of them have responsibility for instruction?

Chapter 3

"The Jewels in Our Crown"

Leadership Demands in High Schools with Pathways

The requirements of leadership in high schools are in many ways greater than those in elementary and middle schools—or, at the very least, different from those that are the usual subjects in leadership preparation. However, when high schools engage in *systematic* reform—not simply hiring better teachers (however "better" is defined), improving guidance and counseling, or engaging in any small improvement within the comprehensive high school, but trying to reshape its basic structure—then there are additional challenges. In this chapter, I concentrate on the leadership demands specific to creating multiple pathways, one of the most fundamental reforms that has been suggested for high schools. They reshape many aspects of priority, purpose, time use, curriculum, and pedagogy, rather than being confined only to structure (such as small schools), to curriculum and purpose (as early and middle college high schools do), or to innovations that reform only a part of the high school (as ninth-grade academies or houses do). There are many different forms that pathways can take, as I emphasize in the next section, but virtually all of them engage in fundamental reform of the traditional high school.[1]

Small size itself has many benefits in the pathways whose leaders we interviewed because it facilitates certain reforms that are virtually impossible in large, complex high schools.

One attribute of all pathways, however, is that they are relatively small—including, in our sample of schools, from eighty to four hundred students. Small size itself has many benefits in the pathways whose leaders we interviewed because it facilitates certain reforms that are virtually impossible in large, complex high schools. Small size is not an end in itself, then, but a vehicle for accomplishing other reforms and facilitating certain practices that, in turn, may lead to improved outcomes.[2] In particular:

- Pathways usually rely on closer working relationships with students to improve student connections to adults and teachers—one of the issues in motivation and engagement cited in chapter 1. Their small size allows leaders and instructors alike to know individual students better. As one principal said,

  > At the big schools, they [students] often respond very obnoxiously to teachers. What's different about a small school environment is that the teachers know the kids, and so there's far more responsibility for kids standing in the hall, to like, say, "Kevin, what are you doing out here?" You know there's this immediate personalization that does not happen in the big schools, and there is more responsibility from teachers.

  Staff meetings discuss individual students and their progress as often as they discuss curricular and pedagogical issues. Instructors can readily see whether the same kinds of problems are taking place in different classes, and principals (or teacher-leaders) can then work more closely with a small group of students and their parents rather than with the impossibly large group that might be necessary in a high school of three to four thousand people.

  Teachers and leaders also claim that small size improve attendance and reduces discipline problems: "I've had teachers come in for pre-observation conferences, and they said, 'The attendance has improved in my classes. It makes teaching easier—I can implement the curriculum easier.'" In the MDRC (formerly Manpower Development Research Corporation) evaluations of academies, increased attendance was one of the clear outcomes, along with lower dropout rates, more credits earned, and more credits in college prep courses. High-risk students seemed more future-oriented, as measured by researching college options, taking the SAT or ACT, and submitting college applications. More generally, the personalization of the high school facilitated by small size is one of the features that improves student advancement through high school.[3]

Closer relationships in turn allow students to discuss problems at home and then facilitate the school's making referrals to appropriate agencies. In some schools, an unanticipated consequence of small size was learning about home problems that the comprehensive high school could not identify: "the more you dig into kids' lives, the more help you realize that they need." And these leaders see the combination of smaller size and theme-based approaches as engaging students more and reducing discipline problems. Particularly in districts that have converted large, dysfunctional high schools into small, autonomous schools, the differences in behavior before and after the breakup was frequently noted.

- Small size also facilitates leaders working with teachers, in professional development and instructional improvement in particular. Rather than the impossibility of working with huge numbers of teachers—"with eighty teachers and one of me, where do you start?"—professional development efforts work not with eighty teachers but more like ten to fifteen. Professional development as a group activity, with continuous discussion within a school about instructional and other issues, becomes possible in ways that it is not in a comprehensive high school.[4] So the smaller scale of pathways is one antidote to the challenges to *instructional* leadership in large comprehensive high schools.
- Small, autonomous schools and schools-within-schools resolve some of the structural problems leading to mediocre teaching. The high numbers of students per teacher, or total student load, is much smaller because teachers typically teach fewer classes, often for longer periods of time (in block schedules or another redistribution of time). In addition, where instructors collaborate on integrating their courses, they

can pay attention to the "whole student," seeing how students perform in different classes and on different tasks, allowing schools to develop more targeted interventions for weaker students. Finally, "it's easier to hide at a comprehensive school," as mediocre instructors escape notice from administrators unable to get around to classroom observations, but that is less true in a small school where teachers and leaders are working together constantly and are more likely to be in each others' classrooms—"in a small school they [mediocre instructors] stick out like a sore thumb," and leaders can then work either to improve their instructional abilities or, if that fails, to dismiss them.

- Pathways focus on the academic and occupational content of the high school, not on the vast extracurriculum, and some pathways and autonomous small schools do not provide an array of extracurricular activities (partly because of diseconomies of small size). (Other autonomous schools do provide a variety of extracurricular activities, as I will illustrate in the first section below, so this is a choice to be made.) This means that the complexity of the comprehensive high school is much reduced, and principals and assistant principals need not be distracted from instructional responsibilities by nonacademic activities. Of course, this comes at some cost because some students and parents like the comprehensive high school for its nonacademic side. Over time, if comprehensive high schools continue to coexist with multiple pathways, we might expect pathways with self-selected students (and parents) to become focused on their learning goals, with neither students nor leaders distracted by fun and games, while some comprehensive high school remain the anti-intellectual and anti-schoolwork places they often are. Developing pathways is therefore one way of restoring academic rigor to the high school, not by the tactic of increasing testing and requiring supposedly more advanced courses,[5] but by enhancing the focus on those aspects that should matter and getting rid of distractions.
- In pathways within comprehensive high schools, the difficulties of the master schedule are largely eliminated because there are many fewer teachers, students, and classes to juggle. To be sure, when pathways exist within comprehensive high schools (but not in autonomous small schools), grouping students and teachers in particular pathways must be done *before* other priorities are considered; without school-wide

agreement on pathways, these issues are unlikely to be resolved. But with this crucial caveat, scheduling dilemmas are much simpler, and master plans need no longer be seen as a malevolent external force.

So, although small size by itself cannot resolve all the problems in high schools,[6] it can create the conditions for addressing many of these problems, especially those of instructional improvement, students' sense of belonging, and improved relations among teachers—as can smaller charter or choice schools or early college high schools with a clear emphasis and smaller size. But with any of these reforms come greater challenges, and—as with the general challenges in high schools—they need to be confronted directly.

THE MULTIPLE FORMS OF MULTIPLE PATHWAYS

As chapter 1 clarified, there are varying ideas about what a pathway is. Some are based on a broadly occupational theme (such as health, information technology, international business, or media and design), whereas others have nonoccupational themes (such as environmental concerns, social justice, or urban issues). The theme can then determine the content of just one or two courses or can influence all courses students take in a small, autonomous high school, for example. What people call pathways can therefore vary substantially, and various definitions may not be consistent with one another.

In the schools where we interviewed, pathways take five major forms:

- A comprehensive high school incorporating several pathways, or majors (to use the terminology of colleges), or strands, where students take a theme-based course for one or two periods a day but take all other courses in the regular part of the high school. The proportion of students in such strands can vary, of course, from relatively trivial to substantial. If pathways or strands include relatively few students and only one specialized course during junior and senior years (for example), and the specialized subjects are not integrated into other courses, then the comprehensive high school is only barely affected. At the other extreme, all students are in a pathway—often called "wall-to-wall pathways"—and the concept of high school starts to change dramatically.

- A comprehensive high school incorporating several pathways or academies, where students take several courses together. In the California Partnership Academy model, for example, four instructors teach together—typically an English teacher, a math teacher, either a science or social studies teacher, and one teacher specializing in the theme of the academy. Sometimes a large high school will have one or two academies, or eighty to one hundred sixty students in a school of fifteen hundred or two thousand, in which case the comprehensive high school is virtually unchanged for most students. At the other extreme, some schools have "wall-to-wall academies," where every student is in an academy. Therefore the importance of pathways compared to "regular" offerings in the comprehensive part of the school can vary substantially.
- One physical high school with several autonomous small schools at the site. This approach has often resulted from districts reconstituting a traditional high school by breaking it into several autonomous small schools, a subject to which I return in chapter 5 concerning district policies. Typically, there is little interaction among the schools at one site. Each small school has a roster of teachers, both in conventional high school subjects and in the school's theme, and each school also has a principal, usually with expertise in the theme of the small school. All principals at one site may meet to discuss issues that face the entire facility, such as maintenance, sometimes scheduling, sometimes graduation, proms, and other campus-wide events. However, they typically have no authority over the other small schools, and there is no one who does except perhaps district officials.
- One physical high school with several semi-autonomous small schools, each with a principal (or perhaps an assistant principal) but with a central administration with authority over all small schools. In one example, a dysfunctional high school was literally demolished, replaced by a lovely new facility incorporating a ninth-grade academy; three themed schools for grades ten through twelve (each with its own principal); and a central office with an executive principal, a budget director, a facilities director, and a coordinator of sports and extracurricular activities. Unlike the case of several autonomous schools at one site, the central office and the executive principal do have authority over the small schools.
- A freestanding small school, again with a theme. Such a school typically reports to district officials. Within the school, both conventional

academic teachers and theme teachers orient their subjects around the theme. Without any other pathways at the site, there are no distractions or coordination problems from other small schools. Sports and extracurricular activities are unlikely to be very important, simply because of the diseconomies of small size—unless the school has found other ways for students to participate in these activities, for example, in neighboring schools.

The administrative structure of these different approaches also varies. Typically, pathways or academies within a comprehensive high school are headed by teacher-leaders or lead teachers, released part-time from teaching responsibilities. They usually report to various assistant principals, with the division of authority between assistant principals and pathway leaders varying among schools. However, in most states teacher-leaders cannot formally evaluate other teachers, so teacher evaluation—which itself may vary from serious to pro forma—must be carried out by assistant principals. Autonomous small schools typically have principals, however, who report to district officials, except where there is a central office and an executive principal.

The importance of identifying different approaches is that some leadership challenges in high schools vary among types of pathways, while others are constant. I will return to advantages and disadvantages of different forms of pathways in the conclusion of this chapter.

The following sections outline nine different challenges that arise in high school with pathways. Some of them are special cases of the challenges identified in chapter 2, whereas others are unique to pathways. But all of them indicate that leaders in pathways should be prepared to play certain roles and to anticipate particular problems for which there is currently no form of preparation except on-the-job training.

THE CHOICE OF PATHWAY THEMES

One special element of all pathways is the theme that orients curriculum and instruction. High schools have tried other forms of personalization—houses and advisories, for example. But breaking up a class into small houses, but failing to give the houses any special roles, creates a meaningless structure; as one house principal for ninth grade noted, "what we didn't do with houses is we didn't create the need for them," so they made no difference to students and to learning. In contrast, a theme responds to a need of some kind, especially the desire of students to enter a broad occupational area or the need of employers for well-prepared workers. In turn, the theme has many consequences—for attractiveness to students and enrollment, for attractiveness to teachers, for the equity of pathways, for the ability of pathways to link with employers and with postsecondary programs—and so it is a decision to be carefully considered.

The themes of pathways may mean different things to different people. One purpose, especially for occupationally themed pathways, is to prepare students for particular careers, either for employment right after high school or for college majors that lead to careers ("college *and* careers"). For another pathway leader, the purpose was college preparation, partly because of a nearby community college where students began taking courses as early as ninth grade: "We are an early college high school with an arts theme." Yet another declared the value of all small learning communities but went on to say that "the themed academies offer direction and support to first-generation college students"—something that the amorphous college prep curriculum does not offer. Another reaffirmed the value of direction and what might be called the guidance function of pathways:

> We're not teaching anybody something that they could go out and get a job with, to be very honest. Our purpose is to use this career focus to expose kids to what their options are, in that way get them connected to their education so their grades and their engagement more reflects their ability ... And the other part is to help propel them into some sort of plan for their future because too many of them drift around with no plan.

For a local business council, a pathway may be a way to develop the workforce in particular ways; one principal said that the local chamber of commerce "gave us a list of 'Here's where we want to develop in a workforce'"—which sometimes becomes the age-old problem of employers trying to impose a narrow, firm-specific curriculum on the school. Others talked about the value of a theme in creating some order out of the high school curriculum, which otherwise has no coherence. And one principal said that "academies are interesting because they are important"—they introduce students to issues that are important, with internships where "students were sort of seeing the real world, and I've seen internships turn kids around because they go, 'oh, maybe I do need to graduate from high school.'" This is a direct counter to

Paul Goodman's (1956, 41) biting critique of high schools: "If there is nothing worthwhile, it is hard to do anything at all." So the purposes of pathways vary, and the occupational focus of many pathways does not necessarily mean that their main benefits are directly occupational—they may relate more to student motivation and ability to plan, the coherence of the curriculum, the opportunities for faculty to collaborate, and other dimensions.

In practice, the themes of pathways in schools we visited were chosen in several different ways. When a district made a decision to break up an anomic high school into several small, themed schools, they sometimes chose existing vocational tracks as the basis for some themes and sometimes selected dynamic individuals with particular interests to serve as principals. In a few cases, the district identified a theme based on the concentration of particular employers in the area who might serve as sources of employment. In others, teachers with particular interests banded together to promote a particular theme. In some cases, strong teachers coalesced around a theme, even if they were not particularly interested in that theme. As one principal of a science-themed school, originally a social studies teacher, mentioned,

> I originally chose to get in with the science house because I liked the English teacher who had also chosen it ... one of the better science teachers was there, and then we collectively brought other, stronger teachers in. It's very much like the strong students band together on a campus: there's no difference in terms of teachers.

The only problem with this approach is that it may create a pathway with a disproportionate number of strong teachers, depriving the rest of the school—an issue of equity in resources that emerges in subsequent sections.

In a few cases, the themes were chosen by students themselves: "When they broke up [a dysfunctional high school], the kids rose up and said we want a school of the arts. So based on student voice they [the district] said, 'let's create it.'" Another gave decision-making power to students as part of the schools' ethos:

> Because we are a youth empowerment school, those are pathways that students came up with themselves. We had a lot of students who were very passionate about music, and that's how that pathway emerged. Many students were really passionate about the law and social justice and students' rights, so that's how the legal studies pathway emerged. So they were youth- and community-initiated concepts.

There is, then, no one way to create an appropriate theme, though there are several bad ways. One is that teachers don't want a theme that isn't theirs: "they don't wanna have a scripted curriculum [or a pathway] that is not their curriculum." Another complained about a principal who "chose it [the theme] in a back room":

> Let's be frank; he did it because he heard the rumors that they were going to put in another school here totally incongruent with the [existing] School of the Arts. So he created this Academy of Arts and Sciences and a school of the arts ... It wasn't just because we wanted to offer kids an arts- and science-based education. No, no, no, make no bones about it. It was to block another school from coming in here.

So a lack of transparency in choosing themes is another problem. Ideally, then, district officials, the principal, teachers, and students are all convinced of the value of a theme.

Rather than allowing a variety of themes to emerge, some proponents of pathways have created orthodoxies about themes. For example, to be funded by the California Partnership Academies, themes must be occupationally oriented. ConnectEd, an advocacy group in Berkeley, has also followed the idea that pathways must be "industry-themed." The academies sponsored by the National Academies Foundation focus on finance, hospitality and tourism, information technology, or engineering, and the travel and tourism academies supported by American Express all have particular themes connected to their sponsors. Others have asserted that themes should be nonoccupational (Raywid 2006), and some high schools have also forbidden occupational themes for fear that they will degenerate into traditional vocational education. Unfortunately, this particular debate—between occupational versus nonoccupational themes—replicates the division between academic and vocational education that has plagued the American education system since the 1880s. A more Deweyan, both-and solution would be to develop *both* occupational *and* nonoccupational themes, and then see how students and parents choose among them, what the advantages of different themes are in establishing internships and postsecondary connections, and whether there end up being differences in student outcomes based on the themes chosen.

The choice of a theme is not just an issue of finding a topic around which different individuals can coalesce. In most districts, open enrollment and the development of both public and private charter schools means that there is some competition among high schools. Students (and their still-influential parents) choose in part on a school's reputation, in part on its neighborhood (especially its location on the right or wrong side of the tracks), and—inevitably—on the racial and class composition of the school. But the theme also makes a difference in competing with other schools. One district official noted that a school got a grant to start a law academy: "they're totally thrilled because they feel like they need to compete . . . they're feeling this pressure: If they don't have a hook, they're going to lose kids to the charter schools." In other cases, principals noted adopting a high-status theme—biotechnology, for example, or information technology—as a way of competing not only with other theme-based schools but also with a high-status comprehensive high school. In one district, "they perceive [a particular high school] as a sort of ghetto high school—you send your kid there, and he or she is likely to get jumped by a gang or influenced to join a gang," so parents were angry when the district located a popular pathway at the "ghetto school" in order to attract more students there. Conversely, the "wrong" theme can doom a pathway to low status, to uncertain or dwindling enrollments, and to retracking or an "undesirable" mix of students—possibilities I examine later in this chapter.

Principals sometimes have little influence over the choice of a theme, particularly if it has been determined by a district, by locally dominant employment patterns, or by students themselves. However, one responsibility of a principal is to make sure that the subject of a pathway remains appropriately broad—precisely so that it does not become a low-status pathway, or attract only a certain group of students, or replicate the low-quality curriculum of traditional vocational ed. For example, an automotive academy could develop a broader transportation focus; a health academy should not be allowed to degenerate into preparation for dental technicians, as one pathway I visited did. Principals and teachers should also resist student pressures to create narrow or low-status academies; when I expressed some dismay at a cosmetology pathway, the principal explained that "the girls like to do hair"—probably not the kind of student "preferences" that should be respected. Precisely for these reasons, some principals will not allow occupational-oriented pathways for fear that they will degenerate into low-status versions of traditional vocational ed. And in the choice of pathways, as in many other aspects of high schools, the current preferences of students must be balanced against long-run interests they may not fully understand, and preparing girls to "do hair" or boys to work on cars surely does not open up many future opportunities (including postsecondary education) to them.

The choice of a theme also has substantial implications for the development of curriculum. In some cases—the Academies of Travel and Tourism sponsored by the National Academies Foundation, sometimes "green" academies—the sponsoring organization has invested in curriculum development appropriate to the theme. A school of the arts whose principal we interviewed had adopted materials developed by Project Zero at Harvard University, including a course called "Studio Habits of Mind" and another called "Visual Thinking Strategies." But where a theme has developed in response to a local employer, or the interests of students, or a group of teachers with similar approaches and interests, then it's unlikely the pathway can find a ready-made curriculum. Indeed, the vast majority of the pathways we observed did not use off-the-shelf curriculum. These are situations where the cooperation of teachers in *developing* a curriculum—including the participation of conventional academic teachers in molding more integrated approaches to such conventional subjects as math, English, and social studies—is a necessary dimension of the pathway. In two schools we visited, the teachers were developing the curriculum with the help of the local community colleges; one example came in biotechnology, not normally a subject that would be offered in high schools. Such cooperative curriculum development obviously helps in creating a pathway into the community college.

In addition, a pathway implies a progression of courses, not only in such standard subjects as English and math but also in the subject of the theme—the scope and sequence of what students are doing in each grade. Again, in most cases these have to be developed by teachers working together to create such a sequence. As a principal of a school with several pathways noted, "Each pathway is designed to have a four-year sequence of courses, each one being a higher level from beginning to intermediate to advanced." This kind of sequencing is achieved in conventional academic courses either by state standards that specify which specific topics take place within each year (though many teachers may be ignorant of these standards) or by textbooks aimed at different grade levels. But for the themes of many pathways, neither standards nor textbooks exist, so it becomes the responsibility of teachers and leaders to create coherent sequences. One district official maintained that the collaboration among teachers in pathways could enhance the transitions from grade to grade:

> You are looking at a scope and sequence of what kids are doing from ninth to twelfth grade in a way that you don't always do as a classroom teacher, where you may just be worried about tenth-grade social science. . . . But I think teacher-leaders and principals are more aware of the kind of scope and sequence: how is a kid going to navigate from the ninth to the twelfth grade, and how do we keep track of that kid so the kid doesn't drop out?

So the need to create a coherent sequence lies ultimately with the principal convening teachers to plan the curriculum.

KEEPING THE VISION

The principal of a school with pathways, as well as teacher-leaders, must be keepers of the vision—advocates for the special advantages of pathways. "It's a mission, not just a job," commented one; statements of being engaged in "a whole paradigm shift" or being "at the revolutionary edge of high school reform" similarly say that developing pathways requires deeper understanding of the non-traditional practices in pathways. In a study of ten districts implementing pathways, the centrality of vision emerged again (Stanford Redesign Network 2009): "It's not enough to lead; you have to lead with vision." District officials also noted the need for an "executive champion" to promote pathways at the district level, and where this person is missing, pathways may suffer. As one coach noted, in a district without an "executive champion,"

> It's a project that they're doing, but it's not clear how it will alter the district in any fundamental way. The vision for the work seems to be lacking.

The principal of a school with pathways, as well as teacher-leaders, must be keepers of the vision—advocates for the special advantages of pathways.

Keeping the vision means communicating the vision and its practices to teachers, especially teachers who have previously taught in comprehensive high schools; explaining pathways to parents and prospective students, who probably know little about pathways and their advantages; explaining pathways to district and state bureaucrats who don't understand them; and fending off efforts (especially from district officials and budgeters) to compromise the vision. Inevitably, with occupationally focused pathways, a central element of vision is clarifying that pathways are not simply a return to traditional vocational education (which parents always distrust) but a new synthesis of academic and occupational education with goals of "college *and* careers." Pathways and courses don't come in standard forms and subjects, and pathways may create new bureaucratic problems or new course names or inconsistencies with traditional high schools—and the vision of a leader is necessary to continually clarify the ways that pathways are different from business as usual. Keeping the vision also means advocating for pathways in budget debates because pathways cost more than conventional high school programs (as examined below) and are therefore vulnerable to being cut back or even eliminated in such difficult fiscal times as the present.

The challenge of keeping the vision arises precisely because pathways are such substantial modifications of the comprehensive high school. As chapter 1 clarified, the comprehensive high school has been developing at least since the 1820s, whereas pathways began only in the mid-1980s. Virtually all parents went to comprehensive high schools, and their image of "high school" is unavoidably dominated by their experiences. Some parents simply won't buy the notion of pathways; as one assistant principal in an enormous high school with a few pathways noted,

> I thought that this campus didn't want small learning communities at all. It really likes its size, the kids like being part of this big school. There are three hundred people in band; band wins every national- or every state-level competition. Color guard wins; our sports teams win; we have a forensics team that takes national titles every year. That's because we're big: there are four thousand kids here. So our job is, how do you make a big school small but keep it big?

But the attractions of the comprehensive high school—which in her version have everything to do with color guard and sports, and nothing to do with academic content—have to be weighed against its many dysfunctional practices, and the advantages of pathways are central aspects of promoting pathways to the community.

The leaders we interviewed were highly supportive of pathways: "Academies are the jewels in our crown," declared one. They recognized that pathways were excellent vehicles for personalizing schools, for establishing cultures more supportive of academic work than of color guard and proms. They spoke constantly of pathways as ways of engaging and motivating students, of making the high school "relevant" and "motivating" to them,[7] and of reducing discipline problems. Of course they are supportive: that's part of their job. But this means that districts have to choose the right kinds of people to be principals and assistant principals in schools with pathways, and in turn these leaders need to be prepared to defend pathways against the powerful forces that might return to the much more familiar comprehensive high school. As Larry Cuban has stressed,[8] advocacy is part of the position.

ENSURING THE SPECIAL FEATURES OF PATHWAYS

Working with pathways is different from working with departments. Most (but not all) pathways include teachers from a variety of subjects, rather than teachers from one disciplinary area; pathways are oriented around themes that can be interpreted broadly and flexibly, while departments have "more rigid agendas," as one leader mentioned, driven by disciplinary issues. Pathways need to think about the trajectory of curriculum from ninth to twelfth grades, but there are few structures in place—state standards, grade-level textbooks—to help pathways develop this trajectory.[9] Most develop their own curricula, sometimes with the guidance of local employers and postsecondary institutions. Leaders therefore need to be prepared to work with different constellations of teachers and subject matter to construct coherent pathways.

Pathways have many special features that make them different from the programs in comprehensive high schools, and all of them make special demands on leaders:

Fostering the integration of course material. One advantage of pathways is that they allow the creation of multidisciplinary approaches to learning, especially with the integration across courses including the integration of academic and occupational content. For this, a minimum requirement is sufficient time for teachers to plan together. One principal in a new pathway articulated his priority:

> We do want to incorporate common planning time because right now it doesn't exist in our schedule and it's like everything is being done in isolation, which we know is not a very good way to do it.... That's the biggie, and I feel like we have willing participants—we just have to give them time in the master schedule.

To do this, one principal created a ninety-minute common preparation time for all teachers at every grade level: "it was the number-one thing I knew had to happen, the first master schedule I ever built, because for me there were nonnegotiables about building the school." Virtually all pathways have developed some method of assuring common planning time, but the amounts vary dramatically; some allow very little, "and they blame it on the fact that it's too hard to make a master schedule," declared a principal—again a reference to the master schedule as an external barrier rather than a device for scheduling priorities. A central responsibility for leaders, then, is to allocate time for planning and to assure that it is sufficient to accomplish the goals of integration.

One of the central goals of most pathways is to allow teachers of conventional subjects—math, English, history or social studies, certainly science, perhaps even languages—to integrate the theme of the pathway into their teaching. This can be done by choosing examples, reading materials, problem sets, projects (either jointly with other pathway courses or separately), and such activities as field trips. Another technique is to develop guiding or essential questions for integrated units; for example, in a pathway focused on education and future teachers, the guiding question for a government or civics class might be "what role should government play in regulating public education?" or a question for history might be "how has inequality in education shaped cultural and ethnic relations in the United States?" (Gurholt 2010). Several guides to curriculum integration are available, some of them developed specifically for pathways (for example, ConnectEd 2010a), and some of them developed for integration and interdisciplinary teaching of any subjects (Jacobs 1989; Jenkins and Tanner 1992). But curriculum integration doesn't take place automatically, simply from the structure of a path; it must be encouraged or facilitated by leaders, and creating planning time may be only one of the requirements for integration.

One of the advantages of pathways is the possibility of integrating the theme into courses in literature, history, social studies, and government—subjects related to the moral and civic purposes of schooling but that students often think of as among the most boring and irrelevant of the entire curriculum. It's not difficult to think how to integrate history with various broad subjects—the history of medicine and health care or of business and government regulation, the history of transportation for an auto-related pathway, even the cultural history of hair and clothing styles if a high school decides it must adopt cosmetology or fashion merchandising. Similarly, virtually every subject appropriate for a broad theme has some policy and regulatory issues appropriate for government or civics courses—the regulation of medical care, the public debates over corporations and their responsibilities, school laws and current policy debates, even the regulation of cosmetologists. And literature could include the novels of rural life for agriculture programs, the novels of corporate life for business, the novels related to medicine (such as Sinclair Lewis's *Arrowsmith*), or the autobiographies of particular well-known individuals working in the area of the theme.[10] The integration of a theme into these subjects might increase their "relevance" and interest for students.

A related issue is that of choosing, or better yet *developing*, teachers who are willing and able to plan together and integrate content across disciplines. As one principal mentioned,

> [The] Irvine [Foundation] has funded a project down at the State University of San Diego, to worry about teacher training—again, with the idea that you are going to have to have teachers that are trained in this kind of cooperation and integration across disciplinary lines. This has several advantages, and I am curious to see what they come up with, because it is clearly one of the challenges in running these theme-based schools.

This statement recognizes, as many principals did, that innovative structures in high schools require different kinds of teachers (just as they require different kinds of principal preparation, discussed in chapter 4, and district policies, examined in chapter 5). The program at California State University at San Diego mentioned by this principal has a multiple pathways emphasis or linked learning "lens" within a conventional single-subject credential program. Students receive the same preparation in academic content areas, but they also learn more about "problem-based learning activities that focus on authentic problems around an industry theme," interdisciplinary planning, the "collaborations and process that accompany cross-disciplinary work," and they are placed in "schools that model the approaches it [CSU–San Diego] is integrating into the teacher education program"—that is, high schools with pathways that will use these special capacities. The program, started in 2008, now includes a network of five additional teacher preparation institutions, and several other universities, both public and private, have expressed interest.[11] Similarly, the San Joaquin County Office of Education has developed the Teachers College of San Joaquin, which includes three multiple pathway labs as part of their core courses for the master's degree in teaching.[12]

Teacher preparation specific to pathways has several advantages over conventional single-subject programs: teachers presumably emerge from the program already familiar with the idea of pathways; they should be more skilled in the process of integrating subjects across disciplines or courses; and they are hopefully less wedded to a rigid idea of their discipline, and more concerned with developing a program around a theme and student interests. Such programs could also be a partial antidote to several problems presented in chapter 2, especially the tendency of high school teachers to ignore instructional methods in favor of content and coverage. Teacher preparation in this country and certification of high school teachers in single-subject programs developed from the 1894 model of high schools divided into isolated departments, and a new kind of high school requires new forms of preparation for teachers as well as leaders.

Guidance and counseling oriented toward future choices (or toward college and careers, in the now-familiar vocabulary), so students have some basis for choosing pathways and for understanding how their programs are related to life after high school. Most schools we visited have strengthened counseling by finding funds for an extra counselor or two, reducing the pupil/counselor ratio from the norm in California (700:1 to 800:1) to something on the order of 250:1. Some of them have also created introductory courses in ninth or tenth grade that review the possible occupations associated with the pathway theme, a targeted form of career education. In addition, the curriculum in occupationally oriented pathways exposes students to a wide variety of future options, whereas conventional counseling does not. As the principal of a small, autonomous high school focused on health occupations commented,

> A lot of people would look at our approach as a massive funnel that eighth graders jump into, and it chokes them down to become a doctor or a nurse. And it's exactly the opposite. What it really is, is this massive group of eighth graders, and the funnel is upside down. They are climbing in the small end of the funnel, and then they are seeing that health care is this vast industry. What we would like is for them to come out with a much broader approach to what the possibilities are ... [In terms of career options] they can work in diagnostics, therapeutics, health informatics, EMT dental assisting, dental radiology tech ... and then if you ask them what they're interested in, it's this big spectrum.

Where there are forms of work-based learning, including job shadowing, and opportunities to attend community college courses, there are still other sources of information about options after high school.[13]

Where pathways have their own counselors, they can become more familiar with pathways, and they are likely to approach counseling in ways different from traditional counselors. Conventional counselors may steer students away from pathways; as one pathway leader complained, "the counselors say, 'no, you better go to the general program because you won't be able to get into college if you stay here in the pathway,' which is a lie." Conventional counselors also tend to be ignorant about labor markets; their training is often in some therapeutic tradition appropriate for *personal* counseling (even though little of that takes place in most high schools). Most of their time is spent on *academic* counseling about what courses to take for graduation and for college. As a result, very little guidance and counseling in traditional high schools is future-oriented, about occupational and education opportunities after high school and their implications for high school programs. In addition, there is all too much anecdotal evidence that counselors engage in tracking students: one pathway leader said that "the counselors tend to make judgments about who is college prep and who isn't," asserting in particular that "kids of color tell me that." Many pathways have found ways around these old and familiar practices by relying on their own counselors, who in turn try to attract students of color rather than telling them they are not "college material."

Of course, there's always the issue of how well adolescents can formulate their plans under a guidance system that asks them to create a long-term plan. One district leader described her ambitions for guidance and counseling:

> We were trying to make it that kids made an informed decision about what they wanted to do, and we are hoping that more kids are choosing based on—"wow,

> that really looks like a cool program." ... But listening to some of the eighth-grade teachers who were there when the kids were filling out their forms, I think a lot of it is that "my friends are going there." I don't know how much eighth graders know about what they want to do ... But what we really want you [students] to do is choose a program so that you can say, "I choose to be here, I should go and be engaged, I should go to class, I should get involved in my projects, I am with other people who also chose to be in their program."

Even if guidance and counseling don't produce highly rational decisions, the element of choice, and trying to promote informed choice, may have its own benefits for motivation and engagement if students become committed to the choices they make rather than resisting a curriculum they did not choose. Another principal admitted that

> We try to develop a four-year plan, but I'll be honest: when you're younger, it's hard to—the next text message is the next best thing, if you know what I mean, sometimes it's hard for them to see into the future.... By the junior and senior year, they definitely start to clue in a little bit more, where they need to make some decisions as to what specifically they're going to be doing.

So even under the best of conditions, it may be difficult to engage young adolescents in such rational planning.[14]

However, a great deal of what principals call guidance and counseling is really *recruitment*, or what one principal referred to as "our marketing," citing videos, brochures, and open houses. In response to questions about counseling and guidance, most responded by describing information sessions with eighth graders and their parents, orientation sessions in ninth grade where all pathways explain their purposes to prospective students, and brochures and publicity aimed at explaining to parents the wonderful opportunities in particular pathways. This may be a necessary element of constructing pathways, particularly because lack of enrollment appears to be the chief reason for pathways collapsing.[15] But advertising and recruitment efforts are intended to attract students to a *specific* pathway rather than others (and rather than the comprehensive high school), not to prepare them to think broadly about their futures and the *multiple* options they face. Recruitment is not, therefore, a substitute for more general forms of future-oriented guidance and counseling.

In the absence of career-oriented guidance and counseling, what appear to be student "choices" are not the expressions of rational interest that we might imagine. One leader of a school of the arts noted that

> I don't think kids know why they're here. They just kind of ended up here, and it's small, and it's nice and it's friendly and it's safe. Our arts programs seem to be where the kids find community. "I am at the academy because I want to get a high school education and I happen to be here, and my parents picked it because they know it is safe." ... But as far as like, "I am at the academy because I want to go into biosciences"—no. "I am at the academy because I want to go into liberal arts and be a journalist"—no. We're still figuring that out.

Virtually all schools with pathways, at least in our sample, rely on intensification of quite conventional forms of guidance and counseling: individual contacts with counselors; career information in introductory courses; information about college application procedures; college trips; and ubiquitous college photos and banners, as if such visual reminders strengthen a college-going culture. But one special opportunity that multiple pathways offer is the chance for students to try out different pathways before they make a choice—to understand the requirements of different broad occupational areas in a way that is more experiential, and certainly less manipulative, than recruitment sessions are. For example, one high school not in our sample, with six pathways or majors, required students to spend nine weeks in each of the six pathways, learning about related careers, about the schooling and academic requirements, and about the kinds of activities that working in these pathways might require. Then they chose two of the six for a second nine-week period, and at the end of tenth grade made a choice of a pathway for eleventh and twelfth grades. Not only did students learn about a variety of occupational areas and pathways but certain stereotypes could be avoided. Most obviously, where young women must take one of these nine-week "exploratories" (the term sometimes used in traditional vocational ed) or "tasters" in every pathway, then they are least exposed to occupations that might be traditionally thought of as "male," such as engineering or (in health-related pathways) doctors as well as nurses. One principal in a school with multiple pathways reinvented this idea in the form of "wheel courses," which might also be an antidote to the instability of adolescent choices:

> You're asking a thirteen-year-old to choose an academic strand that they're interested in, and their interests change quite frequently. As a freshman they may enter, for example, computer technology because they're very much into videogames. By the time they're a sophomore and they're talking to some of their other friends, they want to maybe join health and medicine because it seems more academically competitive.... I would say that the trend is about a third of the students change their small learning communities every year, for three years.... What I've been suggesting, rather than the academy course their freshman year, they could take a wheel course. Each nine weeks, they could take a different wheel course, get a taste of what that academy would be like and then, sophomore year, enter academies better-informed consumers. But nobody has listened. I think that is a great idea, even if it is my own.

Neither her school nor any of the other schools we examined have adopted these "wheel courses" or "exploratories" or "tasters." Nor have they adopted any other innovative practices that we could detect. In effect, these schools with pathways rely on an intensification of conventional counseling and guidance through an additional counselor—and on small size—to provide more direction to students about their futures.

Principals are typically unprepared to think about innovative forms of guidance and counseling. But most critics fault high schools not only with inadequate numbers of counselors—an issue that principals may not be able to resolve without district funding—but also with burdening counselors with administrivia, special ed paperwork, and other bureaucratic functions unrelated to helping students figure out their life courses. And the amount of innovation in guidance and counseling is quite limited: most counselors use trait and factor analysis, in which students are given personality and interest inventories and then provided with information about the occupations for which they are presumably best suited, a procedure sometimes ridiculed as "test 'em and tell 'em." In reality, decision-making is a much more complex capacity requiring at the very least a set of stable preferences that youth in particular may not have, a willingness to weigh a wide variety of options, some understanding of probabilistic events and future options, and some sense of how to evaluate present costs against future benefits. So planning and decision-making are capacities that must be developed in more careful ways than simply providing an "information dump" (Grubb 2002b).

Because preparing students to make schooling and life choices is even more important with multiple pathways, this places a responsibility on leaders to stop burdening counseling with duties unrelated to their ostensible purposes, to learn more about innovative counseling, and to implement a program that can reach all students. The following are among potential innovations, in addition to "exploratories":

- Counseling in culturally sensitive ways, incorporating awareness of how students of color understand the world of work; knowledge of multicultural counseling theory; and the creation of career centers that are welcoming to diverse students—for example, that include counselors of color (Flores and Heppner 2002; Hendricks 1993; Cheatham 1990).
- Developing ways of considering future careers that focus students on alternatives and on the educational paths to these choices. One is the notion of "career construction," with interview methods and storytelling exercises to help students develop "a road map for guiding their clients do on the path of self-discovery and personal fulfillment" (Hartung and Taber 2008). Another is Curry and Lambie's (2007) "counseling portfolio," incorporating career interest inventories, financial aid calculations, research on particular careers, various essays, and a résumé.
- Transforming concepts of what counselors do. For example, in the Puente program aimed at Latino students, counselors provide conventional college and career counseling (though with a smaller student/counselor load than usual), but they also work with teachers to identify academic and personal problems and convene parents to support their students and learn more about the role of schooling in gaining access to future opportunities (Grubb, Lara, and Valdez 2002). The Education Trust and the MetLife Foundation envision counselors as reform leaders in their schools, diagnosing the problems students face and organizing reforms to enhance effectiveness.
- Creating a more developmental approach to guidance and counseling. Perhaps the best example is the LifeMap program at Valencia Community College. LifeMap articulates five stages: the transition from high school to college; the initial period in college when students are taking basic skills courses as necessary and making decisions about majors; the transition to graduation with the completion of coursework and other requirements; the period of progressing toward their degree

> and accumulating the necessary coursework; and gradation and then lifelong learning. LifeMap clarifies students' choices at each stage, as well as the college services provided; it therefore articulates both student and institutional responsibilities. The overall goal is to make students independent: "you will become increasingly self-sufficient in implementing your career and educational goals, until you are totally directing your own learning process." Students can see the entire trajectory of five stages at a glance, in the LifeMap handbook and other materials, so they can envision the entire process as they begin college. The LifeMap program is easily modified for the transition into and through high school (Grubb 2008b) and could therefore be adopted in any high school.

There are, then, many ways that high schools with pathways—and conventional high schools too—could improve guidance and counseling at this crucial stage in students' lives. Unfortunately, counseling has been quite resistant to improvement, partly because it often seems peripheral to academic instruction, and partly because it is underresourced as a result. Correcting this pattern requires new attention by school leaders.[16]

Internships, work-based placements, and service learning so that students have out-of-school experiences to complement in-school learning. In pathways with nonvocational themes, the analogue to work-based placements is service learning, or placements in organizations that work with issues related to the theme—for example, environmental organizations for students in environmental academies, or immigration advocates for students in international academies. Most principals we talked to acknowledged the difficulty of finding sufficient work-based placements. In several schools, internships—where students carry out real work assignments under the guidance of mentors—are reserved for seniors because internships are hard to find; sophomores and juniors may engage in less intensive job shadowing or briefer periods of work experience. The barriers to good placements include the difficulty of finding cooperative employers, especially because high schools have to compete with community and state colleges for such positions; transportation issues; the difficulties of meshing school schedules and work schedules, which are obviously not geared to the school day; sometimes limits on the hours and conditions under which individuals under age eighteen can work; and the fact that some students don't have social security numbers or (in the case of immigrant students) green cards.

As a result of these difficulties, several schools have hired individuals to recruit and coordinate work-based learning, relying on special grants to cover the costs. One principal of a freestanding small school noted that a network of schools and employers was forming *slowly* in his area, with the implicit warning that establishing the close and continuing relationships necessary for strong work-based learning is not something that can happen right away.[17] For the same reasons, it would be premature to require relatively new pathways to include serious forms of work-based learning in their first few years, when they are working on creating the internal relationship and curriculum necessary for a pathway. What is important, however, is for leaders in pathways to understand the importance of work-based learning and to be developing such placements as time and resources permit.

An alternative is to use partnerships with groups outside the school—especially business partners and chambers of commerce—to develop internships. As one district official with many large high schools broken into small, semi-autonomous smalls noted, "the truth of the matter is the internships are valuable and they're important, but they only really happen with outside partners who help get the internships. I don't see the school as having very good capacity to find internships." This is one aspect of pathways I will recapitulate in chapter 5, on the responsibilities of districts.

Connections to postsecondary education represent the efforts in pathways to provide access to *both* college *and* careers—in contrast to traditional forms of vocational education that led to work but not further education and to academic education that prepared for college but not employment. As for work-based learning, what is required of leaders is that they understand the dual purpose of pathways—a part of keeping the vision—and that they seek out opportunities to create postsecondary connections. Virtually all of the schools we visited make sure that all their courses, occupational as well as academic, are eligible for college admission. Most of them have worked to create a "college culture," with activities geared to preparing for college (just as an early college high school might):

> The moment [students] walked in as a freshman to the moment they graduated, depending on what kind of effort they put in and how much parents were involved ... their trajectory during those four years determined where they ended up, whether it was a community or a four-year college. But the expectation was that you were going to go to college—whether it's doing a four-year plan; visiting colleges and universities; doing SAT prep class; having special tutors in the highest level math, science; preparing them for the college application process. Everything about that program was designed with that goal in mind—yes, you are going to college after high school.

Other schools included advisories concentrating on the long process of college application, required courses in college and careers, and various fairs where colleges would come and explain themselves to students. Most of these high schools have dual enrollment agreements with local community colleges, where students enroll in college classes and receive both high school and college credit; often these are reserved for advanced courses that high schools can't provide. Colleges seem eager to create these for enrollment purposes, and the barriers to doing so are not as difficult as they are for work-based learning, though transportation and scheduling issues must still be overcome.

These four elements give pathways their special characteristics. Although schools that ignore some of them—or postpone them, particularly in the case of work-based learning—are still improvements over the comprehensive high school, they may not be realizing the full potential of pathways.

THE QUALITY OF INSTRUCTION IN PATHWAYS

The difficulties of reforming instruction in high schools, examined in the previous chapter, are somewhat moderated in schools with pathways. Principals noted that the effort to have teachers collaborate by itself improves instruction, as teachers develop new ways of integrating their subjects and of sharing the work of students. (In this way, pathways almost automatically create what others have called professional learning communities or PLCs, which many advocates have promoted to create more coherent curricula and improved instruction.[18]) One principal of a small school noted again the usual quality of teaching in high schools and the role of small schools in creating a different culture, including the equivalent of PLCs:

> High school teachers think they are content-area teachers, that they are math teachers, that they are science teachers, that they are teachers of the Civil War. But not necessarily teachers of language, or teachers of critical thinking ... Any type of collaborative work—whether it's trying to create these small learning communities, trying to create these co-teaching opportunities, trying to create these professional learning communities, trying to do any kind of cross-curricular collaboration or planning—you almost always have to overcome that initial type of stereotype of mindset or attitude ... It has taken six months to convince them that it [collaboration] is their job. And when their kids were happy, excited, talking about content, talking about critical thinking—that turned them on completely, and they're going to be our strongest advocates.

Another principal of a pathway noted that "there's a real shared belief in my school that the instructional program is precious and that the minutes in the classroom are precious." When pressed for why this was true, she cited small size—"in the small schools there's an understanding of kids, and it's become more of a student-centered environment"—as well as her selection of like-minded teachers: "my whole goal at the time [of designing the school] was to get together the best group of people I could, that really believed in kids and in serving kids that have the most challenges."

A second consequence of forming small pathways is a process of accountability and self-selection of certain teachers *out* of the pathway:

> Some of the people who had come in just because they had been in jobs and had first rights, they quickly found out that there was a lot of peer accountability ... the majority of teachers that really had a vision for the school were holding those that didn't very accountable and made them very uncomfortable.

The implication is that teachers who did not fit with a culture of collaboration and mutual accountability—*internal* accountability to other teachers and leaders,[19] as distinct from the *external* accountability to state and federal testing regimes—would be more likely to leave. The principal herself also had "some real candid conversations" with teachers who applied for positions but who she felt were unsuitable. So multiple factors—small size, collaboration, selection of teachers by leaders, and self-selection of inappropriate teachers out of pathways—improve the conditions for instruction in pathways. As a district official noted about the advantages, "There's lots of opportunities for teachers, through common planning time, to share best practices with one another. There's a lot of student-centered work that we hope teachers are implementing in the classroom, like project-based learning experiences." But the weasel-word "hope" indicated that the district had done nothing special to ensure that instructional methods would change.

In examining the forty-three schools where we interviewed leaders, we did not observe classrooms—which is the only reliable way to understand what approaches to instruction are taking place. However, the leaders of pathways to whom we spoke were more knowledgeable about instruction than are most principals; they undertook more classroom observations, something that's virtually impossible in the large, comprehensive high school ("with eighty teachers and one of me"), and they talked more knowledgeably about what happens in classrooms. Here are comments describing teaching, from the principal of an autonomous school focused on international business:

> We implement strategies for literacy across the curriculum—typically unheard of in a lot of high schools. I have four math teachers who really believe that students need to understand how to *read* mathematics and to understand mathematics conceptually instead of just algorithmically. They teach vocabulary; they work with the literacy coach who assists them ... It's critical for there to be a lot of student interaction, so in the classrooms you see a lot of Socratic seminars, even in ESL 3–4 class [English as a Second Language at relatively low levels], and they learn to interact with each other there; they're practicing their English skills, they're understanding different points of view ... They are doing projects that are meaningful to them, things that are applicable and connect the learning to them ... All those things are probably more specific to the pathways or the small-school feel, but the idea that kids are active in their learning is really important.

Although she might not use this vocabulary, she refers to several dimensions of constructivist teaching promoted by small size, teachers selected for their approaches, and a school-wide belief about instruction. The evidence indicates that movement toward constructivist teaching, or toward "balanced" instruction combining behaviorist and constructivist approaches, is necessary to enhance learning and the all-important test scores.[20] So these changes in teaching turn out to be precisely what is necessary to enhance learning.

Although conditions in small-scale pathways are conducive to improving instruction, instruction does not improve on its own. The right conditions may be necessary, but they are not sufficient. A small number of leaders—just four out of the forty-eight we interviewed—warned that the emphasis on revising the *structure* of the high school might cause leaders to miss the importance of explicitly improving *instruction* as well. One principal of a school with several pathways noted this directly: "I think they [pathway leaders and teachers] are so full of some structures—i.e., what classes will we offer? What will kids take? What will our student activities be?—they forget the main thing, which is instruction."

Although conditions in small-scale pathways are conducive to improving instruction, instruction does not improve on its own.

Another noted the lack of instructional change in moving to academies:

> Our focus has been academies, but I haven't seen the depth in these academies and that's what worries me … when I go into those classrooms I haven't seen anything different than the general education cases … we are having conversation as to, it just can't have a different name, but it has to look different.

In this case, "looking different" referred to teaching in ways that take advantage of the academy structure, including project-based learning coordinated across four subjects. Another principal of a comprehensive high school with five pathways noted:

> What we found [in trying to create small learning communities] is that you can change the structure, but if you don't change the practice, nothing is going to happen. So next year everybody is going to be in a small learning community, and … we are going to connect science and math and English … teachers will have common planning time and be able to talk in a very knowledgeable way about each and every student.

Another admitted that improvement in instruction might lag behind the creation of an academy structure:

> Up until last year, what you saw in terms of instruction may not have been a whole lot different than it was in the old [school]. So even those so-called good teachers probably would look pretty much the same. I think now it looks

> significantly different. Our teachers use data; collaborate; and sincerely push each other to develop tighter lessons, to look at student work in meaningful ways, to use different protocols to really get at the root of dilemmas and dilemmas they're dealing with, to help improve their instruction.

Another made the link to other reforms that change structure but not instruction: "just like anything else, the academy makes no difference if you don't have good teachers ... We've been trying to get another academy going, and we've been relatively unsuccessful because we don't have the dynamic teachers." So changing the structure of high school, in small learning communities as in pathways, is necessary but not sufficient to improve teaching. In this particular case, integrating subjects, common planning time, and knowing students well were additional elements necessary "to change the practice." Another principal, with experience with pathways as well as middle schools, noted that "as we know, structures can only do so much; there has to be a big cultural shift" in attitudes toward students and teaching.

The inadequacy of structural changes, and the necessity of paying explicit attention to instructional improvement, is a more important issue than the infrequency of this point among our forty-eight respondents would suggest. The same conclusion emerges from my statistical analysis of student performance in high schools, where conditions associated with improved instruction enhance learning and test scores (but not progress through high schools). Elements of personalizing a school—in terms of restructuring, certainly one of the goals of pathways—improve progress through high school but do not improve learning.[21] Alan Bersin, the former superintendent in San Diego, made the same point from experience rather than research. His reforms emphasized restructuring failing schools into charter schools and converting dysfunctional high schools into small schools and pathways. As he finally admitted, after having been dismissed from the district,

> It's about the teaching, in order to improve the learning. We can restructure our high schools as much as we like, but unless we improve the quality of teaching in our schools, we will not see student achievement improve.

The same point has been made more recently about the federal efforts to restructure low-performing schools, where analysts looking at forty-two schools in five states concluded that "no single reform guarantees success," and that schools raising student achievement used "multiple, coordinated restructuring strategies over many years, strategies [that] had been carefully chosen to address the schools' particular needs."[22] Restructuring is not enough by itself; it requires other strategies—curriculum changes, pedagogical shifts, small learning communities, teamwork among teachers, benchmark assessments, and distributed leadership, in one example cited—to improve learning outcomes.

For pathways, the lesson is that leaders need to remember that restructuring "can only do so much," and that improving instruction—moving it in the direction of constructivist or balanced practices—requires specific attention. Otherwise, pathways will look different from the comprehensive high school, but the teaching *within* them will continue to be the dreary, unmotivating instruction that has plagued high schools for more than a century,[23] and students will continue not to learn much. Fortunately, the conditions in pathways make improving instruction easier, and the methods for improving instruction noted in chapter 2—classroom observation and then individual coaching or collective professional development focused on pedagogical content knowledge—are precisely the same in pathways as they are in conventional high schools.

TEACHER RECRUITMENT

A problem related to instruction is the recruitment of appropriate teachers for pathways. Of course, one dimension of recruitment is finding teachers who are committed to student-centered and constructivist or balanced teaching. Another aspect of teachers that guides recruitment, as many principals noted, is the search for individuals who are willing to collaborate and integrate their curriculum with other teachers, rather than individuals who are so wedded to their disciplines that they cannot work with others. However, teachers still need to be certified in subject-specific areas, so the challenge is to find teachers who are conventionally prepared and certified but who are still flexible and collaborative.

The principals of pathways we interviewed were extremely conscious of the need to put together a *team* of teachers who not only had the necessary subject-matter preparation but who were interested in the pathway theme and could collaborate with others. Several of them, quite independently, used the same expression—"who's on the bus"—and they were concerned with assembling a group of compatible individuals "on the bus" before the beginning of the school year, despite obstacles from district hiring practices and union rules.[24]

The capacities for teachers working in pathways include some that are unfamiliar. One individual, a district official, noted that teachers have dual responsibilities when they work in pathways: "They have to balance their work in really trying to hone their craft in their particular content areas, while also thinking about the science department, and the math department, and the CTE [career technical education] courses—how those all work together." One principal suggested a special certification for pathway teaching or a notation on the single-subject credential, recognizing that the demands on teachers in pathways are different from those in conventional high schools—conceptually, what the new program in linked learning at CSU–San Diego is doing. Such an approach is not yet widespread, though other state university schools of education may adopt these practices, and CSU–San Diego is now convening other schools interested in offering such preparation.

Some principals reported more turnover among teachers in pathways because the work is more demanding. This means that principals needed to be spending more time in recruitment—yet another demand pulling them away from other responsibilities, including instructional leadership. In addition, turnover among teachers itself disrupts relations among teachers and leaders, planning and collaboration, and connections with students. One potential benefit of preparing teachers specifically for pathways is that it might reduce turnover among these teachers.

Other special requirements are necessary for those teachers who teach courses in the theme of a pathway. Some theme areas are already covered by existing credentials—for example, music, art, and English for the theme teachers in a performing arts pathway, or business teachers for an international business pathway. Some of these might not be appropriate for a pathway, however. For example, a teacher certified in business might be prepared for a traditional vocational ed program rather than a new program focusing on international business and the International Baccalaureate curriculum. Similarly, a health science certification might or might not be appropriate for a health-related pathway. In addition, many pathways have themes that are completely unrelated to traditional secondary credentials; such themes as biotechnology, digital media, communications, social justice, and environmental issues in "green" academies require individuals who do not fit neatly into states' credentialing mechanisms. Some of these individuals may have been working in businesses or the nonprofit sector, and getting them teaching credentials may pose barriers.

Finally, union rules and regulations created for conventional schools may hamper teacher recruitment in pathways. Responding to a question about stumbling blocks in hiring teachers, one principal of a school of visual and performing arts complained about seniority rules:

> It's the number of years you have in place. And so I have a [union-generated] list of whom I can interview—it's not wide open. If I knew someone was up in north county, and they are a great teacher and I want to get them on board, I can't, because it has to be within the system and then the union has prioritized. I can't pick them because they're not senior ... someone might have experience in the arts, and yet they are not on the list. And the people who are on the list, who just want to come to a school that they think is smaller or easier—they may lack the motivation. So it [the union list] limits you severely.

Another problem related to unions, one that affects all schools, is the procedure in each district for "bumping" rights—the rights of tenured teachers to have first call on vacancies. Sometimes these rules are so complex that they are difficult to understand and they often involve the "dance of the lemons," where mediocre teachers are released (that is, fired) from one school only to turn up at the top of the union's priority list. This is harmful to every school, of course, but it is especially difficult for pathway principals searching for a teacher with the right subject expertise, the right chemistry with other teachers in the pathway, and the ability to work across disciplinary guidelines.

The special problem of recruiting teachers is one of many challenges that arise because pathways are relatively new and inconsistent with the bureaucratic structures that have developed for conventional high schools. If and when pathways become more numerous, teacher preparation should change—for example, in the kind of teacher-preparation program developed at CSU–San Diego with a linked learning emphasis—and it should be easier to find teachers for non-traditional high schools. For the moment, however, principals and other leaders need to work with teacher-preparation programs, with districts, with unions and their contracts, and with state policies to clarify the special teacher needs of pathways.

The special problem of recruiting teachers is one of many challenges that arise because pathways are relatively new and inconsistent with the bureaucratic structures that have developed for conventional high schools.

THE DILEMMAS OF SUCCESS AND "RIGOR"

The goals of pathways are numerous: enhancing conventional learning through more motivating and relevant instruction; increasing students' interest in and commitment to their school programs; fostering progress through high school, completion, and movement into postsecondary education, in part by creating a clear trajectory into college; enabling students to understand the relationships among courses; seeing the options after high school and the contribution of schooling to those options; understanding what problem-solving, critical thinking, and other higher-order abilities (or "twenty-first-century skills" or "deeper thinking") mean in a particular area of application; and developing some of the non-cognitive competencies required in different broad occupational areas, such as interpersonal skills and sometimes kinesthetic, visual, or musical abilities. There are in this sense many more goals, and therefore outcomes and conceptions of success, than in the conventional high schools limited to a fixed set of college-prep courses and to a single goal—graduation and college for all.

Of course, some measures of success are as important in pathways as in traditional high schools. Principals in our sample were highly conscious of the need to be judged by graduation rates, by the proportion of students eligible for and continuing to college, by rates of passing the high school exit exam, and by scores on the SAT as a prerequisite for four-year colleges. Almost all of them made sure that their courses met the standards for college eligibility[25]—in sharp contrast to traditional vocational ed, which has usually offered coursework not eligible for college-going. If pathways are able to show higher rates of completion, mobility into college, and then success in college, that is one way to document their success and "rigor." But in districts with narrow attention to standard test scores, or where superintendents concerned only about test scores take over from those with broader views of success, pathways are under special pressure to show test score improvements.

Unfortunately, under current state accountability systems and No Child Left Behind, success in learning is measured by basic skills tests in reading and math, neglecting other subjects as well as higher-order dimensions of these two subjects, and completely ignoring the wider range of competencies that many pathways foster. Similarly, concepts of rigor are limited to the conventional hierarchy of the high school curriculum, where algebra II or calculus is considered more rigorous than algebra I, or college-prep physics is more rigorous than general science.[26] Therefore, measuring the success and rigor of pathways by conventional measures of learning is limited, if not foolish. Some pathways develop a broader range of competencies than are measured by state and federal accountability exams, particularly when they incorporate non-cognitive abilities required in particular occupations, or when they explicitly develop various twenty-first-century skills. Some pathways don't include conventionally rigorous courses, such as algebra II or British literature, because these subjects are irrelevant to their theme: a performing arts high school has little use for algebra II, and a health-themed pathway might substitute other reading—on the ethics and policies (including current policy debates) in the medical field, for example—for British literature. It is not conceptually difficult to imagine courses related to pathway themes that also raise the classic themes of great literary works, of historical perspectives, and of political battles and social developments, though such courses would look quite non-traditional. They might be about the history and social dislocations of technology, for example, or the literature of agricultural life or work in modern societies, or ethical issues in health or in finance.

As a result of these differences, many pathways have developed alternative forms of assessment that are better suited to their goals. Some have adopted portfolios in which students accumulate their work and present it to teachers and peers as evidence of accomplishments. Others have developed senior projects, an exercise consistent with the student-centered teaching in many pathways and one more closely linked to the theme of a pathway. But these assessments are not accepted in the conventional judgments of school by districts and states, and they are only sometimes considered in college admissions. There are only a few exceptions where there are ready-made tests and certification mechanisms providing alternatives to the SAT; for example, international business programs may prepare students for the International Baccalaureate exams. Even pathways with broadly occupational themes tend not to use existing certification mechanisms because these are likely to be associated with traditional vocational ed programs or lower-level occupations. Pathways therefore have no special ways of demonstrating their rigor except performance on conventional tests, even though pathways aspire to many other outcomes.

Some principals are trying to think of ways to define rigor in different ways, and this is a long-run project. The development of our current standardized tests has taken ninety years, since the development of the Army's alpha tests for World War I, and developing alternative tests and then having them widely accepted is a slow process. In contrast, pathways have been under development only since the late 1980s, and few of them have managed to develop their own standards of rigor and ways to measure them. Over the long run, however, we should expect to see the steady development of alternative assessments linked to different ideas of outcomes and rigor—for example, standards that have arisen in broad occupational clusters or developed by environmental groups (for environmental pathways), urban planners (for pathways focused on urban issues), or other groups dedicated to non-traditional schooling. In the meantime, one role for pathway leaders and their supporters is to continue the search for alternative assessments and to insist that the existing standardized test scores do a poor job of measuring what students might know and do.

THE ADDITIONAL COSTS OF PATHWAYS

There is little question that pathways cost more than conventional high school programs do, and covering these costs is a challenge for pathway leaders. The costs come in several different forms and in different currencies. In speaking with pathway leaders, the most obvious currency is money. Pathways typically spend additional funds for people to carry out crucial roles—most frequently an extra counselor, an individual in charge of work-based learning, sometimes an individual creating and monitoring connections to postsecondary institutions, the higher costs of specialized labs in certain pathways, and sometimes the instructors linked to the special theme. Principals' discussions of costs are full of references to the additional grants they need to keep their pathways running: funds from foundations (especially the Bill and Melinda Gates Foundation for its past support of small schools); the federal government with its Small Schools Grants; federal funding for CTE; the resources provided to some schools by Regional Occupational Centers and Programs

(California's version of area vocational schools); and state support of about $1,000 per pupil for California Partnership Academies.

There is little question that pathways cost more than conventional high school programs do, with costs coming in several different forms and in different currencies.

Some principals spend a great deal of time writing grant proposals. One of the most successful grant-writers in our sample said:

> We have been very aggressive at writing grants to fund teacher development, to meet the career education and skill preparation needs of the students ... We have two counselors for five hundred students ... work-based learning and coordination of the early college model into allied health courses, handled by another person who is funded by grants.

This individual claimed to have raised $1 million for 360 students, or roughly $2,800 per student—the equivalent of a 30 percent increase over the average spending per pupil in that district.[27] Unfortunately, fund-raising is necessary at the same time that it takes principals away from instructional leadership. The need for additional funds may be especially serious in California, which has now sunk to forty-sixth among the states in real (cost-adjusted) spending per student, but there's little doubt that pathways cost more than do traditional high schools in every state.

To be more precise, Parsi, Plank, and Stern (2009) conducted an analysis of ten different pathways in California, calculating the costs associated with the increased time demands. (Some of these show up in additional expenditures per student, but others—the hard work of principals and teachers, for example—do not; therefore additional *time* costs do not show up as additional *money* costs in school budgets.) Their first obvious conclusion is that the extra costs of pathways compared to conventional high school programs vary enormously—from $261 per student to $1,113 for teachers, from $6 per student to $212 for principals, from $39 to $202 for work-based learning (WBL) partners, from $505 to $1,937 for total costs without those of

WBL partners, representing additional costs of roughly 15 to 20 percent over average costs in these districts. One-time start-up costs ranged from $36 to $624 per student, indicating that the kinds of schools from which pathways develop make a substantial difference to start-up costs. One start-up cost was teachers' time for professional development, a cost that would fall as teachers become more experienced—or if teachers were prepared in programs specifically oriented to pathways.

However, another unanticipated but plausible pattern emerges from these data. The additional current costs for pathways starting around 2006 were around $2,000 per student; those starting between 2000 and 2004 were closer to $1,000; and the one pathway started in 1995 cost approximately $500 extra. This suggests that as pathways mature, their additional costs fall, presumably because established pathways are able to rely on well-established procedures to run themselves and perhaps find ways to accomplish their objectives more cheaply. If this is true, then it argues—once again—for stability in the development of pathways because these economies can be realized only over periods of eight to fifteen years. Similarly, districts should recognize that the development of pathways is a long-run investment, and that short-term higher costs exaggerate the costs over the long run.

To some extent, of course, the additional costs of pathways come from diseconomies associated with small size and with additional conventional resources (such as counselors and WBL coordinators) that would be helpful in all high schools. The correct cost comparison, therefore, is not between pathways and comprehensive high schools *without* these resources, but between pathways and smaller higher schools *with* the resources that, arguably, all students should get. With this kind of comparison, the additional costs of pathways would be much smaller than the estimates presented above. In addition, several principals noted that pathways are successful in retaining students and enhancing graduation rates; if the measure of costs shifted to cost per *graduate,* rather than cost per *student,* pathways might look like a low-cost option.[28] But no one has been able to carry out such calculations yet, and expenditure per student remains the dominant measure. Particularly in such difficult fiscal times as the present, districts are constantly searching for ways of rooting out higher costs, and pathways feel vulnerable.

Costs also come in forms other than money. Although some simple resources can be readily bought with money—additional teachers, additional counselors, work-based learning coordinators, lab equipment—other aspects of pathways require resources other than money. Many are what I call compound resources—for example, money for labs or computers *plus* teacher training in how to use them, or smaller schools *plus* the leadership and vision necessary to take advantage of small size (Grubb 2009a; Grubb 2009b). Complex resources are those aspects of schools that involve practices difficult to describe and that are difficult to change. The quality of instruction, for example, is a crucial aspect of pathways, but improved instruction cannot be bought in any "instructional improvement store," and higher levels of spending per student do not lead to better instruction. Instead, schools have to construct improved teaching, through vision, leadership, and cooperation from teachers, through the methods of classroom observation and professional development described in chapter 2. Finally, abstract resources are those that describe characteristics of a school that are impossible to touch or to view but which can be detected by asking participants about conditions within a school. Such resources as trust, the coherence of the curriculum, school climate, relationships between teachers and students and among students and among teachers, and the stability of all participants are examples of abstract resources.[29] As with complex resources, abstract resources cannot be bought but must be constructed by teachers and leaders working together.

Many of the principals and district leaders confirmed the importance of resources other than money. Principals acknowledge that they work harder when there are pathways—"dawn to dusk and beyond"—because there are additional responsibilities, such as those described in this chapter. These time costs do not necessarily show up in higher expenditure requirements, though they do influence the higher estimated costs of Parsi, Plank, and Stern (2009). Teachers also work harder: the collaboration mentioned, particularly in developing an integrated, theme-based curriculum, is a particular abstract resource that cannot be bought but must be developed through a combination of choosing the right individuals, perhaps sending them to a teacher-preparation program such as the one at CSU–San Diego, and leadership (either from the principal or from teacher-leaders) in getting teachers together. As one principal described her teachers,

> They don't really come and say, "There's all of this money—how are we going to spend it?" They just said, "We need to do this." Right now all of the meetings

> that we've had here for high school reform, they've been free—out of the kindness of the teachers' hearts. They pick a day. They say we're going to stay here from three to five and we're going to discuss this," and one of the teachers runs the meetings—and then I meet with her and we set up an agenda . . . so everything has been voluntary.

Similarly, improvements in instruction must be *developed* in ways outlined above, a good example of a complex resource. The vision needed for any pathway is an abstract resource, and the cogency and attractiveness of the chosen theme is another, generating benefits as disparate as adequate enrollments, greater opportunities for internships and college connections, status, and equity. So when we ask what is necessary to make a pathway effective, the answer is only partly the money for additional personnel and materials. It also includes many costless but priceless resources arising from the very nature of pathways.

What emerges from these issues is that the *money* costs of pathways, their *time* costs in the estimates by Parsi, Plank, and Stern (2009), and their overall *resource* costs are all different ways of accounting for costs, and it's difficult to get comparable measures. Districts are more likely to be sensitive to the first, and teachers and leaders to the second and third. But in the end what counts is whether all the additional resources necessary for successful pathways—both money and non-money—can be brought together. This is one of the major responsibilities of leaders in high schools with pathways, though it requires thinking about costs and resources in different ways.

BALANCING THE NEEDS OF PATHWAYS AND OF SCHOOLS: THE MICRO/MACRO PROBLEM

The special demands on leaders I have reviewed so far describe actions and responsibilities of fostering successful pathways. But where multiple pathways are located within larger schools or within districts, then principals have additional responsibilities in balancing the differences among pathways, as well as potential differences between pathway programs and the comprehensive part of the high school. The balancing problem is nicely illustrated by an assistant principal whose workload shifted: she has had responsibility, within three years, for one of five pathways in her high school; then four pathways;

and then one pathway, while other assistant principals were in charge of the remaining pathways. As she described her role,

> [In each pathway] we have an advisory committee, you have a parent committee, you have a student committee, and so you [the assistant principal] are working with all these different areas in a small chunk. But you still have to think about hiring for the high school as a whole; you still have to think about the master schedule as a whole; you still have to think about athletics for the whole school ... So you are really doing this micro to macro view, whereas the team [pathway] leader is just looking micro and can get very caught up in their perspective and their teachers and their curriculum. And they don't always see how the high school as a whole functions. So my role is helping them navigate that micro and macro kind of thing.

Another said simply that "people in their little small areas of expertise don't always remember the large picture," and then some leader above the level of a pathway—sometimes an assistant principal or a principal, sometimes a district official—needs to consider the "large picture."

Many examples of micro/macro conflicts include resources, where a pathway may want a well-regarded teacher but where a principal or assistant principal must be concerned with whether a pathway has scooped up too many strong teachers. When a pathway is created by a group of energetic teachers banding together—as in the principal quoted above who said that "we collectively brought other stronger teachers in"—the sense of a pathway "robbing" the rest of the school may be particularly resented. Another principal went through the calculations about class sizes and then asked, "Is it fair that if you're a good teacher, and you teach in an academy, you have sixteen kids—and somebody else has thirty-two and may not have the same kind of [motivated] kids as you have?" Similarly in the case of technology, a pathway may need more computers to serve its theme (or more lab equipment for a science-based theme), regardless of the whole school's needs. As the same assistant principal mentioned, "We had a whole thing about mobile labs, where this one grant from the district funded all the mobile labs for the small schools and nothing for the two largest [comprehensive] programs—how are they going to raise money for their mobile labs?" Resource issues are particularly difficult because a program with more resources is often attacked by other factions within the school that do not have additional resources—what I call the "politics of resentment." Of course, the academy may compensate for its greater resources with greater student motivation and completion rates, but when teachers and parents are judging what's fair—whether all students get equal treatment—the extra, visible resources in pathways seem decidedly unfair.

Another area where micro/macro conflicts emerge is grading. In one comprehensive high school with five small schools, a war erupted about grade inflation: "the small schools will do whatever they possibly can to make sure that students get a passing grade so they can go to college because it's an equity issue for them." (One might reasonably point out that college-going rates may also be issues of status and success within the entire school.) There ensued charges and countercharges about grades and standards, and the entire mess landed in a local newspaper reporting grade inflation in pathways.

Similarly, micro/macro conflicts surface in the degree of autonomy that schools provide their pathways. In one case,

> the teacher-leaders in the small schools wanted to hire their own teachers.... The big struggle was between giving them some autonomy, but not too much autonomy ... because I just felt like I didn't know if they had the ability to hire really strong candidates. They might hire just friends or people they knew, and I wasn't sure—that might be the best thing for the small school, but maybe not the best thing for [the entire comprehensive high] school.

This assistant principal then went on to acknowledge that such a conflict created one of the stresses in his position: "the experience of almost having two jobs, of having what we called the comprehensive school and the small schools ... like doing two jobs, not like you could do either one really well because of the overwhelming work that had to be done."

Where there is a leadership council composed of the principal and all assistant principals in charge of pathways, there is at least in theory a group that can adjudicate these micro/macro disputes. Similarly, an executive principal with several lead principals at one site with multiple pathways can balance the interests of one pathway against the others. However, with autonomous small schools, whether freestanding or co-existing on one physical campus, there is no such leadership council at the site, and so such conflicts can be reconciled only if the district steps in.

Many micro/macro disputes—especially those about resources—are school-level versions of a much larger problem in American education about the sources of inequality and perceived inequity among schools. In the case of pathways, inequities may exist among pathways, or between pathways and the rest of the high school (or comprehensive high schools in the same district). In other cases, inequities exist among schools within a district, a problem raised in the next section; or among districts within a state, the subject of so much school finance litigation; or among states within the country, an issue that will become a major debate if we move in the direction of national standards. The responsibility for recognizing and then possibly correcting such inequities shifts, depending on what level of our education system is involved. When the inequities exist within schools, as they potentially do whenever pathways are created, then this simply adds to the special challenges of principals with pathways.

Many micro/macro disputes—especially those about resources—are school-level versions of a much larger problem in American education about the sources of inequality and perceived inequity among schools.

THE STATUS AND EQUITY OF MULTIPLE PATHWAYS

When a school or district has multiple pathways, the perceived status difference among pathways, and the consequences for enrollment and equity are potential problems. These issues are somewhat parallel to those of traditional vocational education, which in virtually all high schools has been perceived as a second-best alternative to the academic and college-prep tracks, a "dumping ground" for students who are not academically inclined. One challenge for pathways is to avoid such negative stereotyping because it inevitably leads to low status, then low enrollments, and then possible closure.

The questions of status inevitably arise in schools with multiple pathways, or multiple autonomous schools on one physical site, and many of them involve whether a pathway theme attracts particular kinds of students. Some pathways are of higher status than others or attract certain kinds of students.

Any construction academy inevitably attracts more working-class young men and fewer young women; similarly, a pathway based on auto shop attracted males "interested in cars, not school." Hospitality programs and anything related to homemaking attract more women. One school proposed a cosmetology program—attractive mostly to girls—even though it's hard to imagine how cosmetology could be integrated with academic content appropriate for college. Several principals with responsibility for performing arts pathways noted that they attract more lesbian, gay, bisexual, and transgendered (LGBT) students; more Goths; and more students uninterested in standard academic work, "the artsy kids." Another principal of an arts academy noted that "My school, being the arts school, the kids here don't really want an academic focus—they want an arts focus—so their test scores are lower." In the same complex, the international studies program linked to the IB attracted more academic students with higher grades ("it was always the cream that kept [that school] higher on their test scores").

Here is a principal of a high school with sixteen clusters, describing student self-selection:

> In our networking class and our database class, that's like geek city. Mostly boys—a few girls—and they talk about how they're geeks ... so that's the class you go into and it's painful: they don't want to speak to each other, never mind in front of a group. The video class, as you might guess, and the graphics class has a lot of kind of "out there" kids—I call them the fringe, like Goth. The biomedicine program attracts mostly girls, girls who want to be doctors. We have a class called Psychology and Human Behavior, and we say it's the "psycho" class because, my God, it attracts kids who have therapists, need therapists—it's trauma-drama central.... Our environmental class attracts kids who are very much into environmental issues. We have robotics and electronics, and we have maybe two girls in that class—it's difficult in such a male-dominated environment ... we have telecommunications, which is not necessarily that high-end, but we couldn't get students in it so that program closed.

However, despite this variation, all the clusters were designed to fit a "college-prep environment, so cosmetology would not fit into that environment." Another school created a public safety pathway, which was perceived as a blue-collar program preparing for fire and police protection, and middle-class students would not attend; with a slight expansion, it could have been a public health pathway with broader appeal. In one high school, an academy for English learners quickly became a low-status pathway with few enrollments, for obvious reasons; a principal from another pathway noted that they then changed the name "to get rid of the stigma they'll never get rid of." Similarly, the pathways described in chapter 2, for students "who had bad attendance and behavior problems," became known as a remedial program and was rejected by both students and parents: "it was a great idea that didn't really happen" because of low enrollments. At the other end, in one district, academies became high-status partly because of their themes—in engineering, finance, information technology, and health. A district official noted that "What that does is produce academies that are primarily Asian students, and that sends the wrong message. There needs to be an increased push to get underserved populations into the academies." Several schools noted coming up with high-status themes to attract more students, particularly more middle-class students, especially if they were in competition with other schools.

Most examples of low-status pathways are doomed by their association with certain groups of students or with low-status occupations (such as construction). However, a vague theme can also cause low enrollments; at one school with a leadership program, "the whole purpose or the whole vibe would be the ASB [Associated Student Body]/ROTC/public safety kind of angle, and I'm not sure that their theme has gelled ... thematically I'm not sure it is as coherent, or that it made as much sense to begin with." The same principal also noted that "business as a theme isn't nearly as sexy as the word [when] I use [it] in adult company ... by comparison to science and technology, international studies, media, and performing arts, eighth graders look at business and say 'what's that?'" So a field that seems "sexy" (or at least high-paying) at the baccalaureate and graduate school level isn't clear to the eighth graders who make choices. At the other extreme, some subjects are almost automatically high status: an international academy or international business pathway focusing on preparation for IB exams; health pathways linked to high-demand, high-status medical professions; and pathways with subjects in such "sexy" areas as biotechnology, information technology, and science and technology.

Even with themes carefully chosen to be "high-end" and "college-prep," there is still a great deal of sorting among students, and gender equity in particular is hard to achieve. It's difficult to avoid this kind of segregation because expanding student choice is a factor in student engagement, as well as a motive behind pathways; random assignment of students to pathways, or selection mechanisms where many students do not get their first choice, would destroy one of the attractions of pathways. In this situation, it is important for leaders to monitor the composition of pathways, and to change the theme, reframe the theme so that it is less confusing or more attractive to students, and be ready to recruit more heavily among some groups of students.

The problem with creating pathways of unequal status is, most obviously, "students are over-subscribing in some themes and under-subscribing in others," so enrollment and costs per student vary, and recruitment efforts need to take place to equalize enrollment. The second is that some pathways become dominated by certain racial or class or gender groups, potentially re-creating the inequalities associated with tracking. One assistant principal noted that "At this high school the highest-performing kids end up in the same pathways—one's math and science . . . our creative and performing arts tends to be the lowest-performing students." To some extent students may self-segregate: "kids will talk to kids, and kids will say, 'I feel most supported and most connected to teachers in this [particular academy]' if you're African American. And that leads to parents saying, my kid will go to college if they're African American and they go to this [particular pathway]." As a result, this school, vehemently opposed to segregation of any kind, found itself with a pathway of largely African American students despite their best efforts (for example, admission via lottery) to prevent such segregation.

A second problem is that high-status academies may attract other resources that then reinforce their attractiveness, so that differences among pathways get wider over time rather than narrower. In one district, an international pathway focused on IB preparation not only attracted the most ambitious students, but "you took 90 percent of teachers who were teaching at that level of rigor with it." In another case, a freestanding, autonomous small school has begun to attract national attention and special grants, and so its distance from the rest of the district's schools appears to be growing. It is likely to become a selective (and probably unrepresentative) small school unless the district pays special attention to this gap.

In districts with open enrollment, pathways are often used to attract students to particular schools, thereby becoming elements of competition. One principal declared that his school needed to develop a high-status engineering academy to compete with the health and medicine academy at a neighboring school. In the same district, district officials located some high-status pathways at a school on the wrong side of the tracks (actually, the wrong side of a particular highway that I call Main Street) in order to erase the "Main

Street divide." Other districts have created pathways or autonomous small schools on the campuses of dysfunctional high schools, trying to erase the stigma of the prior school by coming up with new curricula and new names for these schools. Whether pathways can in fact overcome the stigma associated with location in neighborhoods perceived as dangerous, or placement within a high school that has failed, is not clear, but this adds to the pressures for such pathways to become successful.

These equity issues, as with those of resource differences among pathways, require some group above the pathway level to be aware of and potentially to correct any developing inequities. In schools with multiple pathways, this is usually the leadership council or the school site council, including the principals and all assistant principals with direct responsibility for pathways. But with freestanding, autonomous small schools, or campuses that have been broken into autonomous small schools, there is no such group to monitor and correct inequalities except for the district, and district officials usually do not get engaged in the workings of small schools in such detail. Indeed, in one complex we visited—which had been created by breaking a large, dysfunctional high school into five small schools—differences among these five threatened to create wide inequalities on that single campus.

Of course, each individual school has the motivation to enhance its quality and reputation to avoid losing enrollment over time, but whether independent small schools have the resources to do that—the vision, the leadership, and the willingness of the faculty to work collectively, never mind high-quality teachers and additional funding for counselors and WBL coordinators—is never clear. When I turn in chapter 5 to the contributions of districts, monitoring and correcting inequalities among pathways is one of their important responsibilities.

Finally, while there are equity issues in the choices *among* pathways, there are other equity issues in the choice *between* pathways and the comprehensive high school. The great hope of pathways, as I outlined in chapter 1, is that several distinctive features—the possibility of student choice; the relevance of themes; the smaller school-within-a-school and better working relations with teachers; the greater adherence to the principles of motivation and engagement; and the greater availability of experiential learning, including internships—would enable low-performing students to become more engaged in schoolwork and to enhance their learning and progress through high school. Certainly some of the evidence, both from quasi-experimental evaluations and from one random-assignment study, indicates that students in academies show signs of greater commitment to schooling—better attitudes toward schooling, better attendance, more credits earned, more academic subject participation, and lower dropout rates in some studies. But it remains to be seen who benefits the most from pathways because they are too new to have developed extensive information about outcomes. One principal described a kind of triage outcome, where middling students may be the ones who benefit most from pathways:

> The other obstacle is this, which is depressing: the students who are really successful in your pathways aren't your bottom quintile because the students who struggle with school and identity and perseverance, resiliency, discipline, and work ethic, they're not successful in the pathway classes either. So the notion that just because you have pathways, it's going to lead to greater achievement of where your achievement gaps exist, isn't necessarily the case. The kids who end up being the top pathway kids are kids that are C kids anyway; they were already doing not great, but they were maybe doing adequate in school. So that's another challenge, the kids with multiple Fs, are they connecting in the pathway? That's the challenge as well.

No other principals made any statements of what kinds of students benefit the most from pathways, and indeed variation in selection procedures would make it difficult to compare the results across forty-three different schools. However, the conclusion that the very lowest-performing students won't benefit from a reform because of multiple "barriers" to success is widespread because the lowest-performing students—"your lowest quintile"—may have a range of problems that schools can't readily address, no matter what kinds of reforms they institute.[30] This too is an issue that leaders should examine, not necessarily because pathways constitute some kind of magic that will reach the lowest-performing students, but because leaders ought to be thinking constantly about equity issues, including what might work for the "lowest quintile."

PROS AND CONS OF ALTERNATIVE APPROACHES TO PATHWAYS

By now it should be clear that the five approaches to pathways described at the beginning of this chapter are quite different from one another. They all incorporate a theme, either broadly occupational or nonoccupational, which determines some part of the curriculum; they all benefit from small size. But in other respects, they differ widely, and the leadership challenges vary as well. If we judge these five approaches according to several normative criteria, no one approach to or model of pathways is optimal in all respects. Therefore schools deciding to adopt pathways, or districts creating pathways in existing comprehensive high schools, should choose carefully which type of pathway to develop. Similarly, some of the problems now experienced in certain pathways might be resolved by changing their organizational and administrative structure.

The different approaches to pathways vary on at least four dimensions:

- **The visibility and integrity of the pathway:** In autonomous small schools and in most academies, the visibility of the pathway is not an issue: each pathway has a name, a clear identity within the school, "everybody knows what the theme is, everybody tends to work together." Students generally take a majority of their courses within pathways so that—though the extent of integration among courses may vary—the theme can infuse many courses within the pathway, not just "core" courses. But in some comprehensive high schools with multiple pathways, students spend as little as one to two periods a day in courses related to the theme and take other, "regular" courses within the comprehensive high school.[31] Under these conditions, the pathways are not especially distinct because only a minority of coursework takes place in them. The possibilities for integration across subjects is virtually nonexistent, and students may not feel that they are part of a pathway.

  Furthermore, in a comprehensive high school with only a few small pathways or only one or two academies, pathways may become virtually invisible because as few as eighty students (out of perhaps twenty-five hundred, on the average) are in pathways. It's impossible to transform high schools at this small scale, and students cannot become familiar enough with pathways to see them as anything more than curiosities. As the number of students in pathways or academies grows—to the point where a school is "wall-to-wall academies," with every student in one or another—then the visibility of pathways obviously grows as well, and pathways become familiar parts of the high school. So a certain scale—both in terms of the number of courses taken within a pathway, and the proportion of students in pathways—is necessary both to create coherent pathways and to make pathways a real mechanism of reform.

- **Student choice**: One purpose of pathways is to provide students with choice over the theme they pursue, consistent with the understanding that student choice of educational activities enhances their motivation and engagement (National Research Council 2004). As a practical matter, multiple pathways at the same site probably maximize choice because students can consider all the pathways in one place and time—for example, in the "open houses" that such schools usually offer for parents and eighth graders. It may also be easier to change pathways if a student decides he or she has made a serious mistake—although the extent of switching pathways in the schools we examined is quite small. Conversely, with freestanding, small schools or in districts where pathways are by design spread among a variety of high schools, it becomes more difficult for students to learn about the variety of pathways. In physically large districts, transportation problems may also arise.
- **Access to the social side of the high school**: For some students and parents (but certainly not for others), the social side is central to the high school experience: sports, band, proms, clubs, and the other nonacademic activities that have grown up over time. Autonomous small schools, whether freestanding or grouped on one physical campus, often cannot provide many of these activities, and so students for whom they are important are more likely to choose pathways within comprehensive high schools, where such activities are still available.

The value of social activities in the high school is ambiguous. On the one hand, research suggests that students who participate in extracurricular activities have higher educational aspirations and progress through high school and into four-year colleges at higher rates, though their test scores are somewhat lower (presumably because of the time involved).[32] For other students, however, one problem of the comprehensive high school is that its social side detracts from an academic culture and makes it less possible to do serious work—and certainly this is true in extreme cases (such as football culture in small Texas towns). For the moment, we might expect that students and parents will choose different pathways and high schools based on the importance to them of extracurricular activities versus academic content. Over the long run, we might expect certain approaches to pathways, such as autonomous small schools without many extracurricular activities, to draw different kinds of students than do pathways located in comprehensive high schools.

- **Coordination problems**: Our respondents raised two issues of coordination among pathways: the micro/macro problem of balancing the needs of pathways with the needs of the traditional high school; and the problem of differences among pathways in status and, potentially, composition and enrollment. Addressing these issues requires some administrative oversight and cannot be easily accomplished with freestanding, themed schools or with autonomous small schools on a single campus. The implication is that the location of several pathways on a single campus with a conventional leadership team, or on a campus with an executive principal and small central staff, is a better arrangement.

Looking across the five approaches to pathways, the model with the fewest drawbacks seems to be the single physical high school with several semi-autonomous themed schools, each with a principal but with a central administration with some authority over the small schools (including an executive principal).[33] Each themed school can act like an autonomous small school in virtually every respect, including the salience of the theme and the ability to integrate courses, students can choose among the pathways at that campus, students can get access to extracurricular activities because the site as a whole is large enough to sponsor various sports and clubs where students from different pathways mingle, and the central administration can balance the needs and the status of the various pathways and resolve various macro/micro problems. Of course there remain coordination problems *among* high schools in a large district, a district responsibility to which I return in chapter 5.

If the approach of several semi-autonomous themed schools on a larger physical campus indeed has advantages over other structures, we might expect it to emerge over time as a dominant approach to pathways. But in an educational system of enormous diversity of parent and student preferences, as well as of teacher and administrator prerogatives and of district perspectives, we might expect varied approaches to pathways to persist.

QUESTIONS FOR CHAPTER 3

These questions are designed to be answered by those with leadership responsibilities for specific pathways.

1. What is the structure of your pathway? Is it a school-within-a-school or a freestanding school? Is the pathway leader a principal, an assistant principal, or a teacher-leader, and to whom does the pathway report? What are the advantages and disadvantages of this structure?

2. How was the pathway theme determined? What are the advantages of this theme? The disadvantages, including possible underenrollment, lack of appeal to certain students, and difficulties in finding internships? Could these disadvantages be reduced by modifying the theme slightly?

3. Does the theme lend itself naturally to both employment and college after high school? Are there local programs in two- and four-year colleges corresponding to the theme?

4. How much common planning time do teachers have? How much progress has there been in integrating content across courses and developing common projects or issues?

5. What changes or improvements to guidance and counseling have taken place in response to multiple pathways?

6. What programs do you have to improve approaches to instruction for teachers within the pathway? Are they available to all teachers in the pathway? Or confined to a subset of teachers, such as particular subjects or grade levels?

7. What fraction of pathway students now participate in some form of work-based learning, service learning, or other experiences outside the school?

8. How does the pathway define rigor? How does it then measure rigor?

9. What are the additional *financial* costs of this pathway, above the regular costs per student in this district? What revenue sources cover these additional costs?

   What are the additional *time* costs of this pathway?

   What other costs does this pathway incur?

   Is there reason to think the additional costs may go down in the future?

10. If the pathway is a school-within-a-school, in what ways (if any) do the needs of the pathway and the needs of the school conflict? Who adjudicates these conflicts?

Chapter 4

"Opportunities Together, Opportunities Separate"

Improving the Preparation of High School Leaders

Given the special challenges facing high school leaders, one implication is that preparation programs—both pre-service programs before working as assistant principals and principals and induction programs as they become novice leaders—should contain a number of elements focusing on these particular challenges. As one leader of an autonomous small school with experience in two districts admitted, existing programs are not adequate to the special challenges of high schools:

> To have a principal position you need to have an administrative credential, and I feel that people in both districts think, "OK, they have an administrative credential; they're ready." And the training program in both districts I have always referred to as, "Here's your chair." I don't really feel that there is much of a training program. Any high school principal, I'm not sure they get the support, the training.

Furthermore, though many challenges examined in chapters 2 and 3 could be addressed in pre-service and induction programs, many leaders argue that there is no substitute for experience. Many aspects of the principal's position can be learned only through on-the-job training. But rather than leaving such experience to the idiosyncrasies of what individuals do before becoming high school principals, such experience could be consciously shaped by districts, both through induction programs and by structuring the experiences of teacher-leaders and assistant principals before they become principals. In this chapter, therefore, I discuss a number of approaches to improving the preparation of high school principals and leaders for pathways. Indeed, for anyone who agrees with the research of the Consortium on Chicago School Research—that change-oriented leadership is the most important of five essential supports (Bryk et al. 2010)—strengthening the preparation of leaders is necessary for any significant reform, at any level of schooling.

In thinking about improving preparation, I was fortunate that approximately half of the principals we interviewed were graduates of the Principal Leadership Institute (PLI) at University of California at Berkeley. The interviewers, all coaches in the PLI, were intimately familiar with what the program does. They routinely asked the interviewees what the PLI program could do specifically for high school principals, and I summarize these comments in the first section of this chapter. It turns out that even the most carefully constructed preparation program cannot get around to everything—just as most principals cannot get around to all the responsibilities they would like to fulfill. The obvious implication is that leadership preparation must extend beyond pre-service preparation into induction programs and subsequent professional development for both novice and experienced leaders.

This chapter focuses on improvements in preparing high school leaders, and chapter 5 examines the ways districts can support—or fail to support—high school reforms and pathways. Inevitably there is some overlap because districts can support their schools by improving the quality of leadership. Astonishingly enough, most districts in the country have no leadership policies at all: when a vacancy occurs, they simply post a job announcement and hope that the resulting pool of applicants will yield someone qualified for the job. The alternatives to this non-policy—we might call it leadership development by trial and error—are both to create truly developmental approaches to leadership preparation and to structure the experiences of individuals preparing to be high school leaders in careful ways. I cover both these potential district policies in this chapter, leaving for chapter 5 the many other ways districts can support high school reform including pathways.

PRE-SERVICE AND IN-SERVICE LEADERSHIP PREPARATION

From the comments of the leaders we interviewed, as well as the complaints in the commission reports reviewed in chapter 1, all high school principals and assistant principals need additional preparation in topics that are relatively less important in elementary and middle schools. These could be incorporated into pre-service programs in modules designed for those intending to work in high schools; into induction programs, especially as individuals move into administrative positions in high schools where they need to wrestle with these issues; in summer institutes and other forms of short-term professional development; and in the professional literature—"how to" books with more connection to experience than to research. To be sure, district hiring practices may partly determine where these modules or courses might be placed: if districts don't distinguish among pre-service programs, then there is no point in creating differentiated programs if those participants with a high school focus or emphasis are then hired into elementary or middle schools.

All high school principals and assistant principals need additional preparation in topics that are less important in elementary and middle schools.

The topics could include the following:

- Improving instruction in the high school: this topic would recognize that it is more difficult in high schools to allocate time for instructional improvement. Also, the conditions for improving instruction in high school are challenging—partly because of teacher preparation in single academic disciplines but also because of the many demands that draw principals away from instructional improvement. Some of the challenge involves establishing priorities, or at least negotiating among different priorities. As one graduate of the PLI said,

> What would have helped me more is how to provide customer services [to parents, grandparents, and teachers] and yet also do the instructional leader part of the job. And they [PLI instructors] emphasize it, they absolutely emphasize that we must prioritize the instructional leader part of the job. When you're here [in the school], sometimes it's disappointing because there are times when I feel I can't do that. So how do we really do that?

How principals "really do that" requires an understanding about setting priorities and figuring out mechanisms for sticking to them, and it doesn't happen without explicit attention.

- Preparation for college, the many dimensions of "college readiness," the elements of a "college-going culture," and the instructional approaches necessary to prepare students for college-level work (Conley 2007). This would be an alternative to what so often happens, preparing students for *access* to college but where they either have to take remedial courses, or they fail to complete college programs because they are not in fact ready for college demands. The pathways we examined rely on preparing students in courses meeting college entrance requirements, but this is only one element of "college readiness."
- Alternatives to conventional guidance and counseling, both for the general purposes of preparing all students to consider options after high school and for the specific purposes of making choices among pathways. Additional resources in counseling, and attaching counselors to specific pathways, are valuable steps, but other innovations mentioned in chapter 2 (including "exploratories") exist with the potential for helping students make crucial decisions during high school. And principals should not mistake recruitment in pathways as a substitute for genuine future-oriented information and guidance.
- Alternatives to conventional discipline, recognizing the special difficulties of behavior among teenagers. Although a number of alternatives to conventional behaviorist disciplines have been developed, including restorative justice and other more student-centered alternatives, they are not widely known and even less frequently practiced.
- Adolescent development, both to understand the sometimes bewildering behavior of adolescents and to be able to interpret (or judge) proposals for discipline, student participation, and nonacademic support services.
- Potential sources of nonacademic support services, such as personal counseling and health and mental health programs. In addition, the

issues involved in linking the school's culture to the culture of service providers—either providers in the community at large or providers in a school-based health center—are important because there is often a clash of cultures between school personnel and those working in health and mental health. A concern with the nonacademic conditions of students' lives should also include a diagnosis of whether the school itself contributes to various mental health problems because of its instruction, climate, or treatment of students (Grubb and Anyon 2010).

- The issues involved in sports and other extracurricular activities, including the conditions under which these activities support the academic mission of the school and when they detract.
- The logic and intricacies of master scheduling.
- Preparation for accreditation reviews.
- Information about "what works" in high schools, with a special emphasis on those interventions that address the "ninth-grade dilemma" of students who are behind grade-level norms, of those who fall behind in credits, and of those who are at high risk for dropping out. (See also the proposal for an Educational Extension Service in chapter 5.) Such materials would also include information about the effectiveness of credit recovery programs, particularly because many of these programs seem academically fraudulent and thus serve students poorly over the long run.

Virtually all principal preparation programs create a generic curriculum, providing the same subjects to all aspiring leaders.[1] The solution to preparing high school principals more appropriately is surely not creating entirely separate programs for high school leaders. Rather, the way may be through developing a "core and elective" approach where aspiring leaders take a core of courses and experiences appropriate for all leaders and then take some electives according to the kind of school they may elect or to other forms of "specialization," such as special education or schools with high concentrations of immigrant students or of students of color. As one PLI graduate said,

> I remember sitting in our group of six among sixty [the first summer of PLI] and thinking that doesn't apply, that doesn't apply [to high schools]. But I think it is important to hear what are the needs of elementary and middle schools because eventually students end up with us. So there has to be articulation—that's a must. But I think that the issues that pertain to secondary [education]

> are different enough that there need to be opportunities when they are together and when they [aspiring high school leaders] are separate.

To be sure, this is made more difficult where districts hire new principals without regard to their preferences and preparation—where a new graduate is equally likely to end up at any level of the schooling system. But specialization might become part of district policy, as I illustrate in chapter 5.

The solution to preparing high school principals more appropriately is surely not creating entirely separate programs. Rather, the way may be through developing a "core and elective" approach where aspiring leaders take a core of courses appropriate for all leaders and then take electives according to the kind of school they may elect.

For principals in high schools with pathways, an additional set of topics is appropriate. Again, these could be included in pre-service programs, in induction programs, or in other forms of professional development. In one case, a principal who had been both a middle school and high school principal described an approach where the district had cooperated with the local state university to develop programs fitting the district's needs. Because the district was in the process of breaking large, comprehensive high schools into smaller, themed schools, one element of the program involved the issues in creating small schools.

Among the important topics related to pathways are the following:

- The basic rationale and advantages of pathways; the evidence about effectiveness; and other material necessary to keeping the vision and communicating it to students, parents, district officials (especially as they come and go), and board members. One principal in a high school with several themed schools-within-schools clarified the importance of vision:

    > If a principal program does not talk about vision and values, then I think they are leaving that person shortchanged. You really have to

go in with a belief system that you will stand by. So when the waves come, you will stand in the storm.

- Improving instruction in pathways as a challenge distinct from restructuring a high school. As the principal of a small school-within-a-school declared, "If you don't improve instruction, if you don't improve students' learning, then you haven't really done much of anything." In particular, given the special challenge of integrating content and projects across subjects, leaders should be familiar with different approaches to integrating curricula.
- Choosing what pathways to offer, involving issues of equity and status differentials; the clarity of the theme for any pathway; linkages to academic subjects and to "modern" occupations (rather than the occupations of traditional vocational education, such as retailing, secretarial work, auto repair, and cosmetology); student interest; faculty expertise; local employers and their willingness to participate; and natural connections to local postsecondary institutions.[2]
- Finding internships and other forms of work placements and of learning more about the many ways that work-based learning can enrich the school-based part of a pathway. For example, internships provide different forms of learning, from supervisors and coworkers who are quite different from teachers; they encompass many competencies better taught on the job than in school settings, including nonstandard forms of academic abilities. Furthermore, the experiences in internships can be brought back into the school setting for further examination by creating seminars for students to discuss their disparate experiences and their implications for schooling, much as LaGuardia Community College has done in its mandatory internships (Grubb and Badway 1998).
- Developing alternative forms of assessment, including different ways of showing the success of pathway programs other than conventional test scores.

The issues that aspiring high school principals and leaders in pathways face, quite different from their peers in elementary and middle schools, are numerous, at the same time that some issues are generic to all forms of school leadership. So the suggestion of "opportunities when they are together and when they are separate" makes a great deal of sense.

ON-THE-JOB EXPERIENCE, INDUCTION PROGRAMS, AND PROFESSIONAL DEVELOPMENT

Many principals we interviewed don't believe that pre-service programs can prepare high school leaders adequately. They stress instead the requirement of experience and learning on the job. As one principal noted about her leadership preparation program,

> Well, I wouldn't say that none of it matters, but it all fades very quickly compared to the actual experience of being on the job. And there's nothing like screwing up on the job to teach you the really hard lessons about how to develop consistent practices and to be able to implement in the face of controversy or challenge.... It's all a lot of talk until you're on the job.

Another reinforced this point:

> There's nothing that can prepare you for being an administrator at a high school other than shadowing, interning, spending time—finding a way to force [education] students who are interested in being high school administrators ... into high schools during that time. That hands-on experience—you can't do any better than that.

The recommendation for "hands-on experience" leads in at least three different directions. One, of course, is to incorporate internships, job shadowing, and other experiences within schools into pre-service programs. This is a common recommendation for all professional programs, articulated over a long period of time, and is no different conceptually for teachers and for principals, for doctors and engineers.[3]

However, it seems to be difficult for many principal preparation programs to find time in the schedules of their students for internships, or for their schools to release them for long enough periods to carry out meaningful internships. (Indeed, one of the powerful advantages of districts creating working relationships with preparation programs, discussed below, is that they can then structure internships in ways that fit the district's needs.) Where serious internships are not possible, an alternative is to structure various leadership activities that aspiring principals can carry out in the schools they teach in—for example, community mapping exercises to understand the community conditions of their schools; analyses of the micro-political alignments in their schools;

or action research projects in which students examine a problem, develop a solution, implement the solution during a semester or more, and then assess the effects on the original problem.[4] These may be second-best alternatives to having more extensive internships in a variety of schools in order to understand a variety of conditions, but at least they involve aspiring principals in more experienced-based learning about how to shape school conditions.

A second direction emerging from the recommendation of "hands-on experiences" is to shape the experiences that new assistant principals have in their early placements. All too often, assistant principals are assigned to discipline or to one area of a school, and then they fail to learn about all the aspects of a school that they will need to know as principals. One assistant principal noted:

> In my past experience I had a position where responsibilities were divvied up, so it didn't matter who we were. I did have the title of "curriculum and instruction," but I also had some responsibilities outside of that—I think that's necessary for assistant principals to know all facets of this role. I have no experience in sports, athletics, student activities, facilities management. I think if you ask my counterpart, she would tell you the same thing about curriculum—she has little experience with master scheduling, counseling, scheduling students, how many sections of this, testing. So I do believe that rather than having specialization as the system currently stands, it's better to divvy up responsibilities so all assistant principals have a similar experience.... I was lucky that I came into this district already in this seat, the AP for instruction, but it's difficult for a person in the AP for administration to move into the instruction position. Because this position is the core of the school, and the AP for administration is more management.

Where schools have adopted a conventional leadership team—with one individual in charge of discipline, another overseeing facilities, one in charge of extracurricular activities, one in charge of curriculum and instruction—this means that many assistant principals get very little experience with the instructional side of the school, yet another reason why some principals are poorly prepared to improve instruction. As one high school principal who had gone through a variety of assistant principal positions complained,

> I think the drawback of the specialized APs is that you just become a manager. In other words, you do the discipline, you do the safety, you do a certain number of teacher evals, but you're not as much as you should be looking through the lens of overall curricular achievement and student achievement. What happens

> is one person perhaps, which I was fortunate [to be], gets the benefit of looking at schools through the lens of achievement, and the others maybe do not.... At our school what we're trying to do as a team is to keep, through the meetings and through the activities and through the evaluations, focusing on overall achievement, looking at achievement gap issues ... Our team has struggled as assistant principals to see themselves as less just managers of daily operations, and [more] being curricular leaders.

There are various solutions, both individual and collective, to the challenge of accumulating the right kinds of experiences. One principal noted that she had put together a sequence of positions for herself that amount to a program of experience-based preparation, but she was clear that was her own doing. Another assistant principal noted that others in her high school were rotated around several different positions, and "I'm developing in a breadth of areas that will support my movement into a principalship—but there are other areas of the school that I'm not getting any real experience with, and that concerns me." But these planned paths into the high school principalship are very much the exception; most principals we interviewed did not have much control over their placements, and most principals in our sample acknowledged that they did not have enough experience before they began their demanding jobs. Districts tended to assign them to openings without considering the breadth of their experiences. That is, the districts did not have a *developmental* concept underlying how they assigned new administrators.

It would also be possible for districts rather than schools to structure the experiences of assistant principals and principals so that they develop appropriate capacities. One principal in northern California contrasted her recent experiences with those in a large southern California district:

> That was the only place in my career where I got some active, deliberate training in how to be an administrator. Starting my second, third year teaching: "So you want to be a principal?" Support groups. Training programs. Formal opportunities where you could shadow, where you could experience. When I was in [that district], the principal knew that her primary job in having an assistant principal was to train us to be principals.... In-house programs, after-school, Saturday seminars. But I have not seen any inkling of that any place up here [in northern California].... There's no formal direction, not even mentoring, not even a veteran principal. Whereas that [training] was part of the culture [in southern California], and I felt very supported. It was kind of like the people were aware that this was a thirty- to forty-year job and supporting you along the way.

In effect, this principal was describing a district attempt to create a developmental approach to principal preparation, like the one outlined near the end of this chapter. It's impossible to say how frequent this practice is—this was the "only place in my career" where this happened—but it appears to be quite rare.

Districts rather than schools could structure the experiences of assistant principals and principals so that they develop appropriate capacities.

Another example of the strategic use of experience was a practice reported in one large district, also in southern California. There, aspiring high school principals would be rotated through an initial position as an assistant principal in a middle school, then an assistant principal in a high school, then a principal in a middle school, and finally a principal in a high school. In this pattern individuals moved from smaller and less complex institutions to the larger and more complex high school, and from positions of less responsibility into the principalship—one solution to gaining the kind of experience required in high school. Unfortunately, a new superintendent eliminated this program, under the assumption that all principals face the same challenges, without putting anything similar in its place.

A third example may be the approach of the Houston Independent School District. This program, which operated for three years in the late 1990s, involved cohorts of fifteen students chosen jointly by the district and the University of Houston. They completed coursework for a master's program in courses sometimes co-taught by both university faculty and district administrators. During the second year of the program, aspiring principals served a year-long paid internship, at the student's current teacher's salary, and interns were matched with high school principals through a "speed dating" process, where in most cases principals and interns received their first or second choice. The interns functioned as administrators in these schools, taking on special assignments in researching and planning small schools as well as day-to-day administrative practices. The program was apparently well respected by all participants and certainly provided better preparation for high schools with small schools-within-schools than did conventional principal preparation. Unfortunately, a new superintendent at the district and a new dean and department chair at the university failed to maintain good working relationships, and the program ended after three years.[5]

These examples illustrate that a district mindful of the requirements of high schools, and the even greater challenges of pathways, can create programs of preparation *and* experience that develop the appropriate capacities. Unfortunately, these examples also illustrate that unconventional practices are all too fragile and can be readily dismantled with changes in district leadership.

A third direction stemming from the perceived need for hands-on experience is the development of induction programs for novice administrators—analogous to induction programs for new teacher. These provide further education and support as individuals experience their first leadership responsibilities. They can draw on real experiences ("there's nothing like screwing up on the job to teach you the really hard lessons") rather than—as happens in university-based programs—imagined experiences or those drawn from other students. Real experiences in the early years of administration are often freighted with emotions that cannot be simulated in a university-based program—the emotions of angry parents, the acting-out of frustrated students, the reactions of recalcitrant teachers. Induction programs can review the decisions that novice administrators make in their own schools, rather than relying on case studies or decisions made in other schools.

For example, the induction program for the Principal Leadership Institute, the Leadership Support Program, provides new leaders with three years of support, including coaching at their schools and monthly meetings in which these leaders discuss various issues and engage in common problem-solving. These meetings incorporate a variety of more specific activities:

- Using a process of narrative analysis, in which individuals audio- or videotape their reactions to school dilemmas and then analyze their responses with the help of others. The results can help uncover unconscious or unarticulated attitudes of these fledgling leaders about the roles they play in their schools, their unconscious biases, the ways they make decisions, the emotional content of their work, and their interactions with coworkers and students (Brill 2008).
- Reinforcing the importance of instructional leadership and ways to help fledgling administrators think about improving instruction.

- Prioritizing time, especially carving out time for instructional leadership from the many external demands on leaders (especially in high schools).
- Understanding the trajectory of administrators from novice to expert, concentrating on the issues that participants are facing at their early stages of leadership.
- Promoting a problem-solving approach to leadership, focusing on three issues that assistant principals usually face: discipline; evaluating teachers; and engaging in hard or "courageous" conversations (Singleton 2006) about race, class, other dimensions of student backgrounds, and teachers' own prejudices.
- Reinforcing the importance of equity in all dimensions of urban schools, including practices to improve outcomes for low-performing students.
- Developing an inquiry project, similar to action research during the PLI itself, in which participants take a problem, develop actions to resolve it, and examine the effects. At this stage in their development, leaders have more positional authority than they did when they were PLI students, and so outcomes are likely to differ.

In effect, the preparation program itself translates theory into practice, whereas the induction moves practice—the actual experiences of novice leaders—into theory, or more precisely into more general understandings of dilemmas in schools. Such induction activities represent an integration of experience and learning or reflection, a both-and rather than an either-or approach and one that avoids the false invocation of John Dewey as supporting learning by doing only.[6]

A principal preparation program translates theory into practice, whereas an induction program moves practice—the actual experiences of novice leaders—into theory or more general understandings of dilemmas in schools, an integration of experience and learning or reflection.

To be sure, some elements of induction programs could be quite informal and easier to establish than a full-fledged program. One principal said that

> It would be really nice to have, once a month, a high school principals' round table. That doesn't cost anything. Let's have a topic or two topics and just hear different approaches, how somebody else works with the same thing. I mean, that's not rocket science.

Another principal with experience on a campus including three small schools noted:

> We try to get job-alike meetings . . . where I can host three career teachers or five different schools that have career pathways, they can come together at my school and share best practices and use protocols, like we get together and we go, 'OK, these are my five challenges.' . . . You've got to do that on an ongoing basis, to share best practices, and be creative and not reinvent the wheel on your own.

Unfortunately, either informal roundtables or full induction programs for leaders appear to be rare. A few states—Pennsylvania, South Carolina, and Colorado—require them, but the programs themselves are short, more like workshops than continuous support over several years.[7] So one way to enhance the preparation of principals—and the more specialized preparation that high school principals and those in pathways need—would be to make the experience of induction programs universal and to provide some specialization so that high school principals and assistant principals could focus on the special challenges in high schools.

Overall, I suspect that the advocacy among some principals for experience *rather than* pre-service is somewhat misplaced. As one principal put it, "[pre-service education] fades very quickly once you're on the job." To return to a Deweyan perspective preferring *both-and* to *either-or* approaches, many forms of experience, or structured experience, promoted by the principals we interviewed amounted to using experience in the context of a school or school-like setting—such as a workshop or institute removed from the schoolhouse. In such situations, experience *and* reflection, doing *and* learning can take place. The creation of internships during pre-service programs, such as the Houston internship in the second year of pre-service education; induction programs that capitalize on concurrent experiences examined in a school-like setting; and professional development designed for novice leaders all combine experience with reflection and analysis away from the school itself. All these enable novice leaders, and even veteran leaders, to learn more from their experiences than they could on their own. And experience by itself is not always the best teacher: those assistant principals assigned to discipline, extracurricular activities, or another area of specialization don't have the breadth of experiences necessary for a principal.

A DEVELOPMENTAL APPROACH TO PRINCIPAL PREPARATION

A more general problem with preparing high school leaders—in fact, *all* school leaders—is that most districts do not have any policies for *developing* principals. When there's a vacancy in a school, district officials post a job listing, interview the applicants, and choose the finalist—often without much participation by teachers in the school or by parents and other community members.[8] These conventional hiring practices rarely consider the history of the school, its parents and students, and whether a new principal will continue (rather than reverse) reforms already in place. To make matters worse, some districts rotate their principals after a certain period (e.g., two years), ensuring that principals never get to know their schools and communities well. The anxiety teachers have about new principals (and also new superintendents) is in part a fear that previous reforms will be reversed rather than continued. This is a special problem with pathways because they take time to develop; a process in which pathways are developed and abandoned, rediscovered and then abandoned, cannot possibly contribute to the long-run development of this complex reform.

The alternative to the current lack of district leadership policies would be a *developmental* approach.[9] This would involve several stages:

- identifying teachers suitable for and interested in becoming leaders, while they are still teachers;
- placing these promising leaders in various positions of teacher-leadership within their own schools, to begin developing their abilities;
- enrolling these teacher-leaders in pre-service programs, especially those with some connection to the district and its policies (as in the Houston approach described above);

- ensuring that their initial placements are in schools where principals will rotate their assistant principals among different responsibilities (rather than, as is often the case, sticking a new assistant principal with responsibility for discipline) and will continue to provide mentoring and guidance;
- ensuring that initial placements are in schools that are reasonably competent, rather than placing new assistant principals or principals in the most dysfunctional and chaotic schools and expecting them to "turn around" these schools when they have the least experience;
- creating induction programs for novice administrators or relying on a school of education operating with the cooperation of the district to address the specific practices, priorities, and problems of the district, whether these are reshaping failing schools, introducing special intervention programs, developing school-based budgeting, or any other priority of the district; and
- continuing to provide support for veteran principals, including the expectation that they would in turn be mentors to new assistant principals.

For high school principals, a pre-service program with some modules focusing on the special challenges of high schools, a planned sequence of experiences of ever-greater complexity culminating in a high school principalship, and an induction program focusing in part on high school issues would create a complementarity among pre-service, in-service, and experiential preparation.

A developmental approach to leadership would involve several stages, from identifying teachers to preparing them in pre-service programs to providing induction programs to placing them in appropriate schools.

In the schools where we interviewed, and in the high schools I have visited over twenty years, only a few pieces of this developmental sequence have been put in place. Some districts have mechanisms for identifying promising leaders and referring them to in-service programs, but that's all. Some districts—Houston, District 2 in New York—have partnered with schools of education to develop in-service programs tailored to their needs, but these are either rare or short-lived (as in the Houston case). *Planned* sequences of experiences are rare, and induction programs tend to be both rare and short. These developmental approaches cannot be created by individual schools; they can be initiated and sustained only if districts are able to develop such policies and then to implement them consistently over time. When I turn in the next chapter to the ways in which districts can support high school reforms in general and multiple pathways in particular, their responsibility for leadership preparation will be one of the many ways they can support—or undermine—pathways.

RESTRUCTURING THE PRINCIPALSHIP

So far I have discussed ways of preparing *individuals* for the position of the high school principal. An alternative, or perhaps more appropriately a complementary reform, would be to *restructure the job itself* so it isn't so complex. There has been relatively little thought about how to do this, but there are several alternatives to consider—all of which need to be developed through district policies as well as in preparation and induction programs.

One idea is to consider having multiple principals within one school (Grubb and Flessa 2006). A relatively small number of schools operate with two or even three principals. As long as these multiple principals are in constant communication with each other, they can serve as perfect substitutes for one another, and members of the school community (including parents) learn that they can go to either principal with their problems. The creation of dual principals in effect increases the resources in the position, and these additional resources are often used for responsibilities that principals cannot get around to—"you can never finish everything you do." In several schools, the additional administrative time was spent on instructional improvement and assuring the provision of nonacademic support services.

A similar effort to increase resources in administration is the effort of the Wallace Foundation to create a school administration manager (SAM). The idea is to separate the purely administrative or managerial aspects of the principal's job and allocate them to a SAM so that the principal can spend more time as an instructional leader. This is also a way to create a role for an individual with more specialized training in management; for example, part of a SAM's preparation might be in a business school. In the early implementation of this project, principals who participated for at least a year increased the time devoted to instructional tasks by fifty-eight minutes a day, and their time on such administrative tasks as building management, student discipline, and office work decreased. To be sure, creating more time for instructional leadership does not necessarily mean that instruction improved, and the evaluation suggested that principals need additional support in becoming instructional leaders—presumably that could be provided during pre-service and induction programs. However, creating positions for SAMs may be a useful first step for improving instruction, especially in large and complex high schools.[10]

Something similar happens when high school principals structure their leadership teams. Typically in the schools we visited, different assistant principals are assigned to curriculum and instruction, to building management, to discipline, and to sports and extracurricular activities; these kinds of specializations can be viewed as ways of relieving the principal of administrative tasks so he or she can pay more attention to instruction. However, the conventional allocation of responsibilities means that only one or two people on a team are responsible for instruction, and as a practical matter that individual may spend more time on curriculum than on the quality of teaching. An alternative, mentioned in chapter 3, is to make sure that all members of the leadership team have some instructional responsibilities as well as other duties—so that the group engaged in instructional improvement becomes larger, not smaller. For example, a school with multiple pathways may assign different assistant principals to different pathways so that all assistant principals are concerned with instruction and the creation of integrated curricula.

In a similar way, high schools that are serious about providing nonacademic support to their students could develop a tripartite division of labor. In addition to the academic high school with its leadership team, a school-based health center (SBHC) would provide a variety of physical and mental health programs, other workshops and seminars related to adolescent development, and support to both teachers and students about nonacademic problems that stand in the way of academic progress. Another individual would be in charge of after-school programs, including traditional sports and extracurricular activities but extending as well to remedial efforts, to internships and service learning placements, and to other activities that take place during nonschool time (Grubb and Anyon 2010). The trio of the principal, SBHC director, and the after-school director would consult periodically about interactions among the three units, about potential new activities to undertake, and about lessons learned about student needs. This is again a way of dividing leadership tasks so that the principal and his or her leadership team need not spend so much time on nonacademic or managerial issues, including those related to sports and extracurricular activities—"nothing to do with academic achievement, but a huge time drain that takes away from paying attention to instruction."

All these ways of restructuring the principal's role in some way provide more resources for the position—more time, especially on such neglected aspects of high schools as instruction; more focus; more consistency; and more specialized expertise (for example, when a SAM or SBHC director is involved). They might also require more money, especially for more administrative time, and spending on administration rather than instruction has sometimes been viewed as waste or "administrative bloat." But administration and the multiple roles of the principal are not necessarily "bloat" if time is spent on instructional improvement, enhancing a school's climate, directing resources to more effective uses, and other actions that improve outcomes for students. The value of administration depends on what it accomplishes, and these ways of restructuring the principalship are all intended to improve the effectiveness and equity of high schools.

CONCLUSION: DIFFERENTIATING PRINCIPAL PREPARATION

There are, then, many ways to improve the preparation of high school leaders and to focus at least part of in-service and induction programs on the special challenges of high schools. However, virtually none of these practices is widespread. Some reasons are obvious: the larger numbers of principals in elementary and middle school, forcing preparation programs to focus on those levels of education; the tendency for leaders to move around different levels of the education system so that neither individuals nor pre-service programs can predict what placements aspiring principals will get; and the tendency to view leadership as a generic capacity with many of the same attributes in all kinds of schools, in business, in government, and even in the military. The lack of a knowledge base specifying what principals at different levels need to know—for example, for high school principals, the ways of addressing the ninth-grade transition and of preventing dropouts—has been another barrier addressed in this chapter. And the lack of any coherent district policies about leadership development has meant that changing leadership programs without district participation may be ineffective; for example, creating special modules for aspiring high school leaders is pointless if district hiring practices ignore such specialization. Most districts need to start at the beginning in developing their own coherent approaches to leadership development.

So it's possible to imagine leadership preparation that is partly differentiated. Aspiring high school principals would take certain modules and workshops that others don't. Elementary principals would concentrate on issues—relationships with early childhood programs, addressing the "whole child," the foundations of early literacy and numeracy—less appropriate at other levels. Middle school principals would concentrate more on early adolescent development and perhaps early versions of high school issues. Finally, heads of specialized schools, such as continuation high schools or schools for special education students, would engage in their own specialized preparation. To do this, however, we must first recognize the particular challenges at each level of schooling.

QUESTIONS FOR CHAPTER 4

1. Have any local leadership programs developed separate modules, problems, or readings specifically addressed to aspiring high school leaders?
2. Are there induction or early in-service programs required of or available for new administrators? How long and how intensive are they? Do any of them incorporate any content specific to high schools?
3. What does your school or district do to provide novice administrators with experiences appropriate for their development as leaders—for example, placement in schools with strong principals or where assistant principals will be rotated among different roles?
4. In your district, are there any ways of restructuring leadership roles so that leaders can spend more time on issues of instruction, equity, and reform?

Chapter 5

"Some Joke Show"

District Support for High Schools and Multiple Pathways

We started our work concerned with leadership and multiple pathways in *schools*. However, as we talked with principals and district officials, we became aware of the importance of *districts* and their support, or more often their lack of support. Most school-initiated reforms need the approval of districts to survive, and even the most talented principals will fail if the conditions created by the district don't reinforce their efforts. These conditions include, at a minimum, developing a coherent strategy for focusing on instructional improvement; backing up the principal's role as instructional leader (rather than undermining that role by imposing specific curricular methods or instructional approaches, or by imposing too many administrative burdens); giving principals sufficient authority for school-based decisions, including potential control over their budgets in school-based budgeting (SBB); developing a collaborative partnership with schools, in a *district* version of distributed leadership, rather than imposing district decisions on schools; and tailoring support to the needs of individual schools.[1]

In addition, our interviews clarified that particular kinds of district support are necessary for such major reforms as pathways. Financial support is crucial because pathways cost more, particularly in the short run. Schools with pathways need to be able to hire the right kinds of teachers, including teachers with expertise related to the themes, rather than having teachers imposed on them by district practices and union rules. Pathways need to develop their own integrated curricula, rather than having curricula imposed on them (as happens in many districts with scripted curricula, particularly under No Child Left Behind). Conversely, a district initiative contrary to pathways—a greater emphasis on multiple-choice test scores in English and math or on conventional conceptions of academic rigor or an abandonment of small schools on fiscal and bureaucratic grounds—would make pathways impossible to sustain. A school might be able to continue its pathways despite district opposition, as long as it kept its test scores up and its spending per pupil down to the district average, but that might be difficult—and it would certainly not allow consideration of other potential benefits of pathways, including their influence on motivation and engagement, their ability to teach a broader range of competencies such as twenty-first-century skills, or their potential effects on graduation and college-going rates.

District support and its opposite, district barriers to multiple pathways, come in many different forms. These range from support in principle—where districts initiate or encourage pathways as solutions to various education problems—to support in practice, in the myriad details of daily interactions with schools.

District support and its opposite, district barriers to multiple pathways, come in many forms. These range from support in principle—where districts initiate or encourage pathways as solutions to various education problems—to support in practice, in the myriad details of daily interactions with schools. Districts can support high school reform and pathways, even though they often do not—many principals we interviewed articulated some version of the statement that "they're pretty hands-off." Some forms of district support—for developing concepts of leadership described in the previous chapter, for improving instructional quality, or for selecting more effective ninth-grade interventions—would apply to all high schools, not just those with pathways. Finally, there are certain issues—particularly those related to equity—that cannot be resolved without district participation. All in all, *potential* district roles are more varied than those we now see in practice, another clue that—as in the case of developmental approaches to leadership—districts have not been as active as they could be.

SUPPORT IN PRINCIPLE: PATHWAYS AS CRUCIAL REFORMS

In some cases, districts have initiated pathways as mechanisms of high school reform.[2] In one common pattern, a district breaks large, dysfunctional high schools into small, independent schools with themes, a change that simultaneously demolishes ineffective practices, dismisses some weak teachers and principals, and creates the conditions for starting small schools with new approaches. This is a particular kind of "reconstitution," an effort to replace a low-performing school with another, more promising school. The distinction between this case and the forms of reconstitution favored by the U.S. Department of Education[3] is that a new and presumably more effective school structure replaces the older comprehensive high school, rather than relying simply on new teachers and principals working within the old structure.

Some districts have left higher-performing schools as comprehensive high schools, particularly for students and parents who prefer a large school with its varied offerings and active social component. In other cases, reportedly, districts are breaking all comprehensive high schools into small schools. The model described by one principal was a campus of sixteen hundred students broken into four small, themed schools of four hundred students each, with such shared amenities as sports facilities, a library, a career center, and a cafeteria. In these cases, the initiative, funding, and authority for pathways come from the district.

In a variant, a strong superintendent may impose pathways on high schools by fiat. In one district where we visited three high schools, a superintendent committed to project-based learning called all principals together and gave a well-known speech cited by every principal, clarifying that "the train is leaving the station"—that every high school would develop at least some pathways, whether it wanted to or not. Not surprisingly, this heavy-handed approach generated resentment because some teachers and some principals didn't want to be on that particular train.

In other cases, the shift to pathways has been an attempt to reverse inequities among high schools in a district, where high-status schools associated with middle-class students continue to differentiate themselves from low-status schools "across the tracks," or located in low-income areas of town. One district official, explaining the motivation for introducing pathways within a school, commented that

> The other thing we are dealing with, honestly, in this district is that we are bisected by railroad tracks and there is literally a good side of the tracks and a bad side of the tracks. [A particular boulevard] splits it. And one of the things we said we were going to do in our small learning community implementation that we wrote to the federal government was that we were going to try to break this divide.

They did so by introducing pathways with high-tech themes that would attract middle-class students into low-status schools. This is a tactic much like the development of magnet schools to attract middle-class students to schools in undesirable locations.

Where a district divides several dysfunctional high schools into pathways, the conversions may vary in their success—not surprisingly because nothing in educational reform ever works uniformly well. In response to a question about the success of these conversions, a district official responded that

> Kane [a pseudonym] has had the most success. [City] High School has had some. And Carling still suffers. Having visited Carling quite a bit before it converted, I would say yes, [it has progressed] socially. Academically, not so much. Socially they had fights all the time; they had a very brutal climate. Now it's much quieter, calmer—you do see the caring. They're still working on their academic rigor.

So pathways may result in improvement in some areas—in this case school climate, facilitated by the smaller size of these pathways—but not in academic areas. One issue in this particular case is that the themes in Kane were all high-status themes with a great deal of academic content, whereas those in Carling were less so. Kane also had higher scores on the state's accountability exams than the other schools that had been broken up, as well as a strong principal—but also "a very veteran and stagnant staff"—so "Kane had many factors working to its advantage," including its location in a middle-class part of the city. Obviously, conversion to themed pathways is not a panacea, and the various factors including the choice of themes noted in chapter 3 are crucial to the success of any conversion.

When pathways are initiated by districts rather than by schools themselves or some combination of school and district leadership, their well-being is completely dependent on the superintendent, or potentially on some other "executive champion" with a clear vision of pathways: "you can't expect a superintendent to spend so much time doing this, but you can expect the superintendent to deputize someone," commented one community leader (Stanford Redesign Network 2009, 6). This in turn means that the stability of these reforms depends on the stability of the superintendent or of the "executive champion," and urban leadership is notorious for high turnover. One principal in a district that had divided dysfunctional high schools into pathways—herself a strong supporter of instructional leadership and improvement—noted the succession of superintendents:

> The level of support I have felt in my job has been directly associated with who the superintendent is. When [the first individual] was our superintendent, I felt respected. I felt that if needed some help at my school I could get it; if I needed support and mentoring as a principal, I could ask for it. Then we moved into the era of [a second individual], and it became very hands-off, which for a lot of principals was fabulous because when it's hands-off anything goes—you don't have to stress me. For me that was no good. I like the accountability, knowing that I have somebody who believes deeply in me and that I want to impress ... And then [a third individual] came in. I have to tell you, as a professional person I do not feel supported by him. I actually feel disrespected. When I go to meetings, I am constantly being demoralized ... It [the district culture] now is not letting anybody know that you have a weakness rather than that culture of showing each other what we don't know and helping each other. And to me, that is totally counterproductive.

Another mentioned the special problems with explaining pathways, which were still new and unfamiliar to most district officials: "We had so many different bosses, it's been a challenge to create a place where you don't have to explain what you're doing over and over again, and they don't quite understand because they weren't here: 'Why are you a small school? What's that all about?'" In her particular case, certain district offices including the career technical education office was supportive, but not the superintendent's office: "We're not able to tell exactly what they think of us at any particular time and what they're planning to do with us."

When pathways are initiated by districts rather than by schools themselves, their well-being is completely dependent on the superintendent or potentially on some other "executive champion" with a clear vision of pathways.

Stability in superintendents has been lacking in many urban districts, and one serious consequence is instability in basic policies. A few principals noted that the school board was responsible for choosing superintendents and that boards seemed not to care about continuity in policies when they interviewed candidates. Indeed, given the difficulty of improving the performance of so many low-performing students, the dynamic in many urban districts has been to seek new!! superintendents who promise new!! approaches—because the old ones didn't work. In the process, innovations that might work if given time to mature—such as pathways—may be swept away in the rush to the new![4]

A good example of instability in superintendents, followed by damaging changes in policy, occurred in one school where we interviewed. Simply by chance, one of our schools was "Railside," [a pseudonym] written about by Boaler and Staples (2008) as an exemplar of a math department creating its own constructivist approach to teaching. More generally, the school had developed a distinctive culture of collaboration, a celebration of diversity, and a vision of meeting the needs of all students through improved instruction. The faculty worked collaboratively to win a grant supporting teacher-led professional development on literacy, integration of preparation for the state's exit exam into regular classes (instead of in separate remedial classes), smaller class sizes in ninth-grade English and algebra, and summer institutes for collaborative curriculum development. Nearby graduate schools used the school for student teaching because of its reputation for professional collaboration, collective decision-making, and innovative instruction in many subjects, not just math. However, a new superintendent with a hierarchical management style joined the district, and the movement toward small learning communities ceased. The new superintendent has put more emphasis on test prep for basic skills tests in reading and math and on conventional remediation classes. The school has begun more frequent observations of core classes to ensure regular use of textbooks and lesson plans focused on district-approved instruction, leaving little room for the former constructivist or balanced instruction. Small, heterogeneous classes on a block schedule have given way to larger, tracked classes on a conventional six-period schedule. The members of the celebrated math department are leaving for other schools, especially charter schools.[5] It remains to be seen how many innovations at Railside will survive the district changes, but the point is that instability of policies can be enormously damaging to reform—and incredibly wasteful of resources as well because the time and effort put into earlier changes are effectively wasted.

The same problem arises with other district personnel. In one district with substantial investment in pathways, a new director of secondary education came in and created chaos:

> The transition to having a director of secondary education has been difficult. She was charged not only with closing the achievement gap but getting out of program improvement. She decided that what she wanted to do, in about December, was to change our schedule and to go from the four-by-four block schedule to a six-period day. Essentially everything we were doing with the small learning communities suddenly had to stop, and everybody had to have long conversations and fights—that was a huge, intense fight all the way until a month ago [March], when she said "Forget it—we'll wait until next year." And suddenly everybody was looking at me [the district director for pathways] and saying, "How can you expect us to come up with two more themed pathways when we have spent all this time yelling about a schedule?"

This is partly a story about the instability caused by a change in district administration, instability that caused a great deal of wasted time, and by the obtuse desire of some district administrators to change practices without finding out what was working well.

Similarly, changes in principals have the same effects. As one district director complained, "a new principal comes in and then they wipe out the academies." She went on to explain that academies in her district were sometimes led by principals and sometimes by "a community of teachers," but either way, pathways were vulnerable to the directions that new principals may take.

One obvious lesson to districts is that stability—in superintendents, in district personnel and policies, in principals, but particularly in their embrace of pathways—is a crucial resource. *If districts are going to change their policies and practices every few years, then they should not embark on multiple pathways.* These are reforms—as with every other worthwhile reform, including those to improve instruction, to reshape school cultures, to create a "college-going culture," or to create an early college high school—that require substantial time, incremental changes in many institutional practices, and slow persuasion ("buy-in") of individuals who are initially resistant to change. They may also require several years of experience to reduce their additional costs per student, as the cost data for pathways in chapter 3 suggest. Instability destroys any possibility that these reforms can be completed and is therefore a crucial resource for reform, one that money cannot buy.

Stability is a crucial resource because pathways are reforms that require substantial time, incremental changes in many institutional practices, and slow persuasion ("buy-in") of individuals who are initially resistant to change.

There are, however, many districts that have not played any special role in promoting pathways as mechanisms of high school reform. In these cases, districts may tolerate pathways but not do anything special to encourage them. A principal in one such district noted that "the district is not involved in them [pathways], so yeah, they're site-level. I don't think the district is hindering; they're just not actively encouraging—they're not involved." In other cases, districts are willing to tolerate any reform as long as it increases test scores. As one principal of a school with several pathways noted,

> I don't think the school board in this district has had much input [about pathways] either way. They've been a rubber stamp prior to [my] getting here. The superintendent now, he is a big proponent of test scores. He will tell you, if

> SLCs [small learning communities] show better test scores, then I am all for SLCs. What we have seen is SLCs have helped test scores. So he's a big fan of test scores going up.

But in this passage, the superintendent did not care about the other learning benefits of pathways that might not show up in English and math scores, or their effects in motivating students and facilitating their progress through high schools.

Furthermore, there are too many roles that districts *must* play for pathways to thrive—providing additional funding, helping identify the right teachers and principals, developing a coherent policy toward leadership, and other issues noted in the next section—for mere tolerance to work well over the long run. We might expect pathways to survive and thrive—and provide distinct alternatives to the comprehensive high school—only if districts and schools can cooperate on their development and sustenance.

SUPPORT IN PRACTICE: DAILY ADMINISTRATIVE TASKS

Whether or not a district supports pathways in principle, districts have many other interactions with schools, the daily interactions that can either smooth the development of such reforms as pathways or undermine them. These interactions arise in many different ways, so districts that are serious about developing pathways (or any other thorough reforms) need to pay attention to a wide range of their policies—or, in many cases, to the fact that they have not adopted coherent policies or implemented them carefully.

Districts have many other interactions with schools that can either smooth the development of reforms or undermine them, so districts that are serious about developing pathways need to pay attention to a wide range of their policies.

Top-Down District Policies

One problem comes from the historical tendency of districts to operate in top-down fashion, dictating policy without considering the differences among schools. Many principals complained about too much district interference in what they were trying to accomplish; one noted that "we need support, not direction." Another noted the didactic pedagogy of district meetings:

> We have what we call "leadership meetings" in [this district]. We have them every other month, and we all herd into this room, and it's mostly [district] administrators, and it's also program administrators, not just site administrators. And then we have a series of "Here's what's going on with the budget; here's the new law that you must do this; these are the people who are getting their technology refreshed." It's that; it's somebody talking *at* you about something. It's not, "Here's a situation," real or not real, it doesn't matter. "At your table, how would you solve this situation?"

She was asking for a problem-solving session, not information transfer, but information transfer—the basis of conventional didactic teaching—was all she got.

In extreme cases, the actions of an autocratic superintendent (and his or her associates) generate such resentment that every change associated with the person is rejected, even changes that might benefit students. In one district with a history of changing superintendents nearly every year, one superintendent's efforts to establish small schools were so resisted that the small, themed schools and their principals were effectively ostracized by comprehensive high schools, which did nothing to help in the conversion. Years later, individuals associated with the superintendent's administration are still being targeted for removal. Similarly, the superintendent who declared that "the train is leaving the station" alienated many in his district, and some teachers left as a result.

Again and again, principals complained about rigid top-down policies that failed to take into consideration the unique histories and needs of individual schools. One principal in an autonomous small high school complained about professional development:

> Even though we said we had already been through it, they put us back in John Sapphire's effective teacher and effective learning. And I'm sitting there going, "That's not what I need." I need somebody to sit down and explain all these bud-

> get items to me, explain all the operational pieces, because I already had the instructional background . . . In a district this size, you're talking about thirty-five high school principals, and it doesn't matter where you've come from, they stick you in the same place—so I had to figure out all that [fiscal] stuff on my own.

So districts can be both autocratic and rigid—the dreaded problem of policies following "one size fit all."

In effect, the ideas of distributed leadership are as applicable at the district level as they are at the school level. Exemplary districts tend to share decision-making with their schools rather than operate in top-down fashion. As one district administrator said,

> Top-down is not going to last. Top-down is going to be resented. Bottom-up is not sustainable—when personalities leave, it goes with them. How do we meet in the middle and change the system?

Several districts have developed more open communication about reforms so that schools can see what the district is doing and respond from their own perspectives (Stanford Redesign Network 2009, 8). Others try to develop flexibility in their policies so that individual schools can adopt reforms to their histories, students, and teachers.[6] This seems particularly important for pathways because they often have emerged as a result of *school*-level conditions: teachers interested in a particular subject or theme; students attracted to certain themes; a history of prior development, for example, in certain departments that come to be regarded as particularly strong; local employers who can be counted on for support; and sometimes a connection to a department in a local college. These specific conditions matter a great deal to the emergence and the development of pathways, and uniform district policies that ignore variation among schools can only undermine pathways.

The ideas of distributed leadership are as applicable at the district level as they are at the school level: exemplary districts tend to share decision-making with their schools rather than operate in top-down fashion.

The Inefficiency of District Bureaucracies

In addition, districts may create more work for principals with all their demands for accountability. As one principal complained,

> Most of the policies and directions that have come out create more work. They've completely revised the single site plan, and they keep revising it every day ... It looks like someone's trying to create a job for themselves and more work for the principals.

A related problem mentioned by many principals is the bureaucratic ineffectiveness of districts. The bureaucratic apparatus moves slowly, especially in urban districts,[7] so school requests take a long time to fulfill. One noted, "our district is so dysfunctional on a very bureaucratic level," and told several stories of how long it took the bureaucracy to respond to her questions:

> I would think all of these departments down there should be serving the needs of the site, but it feels like it's the exact opposite ... Point A doesn't talk to Point B, and they're literally down the hall from each other. I'll get one answer from somebody and another answer from somebody else, and then I'll get an e-mail saying the exact opposite. We turned in our budgets, and we had at least four revisions to the budget process, and one of them came the day that it was due ... You sit there thinking, "Am I on TV, some joke show?" Because it's so ridiculous.

Another complained that "the budget department is a hindrance rather than a help ... and they cloud your mind when you're trying to think clearly about how to spend your money." She claimed that she had gotten the most help on complex budgeting issues in informal ways that circumvented the district, "when you locate another principal who is savvy, and you communicate, collaborate, work things out with that person." Yet another noted that her district

> has been verbally supportive and visually supportive, meaning that district personnel come to sites when we have Tuesday workshops for kids, or the superintendent came when there was a Saturday workshop for parents on college-going culture ... but the real nuts and bolts of it doesn't feel like it's supportive. We weren't able to get funding from the district to support someone manning our college and career center; "we think it's great that you guys [at the school]

> are doing more things a–g [for college prep], but we're not going to give you anybody—you're going to have to figure that out on your own.

Even a district official with responsibility for high schools acknowledged that the district didn't have any sense of appropriate policies: "Our district hands the most idiotic things to the principals," and went on to tell a tale about a system of accounting for time that baffled high school teachers and principals: "It's like we come up with things that just—you know, I often feel like I'm operating in the theater of the absurd."

Part of district ineffectiveness, in large bureaucracies that develop constituencies around the status quo, is that every decision is so embattled and requires such endless rounds of discussion and negotiation that any change takes much longer—one of the classic problems in implementation. The vignette mentioned above, where a new director of secondary education made a series of changes and then canceled their implementation, was in part about infighting over different concepts of appropriate reforms. So the endless bickering in urban districts, well described by Charles Payne's (2008) book *So Much Reform, So Little Change,* affects all policies and progress in reform, including those associated with pathways.

Other interviewees complained that district personnel—many of whom come from elementary and middle schools—don't know much about high schools. One asserted that "district people doing the hiring" don't know enough to send the right kinds of teachers. Another complained that

> I have an assistant superintendent of personnel who publicly, in meetings, will say "I don't know anything about high school master schedules, and I don't want to learn," and she's negotiating our contracts and she pushes us up to the last minute in terms of hiring for high school people, so we get absolutely the dregs of the world because we can't offer contracts early enough.

Human resource departments tend to view teachers and principals as interchangeable among levels of the K-12 system, whereas principals are looking for precisely the right teachers who fit into a pathway ("on the bus"), who have some knowledge of and interest in the pathway themes, who can collaborate with others, and who are committed to pathways as mechanisms of high school reform. This particular problem is another way of saying that bureaucratic districts usually adopt a policy of "one size fits all," ignoring the particular differences among schools as they adopt pathways.

Another common complaint was that district officials are often indifferent to what happens at the school level. One principal talked about the result of such indifference as a form of independence:

> I'm glad that we have a good administration here [at the school] and we have good teachers because I feel like we can pretty much operate by ourselves here, and if I don't see my assistant superintendent come by ever, it's not the end of the world. I guess if I need things, I can get them, but there's not a lot being offered ... I look sometimes [at the district] and I'm like, "What do you do at the district? You have probably a $100,000 a year job, and we can't keep class sizes down." I don't even know what they do. I don't ever see our assistant superintendent. I saw her maybe like once at the beginning of the year. She doesn't e-mail me to see how things are going.

He then pulled back from this criticism, allowing that the district had been helpful at the beginning of the year. But still, the inattention of the district to an experiment with a small school, while at the same time the district imposed various rules and regulations, was disturbing.

A special but all-too-common case of district-caused personnel problems involves district- and union-negotiated rules on teacher rights. Districts have complex rules about the seniority rights of teachers let go from one school, sometimes so complicated that they almost defy understanding. Furthermore, teachers with seniority may have these rights until late in the summer, so that pathways may have to wait until the last moment before assembling their teams of teachers—"who's on the bus." In one district where we visited three schools, principals have to give priority to laid-off teachers until July 1, and only after that can they hire anyone who has applied. This provides an incentive to wait until July and August to hire the teachers a pathway wants instead of the "lemons" who have been laid off from other schools with seniority rights (as in the "dance of the lemons")—but by summer the best applicants may already be taken by other schools. The problem was exacerbated in this particular district, according to two principals, by the district HR director, who gave the last choice of potential teachers to high schools. As a principal in a different district noted, "Has [the rule on priority] been a issue? Yes. Have the people who have bid in through right of first refusal been problematic? Yes." But she went on to say, "Have they left already? Mostly yes"—because she had persuaded such teachers that they would be better off in another school that required less diligence and cooperation. So "it requires another level of savvy, perseverance, and planning or plotting—whatever you want to call it—to maintain the staff that you want."

In addition, bureaucracies are used to conventional schools and conventional ways of doing things, and the nonstandard practices in pathways—for example, the unusual subjects of many themes or the practice of having integrated academic courses linked to specific pathways—don't fit with conventional ways of coding courses. The result is that pathway principals have to keep explaining the differences of pathways to district personnel and figuring out ways of modifying standard operating procedures.

Bureaucracies are used to conventional ways of doing things, and the nonstandard practices in pathways often don't fit with conventional ways.

Another problem, partly a function of state and federal aid, is that districts provide fewer services and special programs to high schools than they do to middle and elementary schools. Title I funds go disproportionately to elementary schools; many state programs also focus on younger students, especially the "intervention" efforts intended to help students catch up to grade-level norms. One principal complained about the lack of support:

> It's really kind of amazing to me—there's no systematic support [for high schools]. I mean, we have instructional services in this district, [but] instructional services are focused on elementary math and language. And I think it's done there because you get the quicker gains there. And so you've got a sort of institutional shying away from the teenagers—that's so reflected in society.... Institutionally I almost see us as being intimidated by the high schools—and then we complain when nothing's changing there.

A different allocation of resources would recognize that students require support at all levels of schooling, rather than concentrating resources in elementary schools under some kind of "inoculation" theory.[8]

The Special Challenges of Budgeting and Finance

Yet another large class of problems arise because districts don't provide much help with some of the challenging tasks that principals face. One area is budgeting, noted in chapter 2 as an issue that is more complex in high schools. Part of the problem is the sheer size of the budget; most high schools are multimillion dollar enterprises. Another issue is the lack of preparation about budgeting and resource allocation in pre-service programs, and in most district preparation. As one principal complained,

> It would have been helpful as a principal to have learned how the budget works before I got here ... when you're trying to operate with really no knowledge of it, it becomes a huge task in the middle of everything else that you're trying to do ... They [district officials] do like an hour workshop, so it's very basic.

In addition, when the districts do provide training about budgeting, the training usually focuses on "budget categories, budget numbers, teacher salaries go in 1005.59—we have 32-digit budget numbers, by the way." District training is about nuts and bolts and computer commands, not about how to think about the most effective resources in schools, how much money they require, whether a school should shift from some ineffective resources (especially those such as class size reduction that cost a great deal) to more effective resources that cost little or nothing. This is so far not part of the preparation of school leaders.[9]

Knowledge About Effective Programs

Similarly, districts provide little help to principals trying to figure out what effective practices might be. What currently seems to happen is that high schools cobble together solutions to problems on their own, without any access to the research that has taken place or to the accumulated experience of other schools in similar positions. The grab bag of interventions the high schools we visited have put in place for the ninth-grade transition and for remediation illustrate the random ways, often relying on hearsay, in which many schools make important instructional decisions (see also Grubb 2009b, chap. 8). As one district official said of efforts to focus on academic literacy,

> Every school did that a little differently—I don't know that there's been a very cohesive plan in place.... that whole idea of student engagement, we really connected with that one idea—what does that look like and how do you do that? And literacy is definitely part of that. So we just kind of developed this kind of grassroots initiative.

But there's an enormous academic literature on motivation and engagement in high schools, summarized by the National Research Council (2004) in a little-read book, *Engaging Schools,* that stresses the importance of changing basic approaches to instruction. It isn't necessary for schools to develop their own "grassroots initiative," though of course they will need to modify practices from elsewhere to suit their own conditions.

The challenge of moving research into practice, or of having schools consider research as they are developing reforms, is a difficult one. Research and practice have grown further and further apart, as researchers engage in ever more arcane methods and theory of no interest to practicing educators, and as educators have been stampeded into action by the demands of state and federal policies to produce changes immediately. Reconstructing a bridge between research and practice is therefore a difficult task, and the lack of information about effective practice is a problem at district, state, and federal levels. The federal What Works Clearinghouse is biased toward the use of random-assignment and sophisticated statistical studies and is designed to be read only by researchers; its new set of Practice Guides is still based on a limited set of studies rather than a summary of all available evidence. Furthermore, the products of the What Works Clearinghouse provide only a repository of information, whereas the process of innovation requires several more steps in persuading practitioners about its usefulness, in translating evidence into policies, and in implementing those policies given predictable opposition (Rogers 2003); a repository of knowledge may be necessary, but it is not by itself sufficient to affect practice. Most districts and states provide little to no guidance about what effective practice might be. One principal even mentioned that "we need to get rid of districts"—that they are not large enough to be helpful because their small size prevents them from providing expertise on most issues. In California, the state is even misleading: the State Board of Education has an approved list of curricula, which many districts think are "proven practices" even though the research underlying them is somewhere between thin and nonexistent. But moderate to large districts and certainly states could play a role in informing their schools about "what works," and regional clearinghouses could provide the same service for smaller districts.

Finally, to borrow a practice from the Agricultural Extension Service, states, regions, and large districts could create Educational Extension Services to help schools interpret and apply research, with educational extension agents providing help at the school level in translating research into practice (Gawande 2009; Grubb 2010a; Rogers 2003). In the absence of such an effort, districts seem to assume that principals and school site councils have the time and expertise to learn from research on their own, which is usually not true given the press of competing demands at a school site. And there is no guarantee that "grassroots initiatives," practices borrowed from a neighboring school, will come up with effective practices. These are all cases where districts could promote better-informed decisions at the school level.

Yet another area where districts could provide guidance for their high schools, but rarely do, is the area of instructional improvement. Most districts, if they are engaged in instructional reform at all, target resources at elementary and sometimes middle schools but neglect high schools. One district official complained that "in this district, instructional services are focused on elementary [schools]—I think it's done there because you get quicker gains." There's also an "inoculation" perspective widespread in education: if students learn well in their early years, subsequent learning problems will be avoided. However, the large numbers of ninth graders unprepared to do high school work—the issue addressed by ninth-grade transitions mentioned in chapter 2—clarifies that the issues of getting students on track persist all the way to high school, "the end of the line."

The Development of Human Resources

In addition, among the other problems in the lack of any leadership development, most districts pay little attention to instructional leadership when they select principals or provide school leaders with support. Indeed, it may be more difficult for district officials to improve the instructional dimension of leadership than other aspects. As a district official in a district with many small, themed schools explained,

> Most of my good principals are strong instructionally, and some of them are much weaker operationally, and I don't care about that as much. I just try to help

> them.... If they're instructionally strong and I'm watching them do good work with teachers, in some ways I would rather have somebody like that than somebody who knows the bureaucratic system well ... I feel that if it [instructional expertise] is not there, there's just way too much to do for me to take someone who doesn't have it and create it for them.... My strong principals, the ones who really get instruction, will take ideas from those [principals' meetings], and they'll go with them. The people who are weaker tend to go back to their sites, and it's business as usual.

This description of the instructional and the administrative aspects of principals (Cuban 1988) sketches an idealized pattern where district officials work with principals on improving instruction, and in turn principals work with their teachers. But even though some district officials try to make instructional improvement their top priority, the more common pattern is to focus on "the budget, the new law, and who's getting their technology refreshed"; the "billion trillion meetings" that have to take place; and the incredible amount of administrivia that principals contend with. In the chaos, instructional issues usually get lost at the district level, just as they frequently do at the school level.

Finally, to repeat an issue from the previous chapter, most districts have no special policies to *develop* principals, or to *prepare* principals for the special demands of high schools and pathways. The few intentional policies I have heard about—for example, rotating individuals through a series of positions with ever-expanding responsibilities—have been short-lived and have ended with changes of superintendents. Similarly, most districts so far have done little to prepare teachers specifically for pathways, even though the CSU–San Diego program and the Teachers College of San Joaquin mentioned in chapter 3 provide examples. In the end, most districts rely on conventional job searches to come up with high school principals and pathway teachers, rather than a developmental process that they consciously create.

In effect, such a thorough reform as pathways requires different kinds of teachers, principals, *and* districts. High schools are too different from elementary and middle schools for undifferentiated policies to work well, and pathways are too different from conventional comprehensive high schools for "one size fits all." The districts we need should provide consistent support rather than the instability that comes with changing administrations; they should provide technical assistance tailored to the needs of specific schools; they should develop policies that cover such missing pieces as budgeting, expertise about effective practices, and the development of principals; and they should pay greater attention to the competency of their bureaucracies. Until districts can develop such capacities, schools will need to reform without much district support and with the resources they have, not the resources they might want or wish to have at a later time.

NECESSARY DISTRICT DECISIONS ABOUT MULTIPLE PATHWAYS

Some issues about pathways cannot be resolved at the school or pathway level but instead require district attention. One of these is the status of pathways and inequality among pathways, noted in chapter 3. If they are to survive, pathways cannot become new versions of old vocational education, often known as "dumping grounds" for academically unmotivated students and accused of tracking working-class students, or racial minority and immigrant students, into second-class education. To be sure, individual schools have every incentive to avoid creating low-status (or African American, or ELL, or ambiguous) pathways because this usually means declining enrollments and eventual closure. But districts can play a role as well, monitoring the themes of different pathways to avoid low-status or traditional vocational themes and seeking to strengthen pathways when they show signs of declining status or enrollment.

If they are to survive, pathways cannot become new versions of old vocational education, often known as "dumping grounds" for academically unmotivated students.

Similarly, districts must adjudicate resource issues, both among pathways within a district and between pathways and comprehensive high schools—the "micro/macro problem" from chapter 3. Resources include funding, of course, but also such personnel as well-prepared teachers and principals; space and facilities (especially for pathways requiring labs or performance space or special equipment); professional development for both teachers and leaders; and support for the special conditions of pathways, especially work-based learning and links to postsecondary institutions. If districts do not provide these extra resources, then principals are forced to become professional beggars, searching for resources wherever they can find them, and this detracts from their roles as instructional leaders. Furthermore, if districts do not fund pathways equitably, then some pathways—either those with hero-principals, or with themes that link them to larger sources of external funds (e.g., health fields or fashionable subjects such as biotechnology)—will be better financed than others, leading either to status differences or variation in effectiveness, and this in turn may lead to some pathways collapsing while others thrive.

The problem of supporting pathways versus comprehensive high schools poses a tricky issue. In the bad old days, differences in resources among schools were more or less routine, as the schools attended by middle-class and white students tended to have more resources (including better teachers) than those attended by working-class or racial minority students.[10] One result in many districts has been to adopt policies of equal funding, or equal resources, for all schools and all groups, lest any inequalities be attacked as favoritism, or racism, or tracking. But this in turn has meant that variations in funding related to improving schools (as pathways are intended to do), or providing more to students with higher levels of need, automatically generate resentment and then political opposition—the politics of resentment. As one high school principal noted about pathways,

> There were people who were resentful the first year because they [the pathways] got little perks. So I started talking about our community and the needs of the kids and how academies help personalize and connect kids to school and make it relevant. And that's our job to do that, you know?

To justify differential treatment of pathways, therefore, districts as well as principals need to be ready to defend their higher costs—either on the basis of creating more effective high schools, serving some high-need students better, or simply responding to differences in student preferences about the high school they attend.

For some resources, districts have advantages over schools because of economies of scale. For example, district agreements with local community and four-year colleges about early college high schools, dual enrollment, or alignment of high school and college courses means that high schools need not negotiate these individually. Similarly, a district office of internships could, working with a local Chamber of Commerce, recruit positions for work-based learning and service learning more easily than could individual schools. The provision of information about effective practices, or the creation of an Educational Extension Service, is another activity that can more efficiently be carried out at the district (or regional) level. The collection and analysis of data also requires a more centralized operation. So in their roles supporting school reforms, districts ought to examine various resources and activities necessary for those reforms, and take on the ones that benefit from economies of scale.

To justify differential treatment of pathways, therefore, districts as well as principals need to be ready to defend their higher costs—either on the basis of creating more effective high schools, serving some high-need students better, or simply responding to differences in student preferences.

THE FUTURE OF DISTRICTS

As they developed in the years around 1900, urban districts took on particular roles that, in many ways, now seem outmoded. They were by far the largest sources of tax revenue, from property taxes, and so the amount and use of revenues was largely under district control. Today, with the steady increase of state revenue in funding schools and with an increased federal role in directing school reform (if not in funding schools), that is much less true, and in many cases states provide the majority of funding. Districts after 1900 were also supposed to be models of good government, replacing the patronage mechanisms of the old ward politics with a more rational, honest, and transparent approach to public administration. But all too often, the old city machines persisted or were re-created, and so many cities and urban districts are now viewed as corrupt and incompetent and wasteful—and now sometimes require state oversight (and occasional state takeover) to regulate their behavior. Districts circa 1900 became the vehicles for administrative progressivism—the movement in education that stressed efficiency, managerial competence, uniformity, and bureaucratic regularity. But that movement paid little attention to instructional issues—those were the concerns of teachers and of the small number of pedagogical progressives led by John Dewey. The pedagogical progressives in effect lost out to the administrative progressives (Labaree 2010), and the result ever since has been a district emphasis on efficiency and accountability, and relatively little attention to instruction. But instructional improvement has become much more important in the past several decades, so the old idea of the district viewing teaching as relatively inconsequential and the responsibility of teachers only has now given way to a new emphasis on instructional leadership and reform.

Above all, for administrative progressives the district was a conventional top-down hierarchy: district officials created the policies that schools carried out, districts developed mechanisms of accountability and control, and principals were middle managers responding to their district superiors. But many educators now see this hierarchical approach as dysfunctional, particularly when the district bureaucracy is slow and incompetent. New ideas of distributed leadership (or internal alignment, or organic management) suggest new relationships at the school level, and potentially also at the district level, with flatter hierarchies; more cooperation between "managers" (district officials) and "followers" (principals, other school leaders, and school-site councils); more collaboration in the development of policies, with less uniformity in these policies as reforms are modified to meet the special histories and conditions in individual schools; and operating less through controls and more through capacity-building.

The concept of the district emerging from the Progressive Era no longer seems so progressive. Its replacement—to the extent that we can perceive a new concept of the district—is more concerned with effectiveness than with efficiency, more with instructional improvement than with uniformity, more with capacity-building than with accountability and control, and more with collaboration between district and school than with a hierarchical relationship. These are, to be sure, practices that have emerged in a relatively small set of exemplary districts, while many districts continue to operate in the old ways of administrative progressivism[11]—and they generate the complaints cited above about districts being a "joke show" or the "theater of the absurd," as well as the larger literature about district incompetence. But there are at least glimmers of change, and they suggest a concept of the district that is quite different from the one that has dominated for the past century.

The concept of the district emerging from the Progressive Era no longer seems so progressive. Its replacement is more concerned with effectiveness than with efficiency, more with instructional improvement than with uniformity, more with capacity-building than with accountability and control, and more with collaboration between district and school than with a hierarchical relationship.

If districts continue changing in these ways, this creates more responsibilities for principals—and other school-level leaders, including members of school-site councils—than the old top-down hierarchies did. Schools are more responsible for reforms than they used to be, and multiple pathways in particular require a great deal more school control. Schools with pathways also have to be more concerned with hiring teachers to create an appropriate team—those "on the bus"—rather than just accepting teachers sent by the district. Principals are now charged with being instructional leaders, and this is a particularly difficult responsibility at the high school level. They also may need to control the allocation of resources, particularly in cases (like pathways) where the right kinds of resources—teacher quality, teacher leadership, teacher collaboration and integration, and the provision of such new resources as internships and service learning—are so important. Any shift away from a conventional hierarchy places more responsibilities on schools, and leaders must be appropriately prepared.

In the long run, pathways will survive and prosper only if they come to be seen as superior in some ways—or superior for some students—to the comprehensive high school. But it will take some time to establish pathways; after all, they have been in existence for roughly twenty years, compared with the much longer history of the comprehensive high school originating in the mid–nineteenth century. Until they can become well established, districts will need to protect them from the politics of resentment, from the tendency of reforms to revert to business as usual, and from the barriers that districts themselves create.

QUESTIONS FOR CHAPTER 5

For both school-level and district leaders to answer:

1. How consistent has your district's support for pathways been?

You might distinguish among:

Support of pathways in principle, compared with support of the comprehensive high school model.

Financial support, for planning costs and the extra costs of pathways.

The development of human resources, especially teachers appropriate for pathways.

The development of work-based learning opportunities.

The development of connections to postsecondary options.

2. Where is your district on the continuum of top-down policy, distributed leadership, and reliance on bottom-up or school initiatives? How does your district's approach to decision-making affect high schools in general, or pathways in particular?

3. What administrative challenges do schools face from the district? What are potential solutions for *schools* to undertake? For the *district* to undertake?

Chapter 6

"There's Simply More to Do"

The Possible Futures of High Schools

Throughout this book, I have raised the issue of leadership in high schools, a subject surprisingly absent from principal preparation programs, from the multiple commission reports complaining about the sorry state of high schools, and from the voluminous writing on leadership. This book has identified multiple ways in which the challenges of high school leaders are quite different from those in elementary and middle schools, especially in chapter 2, and chapters 4 and 5 went on to outline how principal preparation programs and district policies could strengthen preparation for high school specifically. At the very least, I hope this volume has persuaded others that the special characteristics of high schools should be considered in all forms of leadership preparation and development.

However, the previous sections do not exhaust the issues raised by the high school leaders we interviewed, nor those issues in the larger debate over public schools and reform. The issues raised in this book suggest—though they cannot possibly prove—that past efforts to reform high schools have failed because they have not addressed leadership. Although this might be plausible as a working hypothesis, it merits more careful analysis than it has been given so far—it requires us to think about the influence of leadership among the many other effects on teachers and students. In the first section, then, I will reexamine the claims that leaders are central to reforms and then develop an agenda for examining (rather than assuming) the crucial role of leaders—and, by analogy, the possible role that leaders may play (or fail to play) in reform.

Similarly, while it always foolish to forecast the future, the brief history of the high school presented in chapter 1 at least alerts us to several themes and problems that have consistently faced these institutions. Reforms that fail to provide adequate resolutions of these dilemmas may survive—after all, the comprehensive high school has survived for roughly 150 years despite generations of complaints—but they will always be embattled. So in the second section of this chapter, I outline several future directions for high schools, including scenarios in which many different kinds of high schools are allowed to bloom, in place of the current state where the comprehensive high school is so dominant.

There are, of course, many different approaches to reforming high schools. I have chosen to emphasize multiple pathways as the most promising reform because they address more of the historical dilemmas facing high schools, and more of the recent criticisms, than any other approach. At the same time, we should be careful about claims for any particular reform: the history of American schools has been so full of short-term fads, of excessive claims that have not panned out, that we have to consider that pathways themselves might be ephemeral. The third section therefore examines again the strengths of pathways in responding to both historical and current dilemmas of high schools, and the potential problems that might send this reform the way of life adjustment education, new math, career education, or any of the other failed proposals that litter the history of American education.

Of course no book can tackle all the issues raised by an educational dilemma—here, the dilemmas facing high schools. We could not raise all potential issues with the principals we interviewed—we would have exhausted them. But some unresolved questions are obvious both from their comments and from the landscape of discussion around public education, and it would be irresponsible not to mention them. The end of the third section therefore mentions several of these—the current fiscal crisis facing all public schools; the disjunction between the captivity of the school and the greater freedoms of adolescents outside high schools; the potentially destructive role of youth culture; and the growing inequality in American society. School leaders only sometimes have opportunities to address these issues, given the crush of other responsibilities, but thoughtful leaders should be ready to address them should the occasion arise. Some leaders may decide to play more active roles for one or another of these issues—for example, by becoming champions for social justice both inside and outside of the school, by figuring out ways to examine youth culture and defuse some of its most destructive consequences, or by developing a curriculum that allows adolescents greater freedom as they show they can be responsible.

THE IMPORTANCE OF HIGH SCHOOL LEADERSHIP: NECESSARY BUT NOT SUFFICIENT

After *A Nation at Risk* was published in 1983, the first reaction was to improve—or, depending on one's perspective, blame—teachers, and teacher-bashing persists in many forms. States passed teacher exams to make sure they had adequate content knowledge, researchers accumulated evidence that strong teachers made a difference, and language about "highly qualified teachers" made its way into No Child Left Behind—even if there is still no consensus about what a "highly qualified" teacher is. Then reformers started to think that the structure of schools was to blame for inadequate learning; a number of reforms, including an array of comprehensive school reform designs, were developed, and some of them showed positive effects.[1] Then observers turned to leadership and noted that strong schools require strong principals—one result of the effective schools literature of the 1970s. This evidence in turn rests on case studies of schools found to be especially effective through statistical analysis or the perceptions of other educators. Though much has been made of the "five factors" associated with school effectiveness—strong administrative leadership, high expectations for student achievement, an orderly atmosphere conducive to learning, an emphasis on basic academic skills, and frequent monitoring of student progress—the results have also been criticized as much as they have been celebrated.[2] Other than case studies, evidence about the effectiveness of principals is difficult to come by: statistical evidence is rare, though the evidence of the Consortium on Chicago School Research on the centrality of principals is an exception (Bryk et al. 2010).

Most of the literature on how principals make a difference to school outcomes—for example, the widely cited summary by Leithwood and his colleagues (2004), *How Leadership Influences Student Learning*—is therefore based largely on judgments about what principals do or fail to do.[3] When we look closely at this literature, about what principals do that makes them crucial to effective schools, many of the characteristics are missing in many high schools. These characteristics include setting directions for the school, rather than simply allowing the comprehensive high school to function as it has historically; developing people, most importantly teachers, through various forms of instructional improvement; and redesigning the organization, which certainly happens in pathways and in some small schools but which is missing in the kinds of piecemeal high school reforms—adopting new curricula, requiring "rigorous" courses of more students, adopting houses without any content—that dominate the landscape.

There is, then, little proof about the effects of principals, though—even in the absence of strong evidence—there are good reasons to think that leadership is important. Schools are not just random aggregations of teachers, individually strong or weak. They are collectives or organizations; many aspects of schools cannot be created individually but instead require some kind of collective action—the consistency of teaching; other policies related to the quality of instruction, especially the selection of teachers and their professional development; choices about the curriculum; equity practices, including tracking, "interventions," and other forms of remediation; the school's climate, including trust, many aspects of how teachers and others treat students, and the personal relationships within a school; the ways decisions are made; and the difference between hierarchical control and distributed leadership.

Schools are not just random aggregations of teachers, individually strong or weak; they are collectives, and many aspects of schools cannot be created individually but instead require some kind of collective action.

Many of these are what I call "abstract resources" (Grubb 2009a; Grubb 2009b), and in a large and rich data set, they prove to have significant effects on student outcomes. However, they cannot be bought—they must be constructed by the community of teachers and leaders. Strong teachers are therefore necessary for an effective school, but they may not be sufficient if they cannot coordinate their own efforts to improve these collective dimensions of a school. (This may be possible in very small schools, and it sometimes happens in individual high school departments,[4] but it's unlikely to happen in schools the size of most high schools.) And any structural reform—including multiple pathways or any of the other designs of the comprehensive school reform designs—also requires leadership to implement the design consistently. Of course, weak leadership may not be able to create these collective resources. This kind of logical argument implies that the only way that schools can create the collective resources necessary to be effective is to rely on strong leadership, cooperative teachers, and an organizational structure that permits the collective construction of these resources—the organizational structure known as distributed leadership, or internal accountability, in place of the hierarchical and authoritarian leadership of the traditional principal.

Both these arguments—those that rely on evidence and on the structural argument about the importance of collective resources—therefore imply that leadership in high schools is likely to be especially important. This is particularly because of the large size of high schools, the difficulty of creating collective resources, and the need to organize larger numbers of teachers into cooperating groups or (to use the current jargon) professional learning communities. Therefore, the ways of strengthening the preparation of principals, the subject of chapter 4, are particularly urgent for high schools.

At the same time, it would be inappropriate to boomerang from one extreme to the other, as people often do—from the extreme of emphasizing better preparation for teachers but neglecting leadership to stressing leadership alone, or from putting faith in comprehensive school reforms to neglecting the structure of schools. (Remember John Dewey's epithet quoted in chapter 2: "Mankind likes to think in terms of extreme opposites. It is given to formulating its beliefs in terms of Either-Ors, between which it recognizes no intermediate possibilities" [1938, 17].) Strong leadership itself is necessary but not sufficient (NBNS), and the challenge in developing effective urban high schools is in figuring out what the sufficient conditions are. One, of course, is teacher preparation, and the current form of preparing high school teachers that emphasizes disciplinary or content knowledge at the expense of pedagogical expertise, or pedagogical content knowledge, itself needs to be rebalanced.

Strong leadership itself is necessary but not sufficient (NBNS), and the challenge in developing effective urban high schools is in figuring out what the sufficient conditions are.

Another important aspect of teachers is their willingness to cooperate, both in developing the collective resources of a school and—in cases such as multiple pathways, with unifying themes—in creating a more coherent and integrated curriculum. For this capacity, teacher preparation programs stressing cooperation—such as the California State University at San Diego program cited in chapter 4—would be improvements over the current programs that leave out any collective or institutional responsibilities. Indeed, a great deal of teacher preparation at all levels of education stresses teacher proficiency in the classroom, reinforcing the image of individual teachers isolated in their egg-crate classrooms and individually responsible for student performance. But again, schools are collectives, and teachers need to be able to carry out institutional responsibilities if their schools are to be effective (Grubb and Tredway 2010). Teacher cooperation, the opposite of the teacher isolation that dominates most high schools, is therefore part of teacher responsibility and preparation, even though strong leaders can foster cooperation by such mechanisms as creating professional learning communities.

For those who blame teacher unions for intransigence and rigidity, it's necessary to point out that unions come in several forms. Some follow the model of "industrial unionism" arising first in nineteenth-century manufacturing, which stresses wages and working conditions, protection of workers, and often an adversarial position toward administrators—the school version of the classic battle between bosses and workers. But teaching is not like working in a factory, and teachers aren't cogs in a machine. Instead, they develop sophisticated skills and specialized expertise; unlike industrial workers, teachers share common interests and professional status with administrators, even more so in schools with distributed leadership. Beginning in the early 1990s, a movement toward "professional unionism" developed, with a greater focus on professional prerogatives, the protection and enhancement of *teaching* (not just *teachers*), greater teacher and administrator collaboration, and the shared ownership of reform efforts between teachers and administrators (Grubb and Tredway 2010, chap. 4; Peterson and Charney 1999). Any movement from industrial unionism to professional unionism is beneficial to collaboration at the school level, and district leaders can sometimes work with their unions to provide them more professional prerogatives in exchange for greater cooperation in school reform (Marshall 2008).

Capable leaders also need the support of their districts, the subject of chapter 5. But the concept of the district that emerged from the Progressive Era did not stress support as much as direction: districts developed policies, and principals were middle managers who carried out policy, in turn commanding teachers to adhere to district policies. This kind of top-down approach persists in many districts, though studies of supposedly exemplary districts have stressed greater cooperation between district and schools and more support for what schools decide for themselves (Grubb 2009b, chap. 10). As schools try to reform themselves in non-traditional ways (and multiple pathways represent substantial challenges to the comprehensive high school) they require more support from districts of the kinds I reviewed in chapter 5—both support for the specific reform and more general support for the daily activities necessarily to make schools run smoothly.

In addition, we could look beyond districts to state and federal governments. Many supports that *districts* could offer to high schools—information about "what works," leadership development, the additional costs of pathways, the development of work-based learning, and connections to postsecondary institutions—could also come from states. Indeed, in the recent round of state reforms accompanying accountability, a number states have started to work in novel ways with their districts, with less top-down direction via funding and requirements and more consultation with districts about the resources they need (Grubb 2009b, chap. 10). The federal government could also provide more help, particularly because so little federal funding has gone to high schools. On the contrary, No Child Left Behind has been an impediment to reform because it measures outcomes narrowly in terms of basic reading and math skills, without any possibilities for novel forms of assessment consistent with either theme-based pathways or the conceptual competencies required for college readiness. The What Works Clearinghouse has been virtually useless to educators in schools and districts (as discussed in chapter 5), and this too could be reformed. Employers continue to call for schools to prepare students with the skills of the twenty-first century to enhance our international competitiveness, but they have been much more reluctant either to provide work-based learning opportunities or to pay their fair share of taxes. So in addition to more targeted forms of preparation for principals, as I outlined in chapter 4, *consistency* of support from many different governmental and nongovernmental sources, for both high school reform in general and for pathways in particular, is currently lacking. Without such consistency, high schools will continue to be pulled in different directions, and even strong leaders will not be able to respond to all the conflicting demands.

THE (MULTIPLE?) FUTURES OF HIGH SCHOOLS

Currently, most high schools fit the model of the comprehensive high school, drawing upon the curriculum of 1894—what we would now see as a conventional college prep curriculum—and relying on academic standards from the nineteenth century. Course-taking patterns have been relatively stable despite curriculum battles swirling above the schools. In this sense, critics often complain that the high school is a nineteenth-century institution, "obsolete—they cannot teach our kids what they need to know today," for students facing twenty-first-century challenges. Updating the high school would therefore mean developing an alternative concept of the curriculum and then related standards—precisely what multiple pathways do, but which many other high school reforms fail to do.

But despite this dimension of conservatism, it's quite wrong to say that the high school has not changed. Since 1894, the high school has become a mass institution rather than an elite institution, and this has brought all the diversities of American society to high schools—diversities of class, of race and ethnicity, of immigrant status and language backgrounds, of urban/rural location, of value-laden preferences of what high schools should be, and of political perspectives on equity and social justice. With diversity has come curriculum differentiation, so in practice the relatively homogeneous curriculum of the Committee of Ten has been replaced with a multitude of tracks, some obvious (such as the general track), some hidden (such as the current remedial track), and some of them located in the differences among high schools (including "alternative" high schools, such as continuation schools, or between high-quality suburban and low-quality urban high schools). Over the twentieth century, the high school became increasingly crucial to students' life chances, and students began attending for purely vocational reasons—or to go to college to improve their employment opportunities. The current effort to eliminate drop-outs is at least partly an effort to make sure that all adolescents leave with the capacities necessary for modern employment. Unfortunately, with educational inflation and the move toward college for all, this means that high school is often just a means to get to college and therefore a place where nothing of any intrinsic importance happens.

Although high school has become crucial to the future lives of students, on the other hand there has been increasing competition for their time and attention. Some of these distractions come from extracurricular activities, which have become more important than the official curriculum in many schools, or from the attractions of youth culture since the 1950s, a culture that seems to be virulently anti-school and anti-intellectual. Most recently, competition for attention comes from the explosion of electronic gadgets—with cell phones, texting, roaming the Web, Facebook, MySpace, movies and television on handheld devices—distractions that now occupy an average of seven hours and thirty-eight minutes a day for those aged eight to eighteen, almost what adults employed full-time spend at work (Rideout, Foehr, and Roberts 2010). Quite apart from the question of what these gadgets are doing to the ways young people think,[5] if nothing else they represent a new drain of time, one that is increasing enormously. High schools now have to compete for adolescent attention in new ways,[6] and the theme of boredom in recent commission reports (discussed in chapter 1) indicates that schools are not winning the competition.

So high schools can and have changed, and the question is whether they can deliberately change to resolve some of the historical dilemmas and recent critiques reviewed in chapter 1. A possible response, of course, is that the dominant model of the comprehensive high school will prove too strong to do anything more than tinker with its curriculum and structure. The efforts to impose more rigorous standards, relying in part on new assessments to police the standards, represent a reaffirmation of the historical high school. Similarly, early college high schools simply reinforce the ethic of college for all, trying to make sure that every component of the high school supports college-going and eliminating those elements—the general track, the "treaties" with students that water down the curriculum, the basic-level instruction that cannot prepare students for the conceptual demands of four-year colleges—that impede college-going and success. Charter schools have been increasing, but many of them simply replicate conventional concepts of school without the innovations that charter school advocates celebrate. And, as in all reforms, there are all too many tales of schools that have begun reform but—with a change in principal, or new superintendent with different priorities, a shift in funding, or declining enrollments—have reverted to older, more familiar models. So some reforms are reinforcements of the traditional high school rather than changes, and some changes don't last. The question is therefore whether high schools can be sufficiently reformed to answer the many criticisms in existing commission reports or whether—as has been true in so many other areas of education—we end up "reforming again, again, and again" because of our inability to challenge the well-established comprehensive high school.

The question is whether high schools can be sufficiently reformed to answer the many criticisms in existing commission reports or whether we end up "reforming again, again, and again" because of our inability to challenge the well-established comprehensive high school.

My own view is that the comprehensive high school is unlikely to fade away. Much of it doesn't work very well, even for the successful kids in the highest tracks who can use it as a springboard to the best colleges. But the dreary academic curriculum is leavened by enough other activities to be manageable; the transition to college has been institutionalized (at least for middle-class students) through such mechanisms as the standard array of college courses and SAT and ACT tests; and any institution with that much history behind it creates its own justification, as students and parents alike think of "high school" in conventional terms ("I thought that this campus didn't want small learning communities at all—it really likes its size, the kids like being part of this big school"). But it certainly could be augmented with other ideas of what high school could be—more focused on an imaginative curriculum more connected to student interests and to their futures, with different concepts of equity—horizontal equity in place of vertical equity—that have a greater chance of generating equitable outcomes than the current tracked high school does.

Therefore, a second possibility is that, particularly with the popularity of choice and charter schools, high schools will revert to the mid–nineteenth-century pattern, with a variety of high schools similar to the variety of academies that existed then (Beadie and Tolley 2002). This might mean different high schools for boys and girls or for students of different races (such as Afro-centric schools). It might also mean high schools with different curricula for different groups of students—so-called feminist pedagogies for girls, perhaps a more sports-centered and competitive environment for boys, the distinctive First Nations pedagogy in schools for Native Americans (Stiffarm 1998), high schools aiming solely for elite colleges (e.g., private schools), high schools aiming for a balance of college and career preparation (e.g., multiple pathways), high schools preparing environmentalists and peace activists, high schools with low academic standards but rich extracurricular activities (e.g., ski academies or arts-oriented schools), and on and on. This might be the vision of the small school movement, with many varied small schools; examples of all these school now exist.

But there are several factors limiting such a vast variety of schools. One is expense, reflecting the diseconomies of small scale and of specialization; another is limited audiences, making many of these choices unworkable except in large districts. Another is that many of them do not fit well into the conventional mechanisms of access to college, with their reliance on conventional grade point averages, SAT scores, and standardized courses as college requirements. Just as pathways have to wrestle with alternative ways of establishing standards (as discussed in chapter 3), so would the even greater variety of special-purpose high schools. Finally, any vision of one thousand flowers (or high school models) rejects the "one best system" that emerged from administrative progressives after 1900 (Tyack 1974), for better and for worse. The one best system envisions a schooling *system* with institutions linked to one another in a regular progression, from middle schools to high schools to colleges, with each level composed of similar institutions. But as these institutions diverge, then it becomes more difficult to consider this a *system*, and the transitions among levels—from middle school to a greater variety of high schools, from high school to the infinitely greater number of postsecondary alternatives—become more difficult, implying the need for transition strategies like those explored in chapter 2. This problem becomes more difficult as the number of choices expands; for example, the transition to college has been the latest "crisis" to hit the education system in part because the variety of postsecondary options is so enormous.

A compromise between these two visions—of relative homogeneity versus relative heterogeneity of high schools—might be one where a large number of comprehensive high schools coexist with a large number of schools with theme-based pathways, along with some other approaches, such as early college high schools for those who have accepted the goal of college for all. An advantage of limited variation is that the support for alternative models—teacher preparation programs for pathway teachers; modules in principal preparation for high schools in general, for pathways, and for early college high schools; district administrative procedures appropriate for a larger range of courses and activities (such as internships and college visits)—would be easier to develop compared with more extreme forms of choice and variation. And there are always hybrid approaches—as we saw at the beginning of chapter 3—where high schools contain both conventional curricula and several theme-based schools-within-schools, allowing students the choice of either.

A compromise between these visions of relative homogeneity versus total heterogeneity of high schools might be one where comprehensive high schools coexist with schools with theme-based pathways, along with some other approaches, such as early college high schools.

Of course, with the decentralization of the American educational system and the focus on schools as the unit for reform, we as a society are unlikely to make self-conscious choices about the future of the high school. The direction high schools take, whether traditional or reformed, will depend on many decisions in local communities and districts, only sometimes with state direction (such as the funding of career academies in California) or federal encouragement (such as the comprehensive school reform models). So a system of varied high schools will thrive only if it meets a kind of market test: only if the alternatives attract enough students, only if their outcomes are superior in some ways to those of conventional high schools, and only if what they give up (e.g., extensive extracurricular activities) are balanced by other advantages, such as the opportunities for students to work in more engaging environments.

THE FUTURE OF MULTIPLE PATHWAYS

In this book, I have focused on multiple pathways because they seem more promising than other high school reforms. They come up with novel responses to the historical dilemmas presented in chapter 1, particularly new responses to the question of purpose embedded in the slogan "college *and* careers." Their response to the dilemmas of differentiation and to accommodating student interests allows both to take place by developing horizontal rather than vertical differentiation. Their instruction, oriented around themes that students have presumably chosen, reflects many of the recent calls for enhancing motivation and engagement, thereby promising greater equity of outcomes, such as learning and progression through high school. They potentially allow new ways of defining and measuring standards; provide a clear role for outside activities, such as work-based and service learning; and lead to obvious connections with postsecondary programs with similar themes (or majors, at the postsecondary level). As long as the leaders of pathways remember the importance of instructional improvement, multiple pathways and linked learning provide opportunities for enriching instruction that do not arise in conventional high schools.

Pathways also offer cogent responses to the more recent criticisms summarized in chapter 1. They certainly address the criticism of relevance by tying the curriculum to a theme of some importance, one that students can choose. Again, with the reminder that pathways leaders must focus on the quality of instruction, they provide ways of enhancing motivation and engagement and replace the dreary lectures dominated by teacher talk with more active forms of learning. They certainly address questions of equity—except when themes associated with particular groups (such as auto repair, construction, or personal services) are developed. Their smaller sizes can alleviate the problems of impersonal relationships in the high school, and they moderate the captivity of the high school when they provide students choices about projects; internships outside of the school; and other connections with employers, service organizations, colleges and universities, and other outside groups. Pathways have a great deal to recommend them, especially compared to those reforms that simply reinforce the traditional high school.

On the other hand, pathways might prove to be nothing more than the fad of the moment. The American landscape is littered with promising reforms that passed away: the experiments of the 1930s; the Life Adjustment reforms (though they nevertheless live on in life skills and "soft" skills); the enthusiasm for internships in both the 1970s and the 1990s; career education of the 1970s; and many smaller fads in specific subjects, such as the new math of the 1960s. Multiple pathways might be another one of these fads, particularly because the rational analysis I present—that pathways are superior to other reforms because they respond to historical and current critiques—cannot overcome political opposition; allegiance to a historical alternative, such as the traditional high school; or resistance from the budgeters who resent the additional money costs and the other resources—cooperating teachers, workshops and labs, internships, links to postsecondary programs—that successful pathways require.

Pathways will thrive and provide lasting alternatives to the comprehensive high school only if they adopt relatively strong versions. Their themes need to be attractive to students and broad enough to attract both students bound for college and those who may not initially aspire to college; if pathways devolve into new names for traditional vocational education, they will end up as another dumping ground. The instruction needs to be an improvement on conventional high school teaching, using the potential of their themes, coordinated instruction, and problem- and project-based teaching to make pathways more motivating than conventional high schools. They need to take advantage of their natural connections to potential internships, as well as to related postsecondary programs.

Pathways might prove to be nothing more than the fad of the moment; they will provide lasting alternatives to the comprehensive high school only if they adopt relatively strong versions.

Finally, pathways will need support from other elements of our schooling system. One factor that has made the traditional comprehensive high school so powerful is that many other practices have developed to reinforce it: teacher credentialing programs; college course requirements, stated in terms of the conventional curriculum outlined in 1894; state standards for conventional academic subjects, and now even for some vocational subjects; district bureaucratic mechanisms accounting for courses, teaching loads, Carnegie units, and graduation requirements; and extracurricular activities that provide another source of student commitment. But these standard practices make it difficult for clear alternatives such as pathways to emerge. And so such substantial reforms also require modifications in many of these surrounding practices. Among the most important mentioned in this volume are new forms of preparing teachers so that they are better able to collaborate and integrate their curricula with others—such as the program at CSU–San Diego with a linked learning "lens." New forms of district support, such as those outlined in chapter 5, are also necessary. And of course, new ways of developing principals for high schools and pathways, the subject of chapter 4, would transform such preparation from learning on the job to a Deweyan synthesis of learning *and* doing, of preparing high school principals for the special challenges they face *and* providing them induction programs and other support as they move into administrative positions.

We could move beyond these forms of support to look more carefully at state and federal policies. For example, the accountability systems that states have developed, and that federal policy has reinforced in No Child Left Behind, have created narrow tests of basic skills, unsuitable to measure the competencies necessary wither for college readiness or for theme-based pathways. Several principals we interviewed noted that a narrow system of state accountability has made it more difficult to introduce new and nonstandard subjects into the high school. The concept of "qualified teachers" in No Child Left Behind do not cover the special requirements of teachers in pathways nor the nonstandard backgrounds that many pathways require when their themes—such as environmental subjects, biotechnology, or health occupations—fall outside current credentialing systems. And conventional funding streams from state and federal governments do not cover some of the extra costs of pathways examined in chapter 3. Over time, the well-being of pathways will require these and other policies to change as well, accommodating a broader concept of the high school than now exists.

Of course, these do not exhaust the problems facing high schools. Currently, most public schools are facing financial problems that make reform all the more difficult, and it is unclear when the current recession will end. Even when it does, funding is not the solution educators often think it is because money and outcomes are so weakly linked; better understanding of the roles of money, resources, and outcomes is necessary before the shortage of resources in public schools can be overcome (Grubb 2009a; Grubb 2009b). The role of youth culture, which seems to be increasingly anti-school (especially for African American and Latino students), has not been seriously addressed by many educators, and the disjunction between captivity in school and freedom in youth culture—at least freedom in some forms, freedom from overt adult rules—seems to be growing wider and wider. Perhaps most important, the growing inequality in American society means that the social and economic conditions of school are themselves becoming more unequal, and the various achievement gaps almost surely cannot be minimized without noneducational policies creating greater equality in other dimensions of society.[7]

But these issues were not mentioned by the principals and district officials we interviewed, even though they are well aware of these larger problems when they speak of achievement gaps and unequal performance. They are busy enough with running schools as well as they can, with confronting the special challenges of high schools and of reforms as best they can. School-level leaders have enough to do as it is, "sunup to sundown and beyond," and it must fall to others—academics and advocates, policy-makers and citizen groups—to remedy the larger social and economic conditions within which our schools exist.

OUR HOPES FOR PUBLIC SCHOOLING

The high school began life in the nineteenth century as a monolithic institution, providing essentially one course of study—what we now think of as the college-prep curriculum. Over the twentieth century, it developed much greater variety, including many more courses—electives, the offerings of vocational and general tracks, advanced as well as remedial coursework. It also developed an enormous variety of social activities, including sports, the culture of Friday night football and school spirit, extracurricular activities and clubs of many kinds, proms and dances and other supervised forms of mating, and above all a place to meet friends and try on different identities. By the mid-1980s, the high school could fairly be described as a shopping mall where individuals could find anything they wanted.[8] Some of these options were (and are) closely related to the high school's original academic and civic missions; some of them are connected to the challenges of adolescence and growing up; some of them are debased versions of academic coursework, such as the general track and remedial courses; and some of them are just plain silly. In the process of developing, the high school lost any real coherence, just as a shopping mall has no coherence except for its ethic of consumerism and choice.

Toward the end of the twentieth century, the high school began to be a somewhat less heterogeneous institution. The ethic of college for all and the pressure from standardized tests and exit exams to master basic academic skills began to eliminate some alternatives to the college-prep curriculum. In many schools, traditional vocational education disappeared, and in other places, there have been concerted efforts to eliminate the general track. Many high schools have come to resemble the institution of the late nineteenth century—though with a substantial extracurriculum and social agenda tacked on. This restores some coherence to the high school, to be sure, but it's a coherence that promotes college as the only goal, that provides little choice to adolescents except for the alternatives of the extracurriculum, and that remains stubbornly present-oriented even though it is a place where young people are making crucial (if sometimes unconscious) choices about their futures.

In this dismal situation, with critics continuing to critique high schools, multiple pathways present an option for a new kind of heterogeneity. They provide student choice, to be sure, but they also constrain that choice as long as pathways adopt serious themes. They leave postsecondary education as an option while acknowledging that employment after high school—or the common mixture of employment and further schooling—are also options. Depending on the configurations of pathways, they can provide students with continued participation in the social life of high schools—or allow them to avoid this aspect. Their themes encourage contact with the outside world of employment, public service, and political events, as well as bridges to postsecondary options, rather than high schools remaining self-contained "total institutions." We should not expect the comprehensive high school to die out, but—*if* pathways continue to develop and prosper—we might expect it to be joined by new theme-based schools, by pathways within larger high schools, and by other configurations of pathways that present a challenge and alternative to the comprehensive high school.

Americans hold great hopes for their schools, and have for a very long time. This extends to high schools as well, the "people's college," our "citadels of learning," "whose programs correspond to the educational needs of *all* youth." Even if we have contradictory (or at least widely varying) views of high school, it has over time become more important, not less, as average levels of schooling have increased and as the high school has become a mass institution. It is currently the crucial juncture between the K-12 system, with its origin in the egalitarian hopes of the common schools, and the postsecondary system, arising out of the need for leadership in all our institutions and therefore elitist in every dimension. As the intersection between K-12 and postsecondary education, the high school is the place where students are making decisions that are crucial to their futures, the "end of the line." It cannot play this crucial role successfully without the capacities that all school should have—strong teachers, strong leaders, and structures and purposes more varied than the comprehensive high school.

Appendix

Sources of Information

The empirical basis for this book is a series of interviews with high school principals, assistant principals, and district personnel in charge of high schools. We drew on three samples of people to interview:

1. Graduates of the Principal Leadership Institute (PLI) at the University of California at Berkeley. This sample was convenient to interview, of course, but in addition the emphases of this leadership preparation program—on instructional leadership, distributed leadership, and social justice in urban schools—are well known to the interviewers, who themselves were coaches in the PLI. In addition, the PLI graduates proved to be remarkably articulate about the issues in high schools. Of the twenty-two PLI graduates we interviewed, eleven had experience at other levels of education as well, making it possible for them to contrast high school leadership with administrative roles at other levels. In addition, eleven had experience with pathways in some form.
2. Principals known to be working in high schools with multiple pathways, many of them identified by ConnectEd California. I interviewed eighteen of these principals, ten of whom had experience at other levels of the education system. In addition, we interviewed five district-level officials in charge of secondary education or of pathways more specifi-

cally to understand the district-level understanding of leadership. In these five districts, then, we were able to interview both district- and school-level officials.

3. Marisa Saunders and a research team at the University of California at Los Angeles have been conducting case studies of ten schools with pathways. I provided additional questions about leadership challenges to this group, and in return I obtained permission to review the transcripts of eight leaders from this sample of schools. In the end, however, these interviews provided little information, and they have not been used for the results in chapters 2 and 3.

Altogether, then, we interviewed forty-three principals and assistant principals, thirty-three of whom were in schools with pathways, and five district officials with responsibilities for pathways. Altogether they came from thirty districts. All of them were in California, both northern and southern, partly for logistical reasons, and partly because of our focus on pathways in California. This is, to be sure, a small sample of the high school principals and assistant principals across the country, or of districts; this first effort to understand the leadership challenges in high schools could not possibly interview a random sample or a universe of principals. But this research did get to the point known by qualitative researchers as saturation,[1] when we stopped hearing new perspectives.

We asked these individuals questions about their past experience in schools to determine their basis for comparing high school experiences; about their perceptions of the challenges to high school principals; about the structure of the pathways they oversaw and the special challenges they presented; about instructional initiatives and efforts to create work-based learning opportunities and connections to postsecondary options; about changes in guidance and counseling to allow students to make rational choices among pathways; and about equity issues they confronted, particularly the "ninth-grade challenge" when some students enter high school unready to do high school–level work. We also asked school-level respondents about district support and barriers and asked district officials about the difficulties they experienced with principals. These questions were guided by my long history of research and writing about pathways, particularly in their earlier forms of integrating academic and vocational education (e.g., Grubb 1995a; Grubb et al. 1991) as well as more recent writing on pathways (Grubb 2008a; Oakes and Saunders 2008).

In the end, we had forty-eight interviews, plus innumerable follow-up opportunities with organizations mentioned (such as the Principals' Partnerships), various programs to prepare principals, or districts not in our sample. I coded these in the old-fashioned way, reading through them and noting the themes and conclusions that our respondents mentioned; I did not use computer-based coding techniques because they are likely to miss more subtle points, cannot readily detect when potential issues are missing from the record (especially, in this work, those of reforms addressing class and race directly), and often contribute to uninsightful readings of the results.[2] In the results reported, I note when certain points are made by virtually all interviewees or a substantial majority, an important minority, or a relatively few of these individuals as a rough way of gauging the frequency of different responses. But—particularly for points that are little-known or underappreciated—the importance of a conclusion is not necessarily related closely to the frequency of mentions. For example, only four of our forty-eight interviewees mentioned that restructuring a high school through pathways might not by itself improve the quality of instruction; this signals the potential independence of restructuring efforts and instructional improvement, a division reaffirmed elsewhere and one that has prevented many reforms from improving learning and test scores. Only one individual mentioned reforms tied directly to race and ethnicity and only after explicit questions from me. To some extent, then, I have used these results to draw parallels with problems elsewhere in school reform.

With perhaps one or two exceptions, these individuals were enthusiastic about being interviewed. The premise of the research—that high schools are different from other schools in their leadership demands—was something that they had directly experienced and had articulated to others but that no one from districts, from the school reform community, or from the research community had ever asked them about. They were full of suggestions about how principal preparation could be improved, both through patterns of experience and through pre-service and in-service programs (the subject of chapter 4).

Furthermore, those in schools with pathways were uniformly supportive of pathways and were eager to tell the stories of their advantages: "This is a whole paradigm shift," said one; another commented that "we're at the revolutionary edge of high school reform." Many acknowledged how hard the job is and how much time it took: "from sunup to sundown and beyond," in the words of one executive principal supervising four small schools, and "an impossible job," in the words of another. But they were still dedicated to pathways as one of the few reforms to reshape the dysfunctional high school: "It's a mission, not just a job." Reform efforts need to figure out how to make the job less "impossible," something I cover in chapter 4 about preparing high school principals and in chapter 5 on district support. But there is no mistaking the fundamental support of those in the trenches of the pathway movement for this approach to reform.

Notes

INTRODUCTION

1. Academies are one particular form of pathways, usually incorporating four teachers and a cohort of students for three years. See the description of different types of pathways in chapter 1.

2. See Bryk (2010); Bryk et al. (2010); Leithwood et al. (2004); Lemons, Luschel, and Siskin (2003); and Rice (2010), summarizing a variety of studies. The claim that principals are second only to teachers comes from Leithwood et al., but this is the authors' judgment after reviewing a variety of influences in schools, not the result of any statistical analysis or other decomposition of the variation in student outcomes. The argument that change-oriented leadership is the most important of five essential supports for schools comes from Bryk et al., with better statistical support than other analyses of the effects of leadership.

3. A partial exception is McLaughlin and Talbert (2007), which identifies several high school issues: the structural impediments of subject-matter departments and of too many students each day, the inability of high school leaders to provide much instructional leadership, the professional culture of high school teachers and their lack of responsibility for students, and a pervasive culture of student disrespect for teachers.

4. "Distributed leadership" is the practice of distributing leadership responsibilities broadly among teachers and administrators, often working through committees and school councils, in place of a conventional hierarchy with the principal making all decisions; see Spillane (2006) and Spillane and Diamond (2007). See also the closely related ideas of internal accountability in Carnoy, Elmore, and Siskin (2003); the chapter on the different role of principals in Lemons, Luschel, and Siskin (2003); the concept of "organic management" in Rowan (1990) and Miller and Rowan (2006); and the idea of a "professional learning community." The latter term is in widespread circulation and stresses collaborative decision-making among communities of teachers, focused on student learning and experimenting when current practices don't work (DuFour, Eaker, and Karhanek 2004; McLaughlin and Talbert 2007). Within the business community, the same basic approach—with greater reliance on the decisions of

frontline workers—has been called "high involvement management," to distinguish it from conventional firms with low worker involvement in decisions (Lawler 1998).

5. See Rhodes et al. (2005), who found the quality of leadership an important factor. Indeed, the correlation between a measure of leadership and an index of implementing the reform was .70, though not among the highest correlations (Table A-1). They define the quality of leadership as stability, instructional leadership, maintaining a vision, supporting teachers and soliciting their participation in decision-making (the practice known as "distributed leadership"; see note 4, above), and connecting with students and parents. All of these are relatively generic dimensions of school leadership, though they have special dimensions in small schools and in high schools.

6. See the promising-sounding book by Harris (2006) on award-winning practices of secondary school principals. But all of these practices, such as improving communications, the importance of reading, and collaborating with the superintendent, are generic. On the principalship, see books too numerous to cite in the Library of Congress classifications of LB2831, LB1738, and LB1715. One evaluation of theme-based pathways in Boston did mention that the principals of new small schools with themes were "quite naïve about the challenges they would face in developing the new schools/SLCs [small learning communities]" (Neufeld, Levy, and Chrismer 2005, 42), but said nothing else about the specifics of leadership in pathways.

7. See www.principalspartnership.com. In addition to summer institutes, references to resource materials, and articles about exemplary high schools, this group has published research briefs on topics specific to high schools—after-school programs for ninth graders, career education and tech prep, credit recovery, exit exams, preparing for college, advanced placement courses, dual enrollment, and many more: a veritable "What Works" for high school leaders. How widely these are used is unclear; only one of the forty-eight high school and district leaders we interviewed mentioned this organization, and it is not widely cited in the reform literature. It appears to be the only source of information specific to high schools.

8. An exception is the New York City Aspiring Leaders Program, based on project-based learning, that uses some problems specifically written for high schools. See Stein and Gewirtzman (2003).

9. For the consensus that reforms in high schools have been less successful than in elementary and middle schools, see Hess (2004) and McLaughlin and Talbert (2001). On evidence that reforms in six districts were able to improve test scores in elementary schools but not in secondary schools, see Cuban and Usdan (2003b), Table 7.4. On the resistance to change of high school instruction, see Cuban (1993).

10. Information about high schools has been collected from several sources by the National High School Center in its Quick Stats Fact Sheet, "High Schools in the United States."

11. In the 1990s, a great deal of the work of the National Center for Research in Vocational Education at UC–Berkeley was devoted to understanding ways of integrating academic and vocational education, a precursor to multiple pathways. See Grubb (1978), Grubb (1995a), and Grubb et al. (1991), as well as Lazerson and Grubb (1974), for historical perspectives. For more recent writing, see Grubb and Flessa (2006), as well as National Research Council (2004), chap. 7, "Education Through Theme-Based Learning Communities," of which I wrote the first drafts.

12. See especially Allen, Almeida, and Steinberg (undated); Bloom, Thompson, and Unterman (2010); Kahne et al. (2006); Neufield, Levy, and Chrismer (2005); and Shear et al. (2008).

CHAPTER 1

1. For this history, I have drawn on Angus and Mirel (1999); Cohen (1985); Grubb and Lazerson (2004, chap. 2); Hampel (1986); Krug (1969 and 1972); and Lazerson and Grubb (1974).

2. These statistics come from Goldin and Katz (2008), Table 1.1. Although these particular numbers seem a little high, these authors have worked the hardest to create consistent statistics for the twentieth century.

3. Krug (1969) is one of the best sources on both the Committee of Ten and the *Cardinal Principles.* The National Education Association released a fascinating stream of reports in the first half of the twentieth century, clarifying the extent of discussion about the nature of public education.

4. Cited in Hampel (1986), 40. *Education for ALL American Youth* was one of the most interesting statements about the high school of the twentieth century, complete with iconic woodcuts by Lynd Ward for the endpapers.

5. The Prosser Resolution, quoted in *Life Adjustment Education for Every Youth.* Office of Education Bulletin 1951, No. 22 (Washington, DC: Federal Security Agency, 1951), 15, note 2.

6. See especially Angus and Mirel (1999) on the stability of course-taking patterns.

7. See Lynd and Lynd's (1929) influential *Middletown,* an ethnography of a Midwestern high school, especially chap. 15 on "School 'Life.'"

8. Hampel (1986) provides the history of this development, with the high school as "the last little citadel" providing a refuge against the influences that might cheapen education; see especially the quote from George Stoddard, commissioner of education for New York, on page 40.

9. See especially Krug (1969), chaps. 6 and 12.

10. See the analysis in *Crisis or Possibility* of a discourse of crisis in many commission reports, contrasted with a discourse of possibility that leads to more student-centered and community-centered approaches.

11. See especially Boyer (1983); Cusick (1983); Powell, Farrar, and Cohen (1985); and Sizer (1984).

12. See Olson (2005) for a review of the reports as of 2004; more have come out since then. In the references, various commission reports used for this section are marked by asterisks.

13. The quotes are from Harvey and Housman (2004) and Tucker (2004).

14. See also Hill, Foster, and Gendler (1990), who identify among the "high schools with character" a group that they label "focus schools"—Catholic schools and those with a theme or focus, such as pathways, in place of the diffuse missions of conventional zoned high schools.

15. Speech at the National Governor's Association, National Education Summit on High Schools, February 26, 2005. Available at blogoehlert.typepad.com/eclippings/2005/05/bill_gates_amer.html.

16. And even later: any current educator who sees Fredrick Wiseman's 1968 *High School* is likely to be struck by the harsh and arbitrary treatment of students.

17. On the issues of fairness around discipline, see Grubb and Tredway (2010), chap. 6.

18. See Eccles et al. (1993) and Eccles and Roeser (2009), discussing the person/environment fit within the school. They stress the transition to middle school, but their analysis applies equally to the transition to high school.

19. On reports of the Gates Foundation work with small schools, see Bloom, Thompson, and Unterman (2010); Lichtenstein (2006); Mitchell et al. (2005); Quint et al. (2010); and Shear et al. (2008). Despite spending more than $1.5 billion on small high schools, the Gates Foundation seems not to have issued any report summarizing what it learned from this expensive experiment. Its decision to abandon small schools may have been premature: learning and test scores can be enhanced only by improving the quality of instruction, while a structural change, such as smaller schools, might be expected to increase students' progress through high school and completion but not necessarily their test scores. See the discussion of common versus differentiated resources in Grubb (2009b), 70–72. Indeed, the evaluation by Shear et al. (2008) showed evidence of more supportive climates, better student engagement and attendance, and somewhat more challenging curricula in the small schools compared with comprehensive high schools, but not improvements in test scores. Unfortunately, differences in completion rates were not calculated in that work, though they were in Bloom et al.

20. In early work that then merged into pathways, a number of individuals at the National Center for Research in Vocational Education in the 1990s referred to the multiple ways of integrating academic and occupational education (e.g., Grubb et al. 1991). I called this practice "education through occupations" (Grubb 1995a), a reference to a passage by John Dewey that never caught on. David Stern (1999) preferred to use "college and careers"; career academies refer to specific programs in California and other states, with that name adopted by other programs. Some schools called their pathways majors or clusters. The name "multiple pathways" then became popular (Oakes and Saunders 2008). The most recent terminology is "linked learning" (ConnectEd 2010a), which emphasizes the linkages between academic and vocational courses. What is important is not to become fixated on specific language or to develop particular orthodoxies of what pathways must be, but to understand the core ideas and practices that distinguish pathways from other reforms and to apply them flexibly.

21. The Annie E. Casey Foundation has developed a program of establishing multiple pathways to high school graduation for disconnected youth, stressing the integration of systems of youth services and a bewildering number of possible reforms in high schools and nonschool settings. See Brinson, Hassel, and Rosch (2008). Cohen (2009) argues for pathways in which students can learn at their own pace, for example, completing high school in three, four, or five years.

22. See Oxley (2010), including the description of the Atlanta High School Transformation Initiative; see Allen, Almeida, and Steinberg (n.d.) on creating small learning communities in five Boston high schools.

23. Some intriguing evidence is available from a study of Title I schools—not high schools—that principal training by itself did not improve test scores, but the combination of principal training and preparation of teachers-leaders on creating grade-level teams was effective. The authors concluded that distributed leadership, stability in school settings, and the explicit use of protocols are crucial to effectiveness. See Saunders, Goldenberg, and Gallimore (2009).

CHAPTER 2

1. On the benefits of professional learning communities, see DuFour, Eaker, and Karhanek (2004) and Little (2006).

2. On the benefits of participating in extracurricular activities, see Eccles et al. (2003); Feldman and Matjasko (2005); Grubb (2009b), chap. 2; and Marsh and Kleitman (2002).

3. To be sure, there is differentiation (or "tracking") *among* high schools, particularly in districts where there are honors high schools with admissions requirements, low-status high schools located on the "wrong side of the tracks" or in poor and racial minority neighborhoods, and continuation high schools where students in danger of flunking out or dropping out are concentrated. All these practices reduce the potential heterogeneity of high schools.

4. For empirical corroboration, see Grubb (2009b), chap. 6, on dynamic inequality, or the inequality among students that becomes larger as they progress through schooling. Furthermore, inequality probably does not increase steadily but is likely to "explode" at such crucial transitions as the one to high school. The evidence in chap. 7 (especially Table 7.1) clarifies that the inequality among students in test scores increases dramatically between eighth and tenth grades and increases somewhat less from tenth to twelfth grades; some of this increase is because of differences in family background and in race and ethnicity.

5. Conversely, when there are more resources in administration—for example, when there are dual principals—one dominant use of additional administrative time is increased oversight of instruction; see Grubb and Flessa (2006).

6. See www.wallacefoundstion.org/SAM. The project seems to have paid little attention to the preparation of SAMs.

7. In this particular case, the high school had school-wide mechanisms in place to impose uniform standards precisely to forestall such criticisms—for example, by having departmental tests applied to all science courses, all math courses, and so on.

8. See, for example, the evaluation of the Talent Development High School model, relying heavily on a ninth-grade academy, by Kemple, Herlihy, and Smith (2005); see also Quint's (2006, 30–36) review of the challenge of ninth-grade remediation. The Education Trust's (2005) potential remedies for "struggling students" are all useful and *potentially* effective, but the underlying research—yet another application of the "exemplary schools" approach, starting from dubious test score data—is by no means rigorous. Many high schools have put in place a variety of activities, assuming that a rich roster of activities will be more effective than one or two. However, for the research community enamored of random control trials, it's difficult to evaluate schools with multiple interventions for different problems, so we're unlikely to develop evidence about this multipronged approach.

9. See the negative effects of being in a remedial track in Grubb (2009b), chap. 2.

10. See Siskin (1994), especially chap. 7, on how discipline-based thinking dominates these departments, and Siskin and Little (1995).

11. Ouchi and Goldschmidt (2009) present some statistical analysis, though the regression equations are badly under-specified because they include very few school resources and no measures of family background.

12. For evidence that most reforms have failed to improve test scores, even when they have improved other dimensions of student commitment and progress, see Grubb (2009b), 71–72; see also Cuban and Usdan (2003b), Table 7.4.

13. On the variety of inspections in England, a country that has had classroom observations for 150 years, see Grubb (2000).

14. For statistical work on high schools, see Grubb (2009b) and other papers based on NELS data referenced therein. On elementary schools, see Knapp et al. (1995). For reviews of the literature on instruction, see Bransford, Brown, and Cocking (1999); Donovan and Bransford (2005); National Research Council (NRC, 2004); and Snow, Burns, and Griffin (1998).

15. See Grubb (2009b), chap. 5, on "Students as Resources," and Table B.5. In that work, I have labeled these and other variables as dimensions of student connectedness to schooling, and as a group they have strong effects on many outcomes.

16. See Gosa (2007) and more generally the special issue of the *Journal of Negro Education*, Summer 2005, on "Hip-Hop, Rap, and Oppositional Culture in Education."

17. See Blum, McNeely, and Rinehart (2002); see more generally NRC (2004), chap. 6.

18. For a more extended argument along these lines, see Grubb and Anyon (2010).

19. Restorative justice is an effort to replace conventional rules and punishments, which usually create outcasts, with a system intended to address the needs of offenders and victims and efforts to restore the offender to the community: "how can they make it right? And how can they learn from the circumstances of the incident?" as the principal with the PACT system said. On restorative justice, see the website Restorative Justice Online, www.restorativejustice.org; and the Wikipedia site for information on where it has arisen. Because restorative justice has developed in different places and in different institutional settings, it is a developing practice rather than one that has been clearly codified.

20. See NRC (2004), based on discussions with a few principals; see also Grubb (2009b), chap. 8, drawing on profiles of twelve urban schools.

21. A survey of a few randomly chosen textbooks on principalship reveals that most of them allocate at most a couple of pages to budgeting issues; see Grubb (2009b), 320–321, note 5. On district ignorance about revenue flows, see Roza and Hill (2006).

22. This is the point of Grubb (2009b) and its effort to replace the "old" school finance with new understanding of effective resources and their relationship to money.

23. See Grubb (2009b), chap. 1, for an analysis of the incredible waste in schools.

24. My results with NELS88 data are from 1992, when television rather than computer-based gadgets was still the great distracter. For evidence on the huge amount of time now spent by teenagers on gadgets—texting, phoning, MySpace, surfing the Web, and other distractions of the electronic age—see the Kaiser Family Foundation report *Generation M²: Media in the Lives of 8- to 18-Year-Olds* (Rideout, Foehr, and Roberts 2010).

25. See also Cusick (1983), who described three biracial schools where the main emphasis was on papering over rather than resolving tensions between black and white students.

26. Because we did not observe classes, we cannot be sure about the extent to which racial and ethnic issues are in fact discussed in this social justice course. Note that the principal mentioned "what we want to do," not what the school is currently doing.

27. Informal and formal discussions of race and identity and courses explicitly about diversity and multiculturalism (as black and Latino studies courses might be) provide forums for students to explore racial/ethnic dimensions of identity and to develop the capacity to see different perspectives and make better decisions; see Zirkel (2008).

28. This is a complex argument developed in Grubb (2009b), chaps. 4 and 9, and in the enormous literature cited therein by advocates for students of color.

CHAPTER 3

1. Virtually all but not all: no good idea can escape being undermined sometimes. This can happen when four teachers are thrown together in an academy without their consent or cooperation, or when a "pathway" consists merely of a course during one or two years. These are pathways in name only and look simply like the choice of an elective or two.

2. For evidence that the small schools funded by the Gates Foundation increased the rigor of assignments, resulted in more assignments embedded in real-world settings ("relevance"), gave students more voice in shaping assignments, and provided more feedback on student work, all leading to higher-quality student work, see Mitchell et al. (2005). See also Feldman (2010),

an analysis of how smaller high schools improve instruction by allowing teachers to build relationships with students and with other teachers, to facilitate collaboration among teachers (especially important in pathways or linked learning), and to play important roles beyond the classroom. Bloom, Thompson, and Unterman (2010) provide evidence that the small high schools of choice in New York increased the proportion of students on track to graduate on time and increased overall graduation rates for a broad range of students, including black males and Latinos. The small schools of choice did not necessarily include theme-based pathways, however, though there is very little description in this report of what their special features were. Other work analyzing the Gates small-schools initiative is cited in chap. 1, footnote 19. For several review articles on school size, see *Brookings Papers on Education Policy* (2005/2006).

3. For the MDRC results, see Kemple and Snipes (2000) and National Research Council (NRC, 2004), chap. 7. See also the statistical results in Grubb (2009b, chap. 2) on personalization.

4. For this particular model of professional development, see Little (2006) and many other writings on alternatives to the Friday-afternoon, one-shot presentation.

5. See Grubb and Oakes (2007) for the problems with the reform movement to increase "rigor" in the conventional high school.

6. For evidence on this point, see Kahne et al. (2006). Their examination of small high schools in Chicago found a number of improvements, particularly in teacher trust and responsibility, but there were virtually no changes in instructional improvement (including instructional leadership by the principal)—and therefore no change in learning measured by test scores. Once again, small size is necessary but not sufficient.

7. See again NRC (2004), chap. 7, "Education Through Theme-Based Learning Communities," which clarifies the ways that pathways adhere to six different precepts emerging from the literature on motivation and engagement. The leaders to whom we spoke recapitulated many of these points.

8. Cuban's (1988) historical examination of leaders describes three roles: managerial or administrative; political, in the sense of making value-laden decisions and explaining them to various publics; and instructional. Most principals embrace the first; some are forced into the second; but principals in pathways must be adept at all three.

9. Some states are in the process of developing state standards for pathways. California has a set of state standards for fifty-eight CTE pathways organized in fifteen broad areas, but many of these are in narrowly vocational subjects (such as ornamental horticulture, cabinetmaking and wood products, and welding technologies) oriented to traditional forms of traditional vocational ed rather than pathways integrating both academic and theme-based content. Others are in areas (e.g., performing arts, architecture and structural engineering, biotechnology) that have been used as themes for broader pathways. They contain long lists of competencies to be attained, in both academic and vocational subjects, but—as is usual with subject standards—no sense of how to develop a curriculum to meet these standards. Only one of the schools we visited mentioned these standards, and no pathway was using them—though when pathways make use of existing CTE courses or the courses of regional occupation centers, they may follow these CTE standards.

10. See Koziol and Grubb (1995) for this argument, with examples drawn from high schools and community colleges. Rogers, Kahne, and Middaugh (2008) have made a similar argument, but without any empirical examples.

11. Personal communications, Nancy Farnam, director of the School of Teacher Preparation, California State University–San Diego, June 16, 2009; March 15, 2010. See also Nancy Farnam and Arlene LaPlante, "Overview of Multiple Pathways (Henceforth Referred to as

Linked Leaning) Lens for the SB2042 Single Subject Credential Program," San Diego State University and ConnectEd.

12. See http://teacherscollegesj.org/academics.

13. See especially Ryken (2001) for a depiction of internships as an alternative source of information about future opportunities.

14. Rational planning for decision-making proves to be a more difficult task than most educators appreciate; for the complexities of even the rational decision-making model we have, see Grubb (2002b). A substantial literature in psychology and behavioral economics following the work of Daniel Kahneman and Amos Tversky has stressed that most decisions do not follow this rational model but depart from it in the ways that individuals weigh gains and losses, in the ways that decisions are framed, and in individual assessments of probabilities and consequences. However, the implications of these departures from rationality for schools and for guidance and counseling have not yet been addressed, to my knowledge.

15. The evidence for this is slight, but the principal reason for Career Academies in California's closing is inadequate enrollment (based on information provided by Karen Shores of the California Department of Education).

16. See also Protheroe (2010) for the same point that leaders should make more effective use of counselors, but without many examples of what counseling might look like.

17. This is not the place to review the sorry history of work-based learning in American schools, but it has been extremely difficult to establish such programs over a long period of time. The last major effort to do so—the School-to-Work Opportunity Act of 1994—failed miserably in establishing more work-based learning; see Stull (2003) and Hershey et al. (1998).

18. The most commonly read work for teachers is DuFour, Eaker, and Karhanek (2004). For other evidence on the effectiveness of learning communities, see Grubb (2009b), 224–229, and Grubb and Tredway (2010), chap. 2.

19. On the concept of internal accountability, and evidence that internal accountability improves a school's ability to respond to external accountability, see Carnoy, Elmore, and Siskin (2003).

20. See Grubb (2009b), chap. 2, for the results of analyzing the NELS88 data and the associated references to evaluations of whole-school reforms. See also Knapp et al. (1995) for evidence in elementary schools and the reviews of instructional effectiveness by the National Research Council cited in footnote 14 of chap. 2.

21. Grubb (2010) summarizes this evidence; see also Grubb (2009b), chap. 2, particularly pages 70–72. The most powerful finding is that improving instruction is necessary for improving learning and test scores (but not progress through high school), and personalizing schools in various ways contributes to greater progress but not enhanced learning. Both enhancing learning and progress therefore require personalization and instructional change, and pathways can provide both of these.

22. For Bersin's comments, see Trei (2006); a quick look on Google reveals many articles complaining that Bersin's restructuring efforts failed to consider other crucial conditions in low-performing schools. For a recent analysis of restructuring, see Jennings, Scott, and Kober (2009).

23. See the reports of Joseph Mayer Rice in the 1890s, cited in Cremin (1962), chap. 2.

24. The phrase "on the bus" comes from Collins (2001).

25. Interestingly enough, the a–g requirements allow for interdisciplinary or integrated courses, such as those that might be developed within a pathway. In addition, the UC Curriculum Integration (UCCI) Institute is seeking "talented, motivated California high school

teachers . . . to develop innovative model course outlines that integrate career and technical education (CTE) with the 'a–g' curriculum for use statewide, and to develop a cadre of expert teachers and administrators to further the development of these courses." See http://www.ucop.edu/a-gGuide/ag/welcome.html.

26. On the narrowness of conventional concepts of rigor in the high school, see Grubb and Oakes (2007).

27. This guesstimate is based on average spending per pupil contained in the California Department of Education Ed-Data, http://www.ed-data.k12.ca.us/.

28. Such calculations would depend on pathways having higher graduation rates than comparable comprehensive high schools. The research evidence is mixed: the quasi-experimental evaluations of pathways have found higher graduation rates, but the random-assignment evaluation of career academies found no difference in graduation rates despite evidence of higher levels of commitment to schooling. See Kemple (2001); Kemple and Snipes (2000); NRC (2004), chap. 7; and Stern, Dayton, and Raby (2001).

29. On trust, see Bryk and Schneider (2002); on coherence, see Newmann et al. (2001); on school climate, see Grubb (2009b), chap. 2; on internal relationships, see Payne (2008).

30. This kind of "triage" conclusion—that the individuals who benefit the most from special programs are those in the middle, not the ones with the most barriers nor the ones with the fewest who can make it on their own—emerges in job training programs as well; see Grubb (1996), chap. 5.

31. In an extreme version of this, one district in the Bay Area adopted a set of "pathways" where students took two courses out of forty-eight in the theme subject—one in spring of junior year and one in spring of senior year. These are pathways without much content.

32. See Grubb (2009b), especially chap. 5 and Table B.5. See also Feldman and Matjasko (2005) and Marsh and Kleitman (2002).

33. An issue I will not pursue is that different approaches to pathways imply different architectures. The single high school with several semi-autonomous small schools might have several independent buildings, each with appropriate lab space and space for counselors, while the offices for central administrators are housed in a separate administration building or attached in clever ways (so that they are physically close to one another) to the different small schools, perhaps in a hub and spoke arrangement. The issue of architecture that reflects and enhances the academic purpose of schools has received very little attention.

CHAPTER 4

1. I have found only one exception: a program using problem-based learning where the problems are modified for elementary, middle, and high school leaders. Surely there must be more such examples.

2. Community colleges have largely shifted away from traditional vocational subjects—auto repair, metalwork, construction trades—and toward more "modern" subjects connected more closely both to academic requirements and to four-year programs, including those in health, information technology, engineering technologies, teaching, and business (Grubb 2002a). This shift makes it easier for pathways with serious academic content to create links with community colleges as well as four-year colleges.

3. See the stunning similarities in the reports critiquing all kinds of professional preparation, including the lack of adequate work-based experiences, in Grubb and Lazerson (2004), chap. 2.

4. In the Principal Leadership Institute, these leadership action research projects take the place of a master's thesis. Although they are not always successful—after all, the aspiring principals who carry them out have no positional authority in their schools and cannot control a variety of external factors, from principal indifference to faculty fatigue to district mandates—they always provide substantial information about the specific reform attempted, the process of reform, and the nature of leadership.

5. Oral communication, Patricia Holland, University of Houston, March 11, 2010. See also Holland (2004) for a study of five principals from this program, stressing the compatibility of managerial and professional values (trust and judgment) rather than the special characteristics of the program.

6. See again Dewey's argument against either-or positions in chap. 2. Similarly, he did not, as many people falsely assume, advocate "learning by doing." Indeed, he rejected this idea in *Schools of Tomorrow,* where he and his wife explicitly stated that "Learning by doing does not, of course, mean the substitution of manual occupations or handwork for textbook studying" (Dewey and Dewey 1915, 74). They went on to clarify the complementarity between learning, or "textbook studying," *and* doing, including manual occupations and handwork. The modern formulation is, of course, the integration of academic and occupational content in theme-based pathways or linked learning.

7. We know of only one other induction program in California, run by the New Teacher Center at the University of California at Santa Cruz. There is no national census or listing of induction programs. An informal search on Google reveals a mandatory induction program for new principals in South Carolina, but this is a two-day workshop. Pennsylvania also has a mandatory induction program lasting a total of thirteen days, and Colorado also has a requirement. Otherwise, induction programs appear to be few and far between. For a how-to book, see Villani (2006).

8. In the most absurd case, we discovered a district with dual principals in several schools; but when there was a vacancy, the continuing principal was not part of the hiring committee—so there was no mechanism in place to ensure that the coprincipals would have similar educational philosophies and conceptions of leadership. See Grubb and Flessa (2006).

9. For a brief description of such an approach in Atlanta, see Mezzacappa (2008); for one in Fairfield, Connecticut, see Lachman et al. (2009). Without a census of such efforts, it's unclear how many districts have created their own programs. In addition, it isn't clear even from the descriptions available how many elements of a developmental approach have been incorporated into existing programs. The PLI and the umbrella Leadership Connection for Justice in Education follow many of the practices of developmental approaches, though of course they cannot influence all district decisions.

10. On the SAM project, see www.wallacefoundation.org/Pages/SAM.aspx. For an evaluation of it, see Turnbull et al. (2009). For a journalistic account of adopting SAMs in Larue County, Kentucky, see Holland (2008).

CHAPTER 5

1. These precepts are based on the analysis of supposedly exemplary districts, in Grubb (2009b), chap. 10; and on two analyses of district leadership by the Southern Regional Education Board (Bottoms and Fry 2009; SREB 2010). The Bottoms and Fry report is specifically about providing high school principals with more decision-making power.

2. Because there is no "census" of high schools with pathways, it is impossible to know how frequent this is, but it seems to be increasing.

3. For a review of the issues raised in the Department of Education's approach to reconstitution, see Rice and Malen (2010).

4. See especially Cuban and Usdan (2003a), *Powerful Reforms with Shallow Roots,* where reforms in six urban districts have resulted in a "mixed bag of outcomes" with shallow roots, therefore susceptible to change from new leadership.

5. Information on developments under the new superintendent comes from a student in the Principal Leadership Institute writing her master's thesis on "Railside" School.

6. I review studies of apparently exemplary districts in Grubb (2009b), chap. 10. The recent "exemplary district" literature has many of the same flaws of the "exemplary schools" literature whose methodology it copies. It is never quite clear whether the districts chosen for these case studies are in fact exemplary in the sense of enhancing various student outcomes, even though their policies avoid some obvious limitations of traditional top-down bureaucracies.

7. In the large literature on dysfunctional urban districts, see especially Payne (2008), as well as such classics as Rogers (1968) on New York.

8. The argument for relatively consistent support of students also comes from the view of "dynamic inequality," which continues to increase the disparities among students through all years of K-12 education; see Grubb (2009b), chaps. 6–7.

9. Again, see Grubb (2009b) for different ways of thinking about budgets and resources, and see Rigby (2010) for evidence about one district's attempt to provide training for principals around budgeting. I teach a budget and finance class in the PLI where aspiring principals first diagnose a school's problems (and especially its learning problems), then develop an instructional plan to overcome these problems, then identify the resources in a broad sense that would meet this plan, and only then allocate money to the resources identified—an instruction-oriented budgeting process. Typically when students truncate this process, they start planning how to spend money in a piecemeal and wasteful way—just as schools do when they receive additional funding.

10. It is crucial to distinguish between *funding* and *resources* because resources may be unequal even when funding isn't. For example, in 2003–2004, central city schools spent $7,812 per pupil compared to $7,542 in suburban schools (and $7,268 in all public schools). But this slightly higher level of spending did not lead to more real resources: central city schools had higher numbers of students per teacher (15.0 vs. 14.6), lower teacher salaries ($45,400 vs. $46,100, despite higher costs of living in central cities), a higher proportion of schools with temporary buildings (37.7 percent vs. 34.4 percent), and a higher proportion of schools using common spaces for instruction (21.3 percent vs. 19 percent); see Jacob (2007), Table 1. A more detailed analysis would show many other resources to be inferior in urban schools, such as the quality of instruction, leadership, school climate, and certainly stability.

11. See, for example, the six districts profiled in Cuban and Usdan (2003b), with concentration of power in the district, an emphasis on accountability over capacity-building, and using "successful" business practices to lead reform.

CHAPTER 6

1. See Rowan et al. (2009) as well as the epilogue of Cohen (2009).

2. The effective schools literature is summarized in Clark, Lotto, and Astuto (1984); and Edmonds (1979). For critiques, see Cohen (1983); Cuban (1984); Purkey and Smith

(1983); and Rowan, Bossert, and Dwyer (1983). One problem has been the measurement of effectiveness by conventional test scores; the finding that effective schools stress conventional academic skills and monitor students constantly (with the same standardized tests) is almost a tautology because it says that effective schools as measured by conventional tests stress the competencies required by conventional tests. The methodologies of identifying exemplary schools have also been critiqued, and the case study methods used to investigate schools were often unstandardized and incomplete. Finally, the results of this literature often have been used in a formulaic fashion.

3. The Leithwood book cites Hallinger and Heck (1996), but this summarizes studies of principal effectiveness rather than comparing the effectiveness of principals and teachers. It also cites some of the work that Leithwood and Jantzi (2006) have undertaken about the effects of principals and teachers, but these results vary from sample to sample.

4. See Grubb and Flessa (2006) for a profile of a small school with nine teachers who shared the duties of principal. See Boaler and Staples (2008) and Gutierrez (2000) for descriptions of coherent math departments that developed their own pedagogical approach.

5. See Ong (1982) and the challenge he presents: how do "technologies of the word"—the forms literacies take, first in print and now in a huge variety of electronic media—change the ways people conceive of their world?

6. Of course, there was competition in the early years of the century too, particularly from the lure of the streets and from employment. These weakened as children labor laws were enforced after 1900 and as the Great Depression finally destroyed the youth labor market. Youth culture took over in the 1950s, and electronic gadgets represent a particularly virulent form of youth culture.

7. See, for example, Berliner (2009); Grubb (2009b), chap. 12; Grubb and Lazerson (2004); and Rothstein (2004).

8. See Powell, Farrar, and Cohen (1985), especially chap. 5, a historical chapter by David Cohen.

APPENDIX

1. On saturation, see especially Glaser and Strauss (1967) and Strauss and Corbin (1990).

2. This is a longer debate for another place, but the use of computer-based qualitative analysis methods has contributed, with other factors, to the "bureaucratization of research," the proliferation of research with painstakingly correct methods but trivial and uninteresting conclusions that are also useless for schools.

References

Commission reports on high schools are noted with asterisks.

Allen, Lili, Cheryl Almeida, and Adria Steinberg. n.d. *Wall to Wall: Implementing Small Learning Communities in Five Boston High Schools.* Providence, RI: Northeast and Islands Regional Educational Laboratory.

Alliance for Excellent Education. 2004. *Profiles in Leadership: Innovative Approaches to Transforming the American High School.* Washington, DC: Alliance for Excellent Education. *

American Diploma Project. 2004. *Ready or Not: Creating a High School Diploma That Counts.* Washington, DC: American Diploma Project. *

The American High School Crisis and State Policy Solutions. 2003. Washington, DC: National Center on Education and the Economy and National Governors' Association Center for Best Practices. *

America's High Schools. 2009. *The Future of Children* 19, no. 1. *

Angus, Davis, and Jeffrey Mirel. 1999. *The Failed Promise of the American High School 1890–1995.* New York: Teachers College Press.

Beadie, Nancy, and Kim Tolley. 2002. *Chartered Schools: Two Hundred Years of Independent Academies in the United States 1727–1925.* New York: RoutledgeFalmer.

Berger, Andrea, et al. 2007. *Evaluation of the Early College High School Initiative: Select Topics on Implementation.* Seattle: American Institutes for Research and SRI International, for the Bill and Melinda Gates Foundation.

Berliner, David. 2009. *Poverty and Potential: Out-of-School Factors and School Success.* Boulder and Tempe: Education and the Public Interest Center and Educational Policy Research Unit. Available at http://epicpolicy.org/publication/poverty-and-potential.

Bloom, Howard, Saskia Thompson, and Rebecca Unterman. 2010. *Transforming the High School Experience: Boosting Student Achievement and Graduation Rates.* New York: MDRC.

Blum, Robert, Clea McNeely, and Peggy Rinehart. 2002. *Improving the Odds: The Untapped Power of Schools to Improve the Health of Teens.* Minneapolis: Center for Adolescent Health and Development, University of Minnesota. Available at http://www.allaboutkids.umn.edu.

Boaler, Jo, and Megan Staples. 2008. "Creating Mathematical Futures Through an Equitable Teaching Approach: The Case of Railside School." *Teachers College Record* 110, no. 3: 608–645.

Bottoms, Gene, and Betty Fry. 2009. *The District Leadership Challenge: Empowering Principals to Improve Teaching and Learning.* Atlanta: Southern Regional Education Board.

Boyer, Ernest. 1983. *High School: A Report on Secondary Education in America.* New York: Harper and Row. *

Brand, B., ed. 2003. *Essentials of High School Reform: New Forms of Assessment and Contextual Teaching and Learning.* Washington, DC: American Youth Policy Forum. *

Bransford, John D., A. L. Brown, and Rodney R. Cocking. 1999. *How People Learn: Brain, Mind, Experience, and School.* Washington, DC: National Academy Press.

Brill, Fred. 2008. *Leading and Learning: Effective School Leadership Through Reflective Storytelling and Inquiry.* Portland, ME: Stenhouse Publishers.

Brinson, Dana, Bryan Hassel, and Jacob Rosch. 2008. "Connecting Youth Through Multiple Pathways." Baltimore: Public Impact for the Annie E. Casey Foundation. Available at www.aecf.org/KnowledgeCenter/.

Bryk, Anthony. 2010. "Organizing Schools for Improvement." *Phi Delta Kappan* 91, no. 7: 23–30.

Bryk, Anthony, and Barbara Schneider. 2002. *Trust in Schools: A Core Resource for Improvement.* New York: Russell Sage Foundation.

Bryk, Anthony, Penny Sebring, Elaine Allensworth, Stuart Leppuscu, and John Easton. 2010. *Organizing Schools for Improvement: Lessons from Chicago.* Chicago: University of Chicago Press.

Carnegie Council on Policy Studies in Higher Education. 1980. *Giving Youth a Better Chance: Options for Education, Work, and Service.* San Francisco: Jossey-Bass. *

Carnoy, Martin, Richard Elmore, and Leslie Siskin, eds. 2003. *The New Accountability: High Schools and High-Stakes Testing.* New York: Routledge.

Cheatham, H. 1990. "Afro-Centricity and Career Development of African Americans." *Career Development Quarterly* 38: 334–346.

Clark, D. L., L. S. Lotto, and T. A. Astuto. 1984. "Effective Schools and School Improvement: A Comparative Analysis of Two Lines of Inquiry." *Educational Administration Quarterly* 20, no. 3: 41–68.

Cohen, David, 1985. "Origins." In *The Shopping Mall High School: Winners and Losers in the Educational Marketplace,* ed. Arthur Powell, Eleanor Farrar, and David Cohen, chap. 5. Boston: Houghton Mifflin.

———. 2009. *The Ordeal of Inequality: Did Federal Regulation Fix the Schools?* Cambridge: Harvard University Press.

Cohen, Michael. 1983. "Instructional, Management, and Social Conditions in Effective Schools." In *School Finance and School Improvement: Linkages for the 1980s,* ed. Alan Odden and Lloyd D. Webb, 17–50. Cambridge, MA: Ballinger Publishing.

———. 2001. *Transforming the American High School: New Directions for State and Local Policy.* Boston and Washington, DC: Jobs for the Future and The Aspen Institute. *

Collins, A., J. Brown, and S. Newman. 1989. "Cognitive Apprenticeship: Teaching the Craft of Reading, Writing, and Mathematics." In *Knowing, Learning, and Instruction: Essays in Honor of Robert Glaser,* ed. Lauren Resnick, 453–494. Hillsdale, NJ: Erlbaum.

Collins, James. 2001. *Good to Great: Why Some Companies Make the Leap—and Others Don't.* New York: HarperBusiness.

Conant, James Bryant. 1959. *The American High School Today: A First Report to Interested Citizens.* New York: McGraw-Hill. *

———. 1961. *Slums and Suburbs: A Commentary on Schools in Metropolitan Areas.* New York: McGraw-Hill.

Conley, David. 2007. *Toward a More Comprehensive Conception of College Readiness.* Eugene, OR: Educational Policy Improvement Center.

ConnectEd. 2010a. *Designing Multidisciplinary Integrated Curriculum Units.* Berkeley: ConnectEd: The California Center for College and Career.

———. 2010b. "Linked Learning Pathway Certification Criteria." Berkeley: ConnectEd: The California Center for College and Career.

Cremin, Lawrence. 1962. *The Transformation of the School: Progressivism in American Education 1876–1957.* New York: Knopf.

Cuban, Larry. 1984. "Transforming the Frog into a Prince: Effective Schools Research, Policy, and Practice at the District Level." *Harvard Educational Review* 54, no. 2: 129–151.

———. 1988. *The Managerial Imperative and the Practice of Leadership in School.* Albany: State University of New York Press.

———. 1990. "Reforming Again, Again, and Again." *Educational Researcher* 19, no. 1: 3–13.

———. 1993. *How Teachers Taught: Constancy and Change in American Classrooms, 1880–1990.* 2nd ed. New York: Teachers College Press.

Cuban, Larry, and Michael Usdan, eds. 2003a. *Powerful Reforms with Shallow Roots: Improving America's Urban Schools.* New York: Teachers College Press.

———. 2003b. "What Happened in the Six Cities?" In *Powerful Reforms with Shallow Roots: Improving America's Urban Schools,* ed. Larry Cuban and Michael Usdan, 147–170. New York: Teachers College Press.

Curry, J., and G. W. Lambie. 2007. "Enhancing School Counselor Accountability: The Large Group Guidance Portfolio." *Professional School Counseling* 11: 145–148.

Cushman, K., and Students. 2003. *Fires in the Bathrooms: Advice for Teachers from High School Students.* New York: What Kids Can Do. *

Cusick, Phillip. 1983. *The Egalitarian Ideal and the American High School.* New York: Longman.

Darling-Hammond, L., J. Ancess, and S. Ort. 2002. "Reinventing High Schools: Outcomes of the Coalition Campus Schools Project." *American Educational Research Journal* 39, no. 3: 639–673.

Darling-Hammond, Linda, et al. 2010. *Preparing Principals for a Changing World: Lessons from Effective School Leadership Programs.* San Francisco: Jossey-Bass.

Dewey, John. 1938. *Experience and Education.* New York: Macmillan.

Dewey, John, and Evelyn Dewey. 1915. *Schools of Tomorrow.* New York: E. P. Dutton.

Donovan, M. S., and J. Bransford, eds. 2005. *How Children Learn.* Washington, DC: National Academies Press.

DuFour, Rebecca, Robert Eaker, and Gayle Karhanek. 2004. *Whatever It Takes: How Professional Learning Communities Respond When Kids Don't Learn.* Bloomington, IN: National Education Service.

Eccles, Jacquelynne, Bonnie Barber, Margaret Stone, and James Hunt. 2003. "Extracurricular Activities and Adolescent Development." *Journal of Social Issues* 59, no. 4: 865–889.

Eccles, Jacquelynne, and R. W. Roeser. 2009. "Schools, Academic Motivation, and Stage-Environment Fit." In *Handbook of Adolescent Psychology,* 3rd ed., ed. R. M. Lerner and L. Steinberg, 404–434. Hoboken, NJ: Wiley.

Eccles, Jacquelynne, et al. 1993. "Development During Adolescence: The Impact of Stage-Environment Fit on Young Adolescents' Experiences in Schools and Families." *American Psychologist* 48, no. 2: 90–101.

Eckart, Penny. 1989. *Jocks and Burnouts: Social Categories and Identity in the High School.* New York: Teachers College Press.

Edmonds, Ron R. 1979. "Effective Schools for the Urban Poor." *Educational Leadership* 37: 15–24, 37.

Education Trust. 2005. *The Power to Change: High Schools That Help All Students Achieve.* Washington, DC: The Education Trust. *

Elliott, M. N., L. M. Hanser, and C. L. Gilroy. 2000. *Evidence of Positive Student Outcomes in JROTC Career Academies.* Santa Monica, CA: RAND Corporation.

Elson, William, and Frank Bachman. 1910. "Different Courses for Elementary Schools." *Educational Review* 39: 359–362.

Feldman, Amy, and Jennifer Matjasko. 2005. "The Role of School-Based Extracurricular Activities in Adolescent Development: A Comprehensive Review and Future Directions." *Review of Educational Research* 75, no. 2: 150–210.

Feldman, Joey. 2010. *Teaching Without Bells: What We Can Learn from Powerful Practice in Small Schools.* Boulder: Paradigm Publishers.

Flores, L. Y., and M. J. Heppner. 2002. "Multicultural Career Counseling: Ten Essentials for Training." *Journal of Career Development* 28: 181–202.

Fuller, Bruce, Joseph Wright, Karen Gesicki, and Erin Kang. 2007. "Gauging Growth: How to Judge No Child Left Behind?" *Educational Researcher* 36, no. 5: 268–278.

Gardner, Howard. 1983. *Frames of Mind: The Theory of Multiple Intelligences.* New York: Basic Books.

Gawande, Atul. 2009. "Testing, Testing." *The New Yorker,* December 14.

Glaser, Barney, and Anselm Strauss. 1967. *The Discovery of Grounded Theory: Strategies for Qualitative Research.* Chicago: Aldine Publishing.

Goldin, Claudia, and Lawrence Katz. 2008. *The Race Between Education and Technology.* Cambridge, MA: Harvard University Press.

Goodlad, John. 1984. *A Place Called School: Prospects for the Future.* New York: McGraw-Hill. *

Goodman, Paul. 1956. *Growing Up Absurd: Problems of Youth in the Organized System.* New York: Random House.

Gosa, Travis. 2007. "Oppositional Culture, Hip-Hop, and the Schooling of Black Youth: Hip-Hop's Counter-Narrative and Pro-Schooling Messages." Unpublished paper, Department of Sociology, Johns Hopkins University. Available at www.agi.harvard.edu/ScholarDetail.php?CID=276.

Grant, Gerald. 1988. *The World We Created at Hamilton High.* Cambridge, MA: Harvard University Press.

Grossman, Jean, and Siobhan Cooney. 2009. *Paving the Way for Success in High School and Beyond: The Importance of Preparing Middle School Students for the Transition to Ninth Grade.* Philadelphia: Public/Private Ventures.

Grubb, W. Norton. 1978. "The Phoenix of Vocationalism: Hope Deferred Is Hope Denied." *New Directions in Education and Work* 1: 71–90.

———. 1995a. *Education Through Occupations in American High Schools.* Vol. I: *Approaches to Integrating Academic and Vocational Education.* Vol. II: *The Challenges of Implementing Curriculum Integration.* New York: Teachers College Press.

———. 1995b. "'The Cunning Hand, the Cultured Mind': Sources of Support for Curriculum Integration." In *Education Through Occupations in American High Schools,* Vol. I, ed. W. N. Grubb, 11–25. New York: Teachers College Press.

———. 1995c. "Coherence for All Students: High Schools with Career Clusters and Majors." In *Education Through Occupations in American High Schools,* Vol. I, ed. W. N. Grubb, 97–113. New York: Teachers College Press.

———. 1996. *Learning to Work: The Case for Re-Integrating Job Training and Education.* New York: Russell Sage Foundation.

———. 2000. "Opening Classrooms and Improving Teaching: Lessons from School Inspection in England." *Teachers College Record* 102, no. 4: 696–723.

———. 2002a. "Occupational Education." In *Higher Education in the United States: An Encyclopedia,* ed. James Forest and Kevin Kinser, 437–441. Santa Barbara: ABC-CLIO.

———. 2002b. *Who I Am: The Inadequacy of Information in the Information Age.* Paris: OECD. Available at www.oecd.org/dataoecd/32/35/1954678.pdf.

———. 2008a. "Reforming the 19th Century High School: 'Weak' and 'Strong' Approaches to Multiple Pathways." In *Multiple Pathways to College and Careers,* ed. Jeannie Oakes and Marisa Saunders. Cambridge, MA: Harvard Education Press.

———. 2008b. "SchoolMap! A Developmental System of College and Career Guidance for High Schools." Unpublished paper.

_______. 2008c. "Dreams and Leaks, Reforms and Band-Aids: The Transition from High School to Postsecondary Education." In *The Conditions of Education in California 2008,* 3–48. Berkeley: Policy Analysis for California Education.

———. 2009a. "Correcting the Money Myth: Re-Thinking School Resources." *Phi Delta Kappan* 91, no. 4: 51–56.

———. 2009b. *The Money Myth: School Resources, Outcomes, and Equity.* New York: Russell Sage Foundation.

———. 2010a. "Moving Research into Practice: Proposing an Educational Extension Service." Unpublished paper prepared for the W. W. Kellogg Foundation.

———. 2010b. "The Quandaries of Basic Skills in Community Colleges: Views from the Classroom." Prepared for the NCPR Developmental Education Conference: *What Policies and Practices Work for Students?* September 23–24, 2010, Teachers College, Columbia University.

Grubb, W. Norton, and Yolanda Anyon. 2010. *A Trio of Changes Supporting Students: Integrating School Reforms and Support Services.* Unpublished paper prepared for the Woodrow Wilson Early College High School Initiative.

Grubb, W. Norton, and Norena Badway. 1998. *Linking School-Based and Work-Based Learning: The Implications of LaGuardia's Co-op Seminars for School-to-Work Programs.* MDS-1046. Berkeley: National Center for Research in Vocational Education.

Grubb, W. Norton, Gary Davis, Jeannie Lum, Jane Plihal, and Carol Morgaine. 1991, July. *"The Cunning Hand, The Cultured Mind": Models for Integrating Vocational and Academic Education.* Berkeley: National Center for Research in Vocational Education.

Grubb, W. Norton, and Joseph Flessa. 2006. "A Job Too Big for One: Multiple Principals and Other Non-Traditional Approaches to School Leadership." *Educational Administration Quarterly* 52, no. 4: 518–550.

Grubb, W. Norton, Claudia Lara, and Susan Valdez. 2002. "Counselor, Coordinator, Monitor, Mom: The Roles of Counselors in the Puente Program." *Educational Policy* 16, no. 4: 547–571.

Grubb, W. Norton, and Marvin Lazerson. 2004. *The Education Gospel: The Economic Value of Schooling.* Cambridge, MA: Harvard University Press.

Grubb, W. Norton, and Jeannie Oakes. 2007. *"Restoring Value" to the High School Diploma: The Rhetoric and Practice of Higher Standards.* Tempe, AZ: Education Policy Research Unit, Arizona State University. Available at epsl.asu.edu/epru/documents/EPSL-0710-242-EPRU.pdf.

Grubb, W. Norton., and Lynda Tredway. 2010. *Leading from the Inside Out: Expanded Roles for Teachers in Equitable Schools.* Boulder: Paradigm Publishers.

Grubb, W. Norton, and Carey Watson. 2002. "Engagement and Motivation in High Schools: The Multiple Roles of Guidance and Counseling." Unpublished paper prepared for the National Research Council Committee for Increasing High School Students' Engagement and Motivation to Learn.

Gurholt, Anya. 2010. "Curricular Alignment and Theme Integration in an Education Academy." Master's thesis, Principal Leadership Institute, School of Education, University of California.

Gutierrez, Rochelle. 2000. "Advancing African-American, Urban Youth in Mathematics: Unpacking the Success of One Math Department." *American Journal of Education* 109, no. 1: 63–111.

Hallinger, Philip, and Ronald Heck. 1996. "Reassessing the Principal's Role in School Effectiveness: A Review of Empirical Research." *Educational Administration Quarterly* 32, no. 5: 5–44.

Hamilton, Stephen. 1990. *Apprenticeship for Adulthood: Preparing Youth for the Future.* New York: Free Press.

Hampel, Robert. 1986. *The Last Little Citadel: American High Schools Since 1940.* Boston: Houghton Mifflin.

Harris, S. 2006. *Best Practices of Award-Winning Secondary School Principals.* Thousand Oaks, CA: Corwin Press.

Hartung, P. J., and B. J. Taber. 2008. "Career Construction and Subjective Well-Being." *Journal of Career Assessment* 16: 75–85.

Harvey, J., and N. Housman. 2004. *Crisis or Possibility: Conversations About the American High School.* Washington, DC: National High School Alliance.

Hendricks, F. M. 1993. "Career Counseling with African American Students." *Journal of Career Development* 21: 117–126.

Hershey, A., M. Silverberg, J. Haimson, P. Hudis, and R. Jackson. 1998. *Expanding Options for Students: Report to Congress on the National Evaluation of School-to-Work Implementation.* Princeton, NJ: Mathematica Policy Research.

Hess, Frederick. 2004. *Common Sense School Reform.* New York: Palgrave MacMillan.

High Schools of the Millennium. 2000. Washington, DC: American Youth Policy Forum. *

Hill, Paul, Gail Foster, and Tamara Gendler. 1990. *High Schools with Character.* Santa Monica, CA: RAND Corporation. *

Holland, Holly. 2008. "Out of the Office and into the Classroom: An Initiative to Help Principals Focus on Instruction." In *Improving Leadership for Learning: Stories from the Field,* 12–16. Seattle: Center for the Study of Teaching and Policy, University of Washington.

Holland, Patricia. 2004. "Principals as Supervisors: A Balancing Act." *NASSP Bulletin* 88, no. 639: 3–14.

Jacob, Brian. 2007. "The Challenges of Staffing Urban Schools with Effective Teachers." *The Future of Children* 17, no. 1: 129–153.

Jacobs, Heidi Hayes. 1989. *Interdisciplinary Curriculum: Design and Implementation.* Alexandria, VA: Association of Supervision and Curriculum Development.

Jenkins, J. M., and D. Tanner, eds. 1992. *Restructuring for an Interdisciplinary Curriculum.* Reston VA: National Association of Secondary School Principals.

Jennings, J., C. Scott, and N. Kober. 2009. "Rethinking 'Restructuring': Lessons Learned from Five States over Five Years." *Education Week* 28, no. 31: 36.

Kahne, Joseph, Susan Sporte, Marisa de la Torre, and John Easton. 2006. *Small High Schools on a Larger Scale: The First Three Years of the Chicago High School Redesign Initiative.* Chicago: Consortium on Chicago School Research, University of Chicago.

Kemple, James. 2001. *Career Academies: Impacts on Students' Initial Transition to Post-Secondary Education and Employment.* New York: Manpower Demonstration Research Corporation.

Kemple, James, Corinne Herlihy, and Thomas J. Smith. 2005. *Making Progress Toward Graduation: Evidence from the Talent Development High School Model.* New York: Manpower Demonstration Research Corporation.

Kemple, James, and Jason Snipes. 2000. *Career Academies: Impacts on Student' Engagement and Performance in High School.* New York: Manpower Demonstration Research Corporation.

Kerchner, Charles, and Krista Caufman. 1993. "Building the Airplane While It's Rolling Down the Runway." In *A Union of Professionals: Labor Relations and Educational Reforms,* ed. Charles Kerchner and Julia Koppich, 1–18. New York: Teachers College Press.

Knapp, Michael, et al. 1995. *Teaching for Meaning in High-Poverty Classrooms.* New York: Teachers College Press.

Koziol, Ken, and W. Norton Grubb. 1995. "Paths Not Taken: Curriculum Integration and the Political and Moral Purposes of Schooling." In *Education Through Occupations in American High Schools,* Vol. II, ed. W. Norton Grubb, 115–140. New York: Teachers College Press.

Krug, Edward. 1969. *The Shaping of the American High School, Vol. 1: 1880–1920.* Madison: University of Wisconsin Press.

———. 1972. *The Shaping of the American High School, Vol. 2: 1920–1941.* Madison: University of Wisconsin Press.

Labaree, David. 2010. "How Dewey Lost: The Victory of David Snedden and Social Efficiency in the Reform of American Education." In *Pragmatism and Modernities,* ed. Daniel Tröhler, Thomas Schlag, and Fritz Ostervalder, 163–190. Rotterdam: Sense Publishers.

Lacey, T. Allen, and Benjamin Wright. 2009. "Occupational Employment Projections to 2018." *Monthly Labor Review* 132, no. 11: 82–123.

Lachman, Andrew, Richard Lemons, Margaret Orr, and Mónica Byrne-Jiminéz. 2009. "Developing Instructional Leaders." Providence, RI: Annenberg Institute for School Reform Voices in Urban Education. Available at www.annenberginstitute.org/VUE/developing-instructional-leaders.

Lawler, Edward. 1998. *Creating High Performance Organizations: Practices and Results of Employee Involvement and Total Quality Management in Fortune 1000 Companies.* San Francisco: Jossey-Bass.

Lazerson, Marvin, and W. Norton Grubb. 1974. *American Education and Vocationalism: A Documentary History, 1870–1970.* New York: Teachers College Press.

Leithwood, Kenneth, and Doris Jantzi. 2006. "Transformational School Leadership for Large-Scale Reform: Effects on Students, Teachers, and Their Classroom Practices." *School Effectiveness and School Improvement* 17, no. 2: 201–227.

Leithwood, Kenneth, Karen Seashore Louis, Stephen Anderson, and Kyla Wahlstrom. 2004. *How Leadership Influences Student Learning.* New York: The Wallace Foundation.

Lemons, Richard, T. Luschel, and Leslie Siskin. 2003. "Leadership and the Demands for Standards-Based Accountability." In *The New Accountability: High Schools and High-Stakes Testing,* ed. Martin Carnoy, Richard Elmore, and Leslie Siskin, 99–128. New York: Routledge.

Lichtenstein, G. 2006. "What Went Wrong at Manual High?" *Education Week,* May 17.

Lightfoot, Sarah Lawrence. 1983. *The Good High School: Portraits of Character and Culture.* New York: Basic Books.

Little, Judith Warren. 2006. *Professional Development and Professional Community in the Learner-Centered School.* Washington, DC: National Education Association.

Lucas, Samuel. 1999. *Tracking Inequality: Stratification and Mobility in American High Schools.* New York: Teachers College Press.

Lynd, Robert, and Helen Lynd. 1929. *Middletown: A Study in Contemporary American Culture.* New York: Harcourt, Brace.

Marsh, Herbert, and Sabina Kleitman. 2002. "Extracurricular School Activities: The Good, and Bad, and the Non-Linear." *Harvard Educational Review* 72, no. 4: 464–511.

Marshall, Ray. 2008. *The Case for Collaborative School Reform: The Toledo Experience.* Washington, DC: Economic Policy Institute.

McCalmont, Julie. 2010. *Trials of a First-Year Algebra Professional Learning Community.* Leadership Action Research Project, Principal Leadership Institute, University of California, Berkeley.

McLaughlin, Milbrey, and Joan Talbert. 2001. *Professional Communities and the Work of High School Teaching.* Chicago: University of Chicago Press.

———. 2007. "Building Professional Learning Communities in High Schools: Challenges and Promising Practices." In *Professional Learning Communities: Divergence, Depth, and Dilemmas,* ed. Louise Stoll and Karen Seashore Louis. Maidenhead, United Kingdom: McGraw Hill/Open University Press.

McPartland, James, Robert Balfanz, William Joan, and Nettie Legters. 1998. "Improving School Climate and Achievement in a Troubled Urban High School Through the Talent Development Model." *Journal of Education for Students Placed at Risk* 3, no. 4: 337–361.

Meier, Deborah. 1995. *The Power of Their Ideas: Lessons from a Small School in Harlem.* Boston: Beacon Press.

Mezzacappa, Dale. 2008. "A Better Pipeline to the Principalship: Atlanta Builds Education Leaders from Within." In *Improving Leadership for Learning: Stories from the Field,* 6–11. Seattle: Center for the Study of Teaching and Policy, University of Washington.

Miller, Robert, and Brian Rowan. 2006. "Effects of Organic Management on Student Achievement." *American Educational Research Journal* 43, no. 2: 210–253.

Mitchell, Karen, et al. 2005. *Rigor, Relevance, and Results: The Quality of Teacher Assignments and Student Work in New and Conventional High Schools.* Washington, DC, and Menlo Park, CA: American Institutes for Research and SRI International, for the Bill and Melinda Gates Foundation.

National Association of Secondary School Principals. 1996. *Breaking Ranks: Changing an American Institution.* Reston, VA: NASSP. *

———. 2004. *Breaking Ranks II: Strategies for Leading High School Reform.* Reston, VA: NASSP. *

National Commission on Youth. 1980. *The Transition of Youth to Adulthood: A Bridge Too Far?* Boulder: Westview Press. *

National Panel on High School and Adolescent Education. 1976. *The Education of Adolescents.* Washington, DC: Department of Health, Education, and Welfare. *

National Research Council, Committee on Increasing High School Students' Engagement and Motivation to Learn. 2004. *Engaging Schools: Fostering High School Students' Motivation to Learn.* Washington, DC: National Academy Press. *

National School District and Network Grants Program, Year 2 Evaluation Report. 2004. Washington, DC, and Menlo Park, CA: American Institutes for Research and SRI International, for the Bill and Melinda Gates Foundation. *

Neufield, Barbara, Anne Levy, and Sara Chrismer. 2005. *High School Renewal in the Boston Public Schools: Focus on Organization and Leadership.* Cambridge, MA: Education Matters. *

Newmann, Fred M., BetsAnn Smith, Elaine Allensworth, and Anthony S. Bryk. 2001. "Instructional Program Coherence: What It Is and Why It Should Guide School Improvement Policy." *Educational Evaluation and Policy Analysis* 23, no. 4: 297–321.

Oakes, Jeannie. 1985. *Keeping Track : How Schools Structure Inequality.* New Haven: Yale University Press.

Oakes, J. n.d. *Multiple Definitions of Multiple Pathways.* Los Angeles: UCLA, Institute for Democracy, Education, and Access.

Oakes, Jeannie, and Marisa Saunders. 2008. *Beyond Tracking: Multiple Pathways to College and Careers.* Cambridge, MA: Harvard Education Press.

Olson, Lynn. 2005. "Calls for Revamping High Schools Intensify." *Education Week,* Jan. 26.

Ong, Walter. 1982. *Orality and Literacy: The Technologizing of the Word.* New York: Methuen.

Ouchi, William. 2009. *The Secret of TSL: The Revolutionary Discovery That Raises School Performance.* New York: Simon & Schuster.

Ouchi, William, and Pete Goldschmidt. 2009. "A National Study of School District Centralization and Student Performance." Unpublished paper, University of California–Los Angeles.

Oxley, Diane. 2010. "Building District Capacity for High School Transformation." Session presented at ASCD Annual Conference, San Antonio. Portland: Education Northwest.

Panel on Youth of the President's Science Advisory Committee. 1974. *Youth: Transition to Adulthood.* Chicago: University of Chicago Press. *

Parsi, Ace, David Plank, and David Stern. 2009. "Cost of California Multiple Pathway Programs." Berkeley: Policy Analysis for California Education, University of California–Berkeley.

Payne, Charles. 2008. *So Much Reform, So Little Change: The Persistence of Failure in Urban Schools.* Cambridge, MA: Harvard Education Press.

Peterson, Bob, and Michael Charney. 1999. *Transforming Teacher Unions: Fighting for Better School, and Social Justice.* Wisconsin: Rethinking Schools.

Pole, J. R. 1978. *The Pursuit of Equality in American History.* Berkeley: University of California Press.

Powell, Arthur, Eleanor Farrar, and David Cohen. 1985. *The Shopping Mall High School.* Boston: Houghton Mifflin.

Power, Claude. 1985. "Democratic Moral Education in the Large Public High School." In *Moral Education: Theory and Application,* ed. M. Barkowitz and F. Oser, 219–240. Hillsdale, NJ: Lawrence Erlbaum.

Protheroe, Nancy. 2010. "Making Effective Use of Counselors to Increase Student Achievement." *Principal's Research Review* 5, no. 3: 1–4.

Purkey, S. C., and Michael Smith. 1983. "Effective Schools: A Review." *The Elementary School Journal* 83, no. 4: 436–452.

Quint, Janet. 2006. *Meeting Five Critical Challenges of High School Reform.* New York: MDRC.

Quint, Janet, Howard Bloom, A. R. Black, L. Stephens, and T. Akey. 2005. *The Challenge of Scaling Up Educational Reform: Findings and Lessons from First Things First.* New Work: MDRC.

Quint, Janet, Janell Smith, Rebecca Untermann, and Alma Moedao. 2010. *New York City's Changing High School Landscape: High Schools and Their Characteristics 2002–2008.* New York: MDRC.

Raywid, Mary Ann. 2006. "Themes That Serve High Schools Well." *Phi Delta Kappan* 87, no. 9: 654–656.

Reese, William. 1995. *The Origins of the American High School.* New Haven: Yale University Press.

Rhodes, D., B. Smerdon, W. Burt, A. Evan, B. Martinez, and B. Means. 2005. *Getting to Results: Student Outcomes in New and Redesigned High Schools.* Washington, DC: American Institutes for Research and SRI International.

Rice, Jennifer King. 2010. *Principal Effectiveness and Leadership in an Era of Accountability: What Research Says.* CALDER Brief 8. Washington DC: Urban Institute.

Rice, Jennifer King, and Betty Malen. 2010. *School Reconstitution as an Education Reform Strategy: A Synopsis of the Evidence.* Washington DC: National Education Association.

Rideout, Victoria, Ulla Foehr, and Donald Roberts. 2010. *Generation M^2: Media in the Lives of 8- to 18-Year-Olds.* Menlo Park, CA: Kaiser Family Foundation.

Rigby, Jessica. 2010. "Results-Based Budgeting: Conceptualizing Resources in OUSD." Unpublished paper, School of Education, University of California–Berkeley.

Rogers, David. 1968. *110 Livingston Street: Politics and Bureaucracy in the New York City Schools.* New York: Random House.

Rogers, Everett. 2003. *Diffusion of Innovation,* 4th ed. New York: Free Press.

Rogers, John, Joseph Kahne, and Ellen Middaugh. 2008. "Multiple Pathways and the Future of Democracy." In *Beyond Tracking: Multiple Pathways to College, Career, and Civic Participation,* ed. Jeannie Oakes and Marisa Saunders, 153–170. Cambridge, MA: Harvard University Press.

Rose, Michael. 1995. *Possible Lives: The Promise of Public Education in America.* New York: Penguin Books.

Rothstein, Richard. 2004. *Class and Schools: Using Social, Economic, and Educational Reform to Close the Black-White Achievement Gap.* New York: Economic Policy Institute.

Rowan, B., S. T. Bossert, and D. C. Dwyer. 1983. "Research on Effective Schools: A Cautionary Note." *Educational Researcher,* April: 4–31.

Rowan, Brian. 1990. "Commitment and Control: Alternative Strategies for the Organizational Design of Schools." In *Review of Research in Education,* ed. C. Cazden, 353–389. Washington, DC: American Educational Research Association.

Rowan, Brian, Richard Correnti, R. Miller, and E. Camburn. 2009. "School Improvement by

Design: Lessons from a Study of Comprehensive School Reform Programs." University of Pennsylvania: Center for Policy Research in Education. Available at www.cpre.org.

Roza, Marguerite, and Paul Hill. 2006. "How Can Anyone Say What's Adequate if Nobody Knows How Money Is Spent Now?" In *Courting Failure: How School Finance Lawsuits Exploit Judges' Good Intentions and Harm Our Children,* ed. Eric Hanushek, 235–256. Palo Alto: Hoover Press.

Ryken, Amy. 2001. *Content, Pedagogy, Results: A Thrice-Told Tale of Integrating Work-Based and School-Based Learning.* PhD diss., School of Education, University of California–Berkeley.

Saunders, William, Claude Goldenberg, and Ronald Gallimore. 2009. "Increasing Achievement by Focusing on Grade-Level Teams on Improving Classroom Learning." *American Educational Research Journal* 46, no. 4: 1006–1033.

Shear, Linda, et al. 2005. *Creating Cultures for Learning: Supportive Relationships in New and Redesigned High Schools.* Washington, DC, and Menlo Park, CA: American Institutes for Research and SRI, for the Bill and Melinda Gates Foundation.

———. 2008. "Contrasting Paths to Small School Reform: Results of a 5-Year Evaluation of the Bill and Melinda Gates Foundation's National High School Initiative." *Teachers College Record* 110, no. 9: 1986–2039.

Shulman, Lee. 1987. "Knowledge and Teaching: Foundations of the New Reform." *Harvard Educational Review* 57, no. 1: 1–22.

Singleton, Glen. 2006. *Courageous Conversations About Race: A Field Guide for Achieving Equity in Schools.* Thousand Oaks, CA: Corwin Press.

Siskin, Leslie. 1994. *Realms of Knowledge: Academic Departments in Secondary Schools.* Washington, DC: Falmer Press.

Siskin, Leslie. 2004. "When an Irresistible Force Meets an Immovable Object: Core Lessons About High Schools and Accountability." In *The New Accountability: High Schools and High-Stakes Testing,* ed. Martin Carnoy, Richard Elmore, and Leslie Siskin, 175–194. New York: RoutledgeFalmer.

Siskin, Leslie, and Judith Warren Little, eds. 1995. *The Subjects in Question: Departmental Organization and the High School.* New York: Teachers College Press.

Sizer, Theodore. 1964. *The Age of the Academies.* Classics in Education No. 22. New York: Teachers College, Columbia University.

———. 1984. *Horace's Compromise: The Dilemma of the American High School.* Boston: Houghton Mifflin.

Snow, Catherine, Susan M. Burns, and Peg Griffin. 1998. *Preventing Reading Difficulties in Young Children.* Washington, DC: National Academies Press.

Southern Regional Education Board. 2010. *District Leadership That Works: How the Best Districts Create a Culture That Combines Vision, Autonomy, Support, and Accountability.* Atlanta: SREB.

Speer, N., M. McFall, and D. Mohatt. 2009. "Nourishing Students' Mental Health in a Difficult Economy." *Chronicle of Higher Education,* May 15: A25.

Spillane, James. 2006. *Distributed Leadership.* San Francisco: Jossey-Bass.

Spillane, J., and J. Diamond. 2007. *Distributed Leadership in Practice.* New York: Teachers College Press.

Stanford Redesign Network. 2009. "How Do California School Districts Get Ready for Multiple Pathways? A Synthesis of Planning Challenges." Stanford, CA: School Redesign Network.

Stein, Sandra, and Liz Gewirtzman. 2003. *Principal Training on the Ground: Ensuring Highly Qualified Leadership.* Portsmouth, NH: Heinemann.

Stern, David. 1999. "Improving Pathways in the United States from High School to College and Career." In *Preparing Youth for the 21st Century: The Transition from Education to the Labour Market,* 155–214. Paris: OECD.

Stern, David, Charles Dayton, and Marilyn Raby. 2001. *Career Academies: Building Blocks for Reconstructing American High Schools.* Berkeley: Career Academy Support Network, School of Education, University of California.

Stern, David, Marilyn Raby, and Charles Dayton. 1992. *Career Academies: Partnerships for Reconstructing American High Schools.* San Francisco: Jossey-Bass.

Stiffarm, Lenore, ed. 1998. *As We See . . . Aboriginal Pedagogy.* Saskatoon, Canada: University Extension Press, University of Saskatchewan.

Strauss, Anselm, and Juliet Corbin. 1990. *Basics of Qualitative Research: Grounded Theory Procedures and Techniques.* London: Sage.

Stull, William. 2003. "School-to-Work in Schools: An Overview." In *The School-to-Work Movement: Origins and Destinations,* ed. William Stull and N. Sanders, 3–25. Westport, CT: Praeger.

Tharp, Roland, and Ronald Gallimore. 1988. *Rousing Minds to Life : Teaching, Learning, and Schooling in Social Context.* Cambridge: Cambridge University Press.

Thirty Schools Tell Their Story. 1943. New York: Harper and Brothers.

Timpane, M., S. Abramowitz, S. B. Bobrow, and A. Pascal. 1976. *Youth Policy in Transition.* R-2006-HEW. Santa Monica: RAND Corporation. *

Trei, Lisa. 2006. "California Secretary of Education Says Quality of Teaching Is the Critical Factor." *Stanford Report,* April 18. Available at http://news.stanford.edu/news/2006/april19/bersin-041906.html?view=print.

Tucker, Marc. 2004. *High School and Beyond: The System Is the Problem—and the Solution.* Washington, DC: National Center on Education and the Economy. *

Turnbull, Brenda, M. Brice Haslam, Erickson Arcaira, Derek Riley, Beth Sinclair, and Stephen Coleman. 2009. *Evaluation of the School Administration Manager Project.* Washington, DC: Policy Study Associates.

Tyack, David. 1974. *The One Best System: A History of American Urban Education.* Cambridge, MA: Harvard University Press.

Villani, Susan. 2006. *Mentoring and Induction Programs That Support New Principals.* San Francisco: WestEd.

What Kids Can Do and Students. 2004. *The Schools We Need: Creating Small High Schools That Work for Us.* Providence, RI: What Kids Can Do. *

Zirkel, Shelly. 2008. "The Influence of Multicultural Educational Practices on Student Outcomes and Intergroup Relations." *Teachers College Record* 110, no. 6: 1147–1181.

Index

About the Author

W. Norton Grubb is the David Pierpont Gardner Professor in Higher Education at the University of California, Berkeley. He is also the faculty coordinator of the Principal Leadership Institute, a program to prepare principals for urban schools. In addition to conducting wide-ranging research, he provides workshops for secondary and community college instructors and administrators, presenting different approaches to reform. He has also participated in public policy efforts, such as the California Master Plan Commission and the National Research Council Committee on high school motivation. His recent books include *Leading from the Inside Out: Expanded Roles for Teachers in Equitable Schools,* coauthored with Lynda Tredway (Paradigm, 2010); *The Money Myth: School Resources, Outcomes, and Equity* (Russell Sage Foundation, 2009); *The Education Gospel: The Economic Power of Schooling* (Harvard University Press, 2004); *Honored But Invisible: An Inside Look at Teaching in Community Colleges* (Routledge, 1999); and *Learning to Work: The Case for Reintegrating Job Training and Education* (Russell Sage Foundation, 1996).